"Have faith in God."

DR. CULLIS AND HIS WORK.

Twenty Years of Blessing in answer to Prayer.

A HISTORY OF

THE HOSPITALS, SCHOOLS, ORPHANAGES, CHURCHES, AND
MISSIONS RAISED UP AND SUPPORTED BY THE
HAND OF THE LORD THROUGH THE
FAITH AND LABORS OF

CHARLES CULLIS, M.D.,

OF BOSTON, U.S.A.

EDITED BY

REV. W. H. DANIELS,

AUTHOR OF "D. L. MOODY AND HIS WORK," "THE TEMPERANCE
REFORM AND ITS GREAT REFORMERS," "MEMORIALS
OF BISHOP HAVEN," ETC., ETC.

WILLARD TRACT REPOSITORY:

BEACON-HILL PLACE, BOSTON; No. 239 FOURTH AVENUE, NEW YORK;
813 ARCH STREET, PHILADELPHIA; 39 WARWICK LANE, LONDON;
BOMBAY, INDIA; SANTA BARBARA AND LOS ANGELES, CAL.

ELECTROTYPED AND PRINTED
BY RAND, AVERY, AND COMPANY,
BOSTON, MASS.

CONTENTS.

PART II.

FAITH MISSIONS AT HOME AND ABROAD.

CHAPTER XX.

CHAPTER XXI.

CHAPTER XXII.

CHAPTER XXIII.

CHAPTER XXIV.

CHAPTER XXV.

CHAPTER XXVI.

DR. CULLIS AND HIS WORK.

CHAPTER I.

GOD'S CHOSEN ONES.

" Many are called, but few are chosen."

WHILE the call of the Lord to repentance and salvation includes the many, there is a choice which elects the few to some special post of duty.

This view of that much-disputed text is strongly brought out by the exceptional careers of such Christians as Francke in Germany, Muller in Bristol, Boardman and Barnardo in London, and Dr. Cullis in Boston. These men are the chief representatives of a class of persons whom the Lord has chosen out of the multitudes of his people, that through them he may show forth his power and grace in a striking manner, and to an unusual degree. The Divine plan for laying out the surface of the earth comprises hills and mountains, as well as plains and prairies ; and even the sea finds its level disturbed when God lets loose the winds upon it. So it is with human life.

There is a vicious extreme into which certain lines of theology sometimes run, — that, in order to treat his children fairly, he must treat them all alike. "Liberty, equality, fraternity," may answer well enough for a commune, but it is out of place in the Church. A diversity of gifts, and a gradation of powers and places, is as plainly taught in the New Testament, as is the doctrine of free and full salvation; and the call of certain individuals to extraordinary work, and experience above the plane of the lives of the mass of Christian believers, is just what ought to be expected under the personal and absolute government of King Jesus. That one man or woman out of ten thousand should be able to heal the sick without medicine, or to maintain a great hospital or orphanage with no other treasury open to them except the bank of Heaven, is by no means incredible: the inability of the other nine thousand nine hundred and ninety-nine to do the same, and the failure of some of them who attempt it, is no argument against the exceptional fact. Here and there is a mountain that pours out fire from its summit; and it is no argument against volcanoes, that the vast majority of mountains do not smoke and burn.

In order, then, to find the largest profit from such histories as this, let it be constantly borne in mind, that, while there are common duties which, like "common prayer," may be taken up by hands and hearts at will, there are also special Divine appointments to great and rare works in the kingdom of Christ, — appointments which he makes by his own sovereign pleasure, with which he bestows exceptional opportunities and powers, and for which he never condescends to render a reason or lay down a rule.

One of these special works, God was pleased to lay upon the heart and hands of a young physician in the city of Boston, U.S.A., in the early part of the year 1862, — a work which has grown and multiplied until it has become a constellation of charities, the fame whereof has gone forth into all the earth. From all the continents come words of cheer and gifts of money; and to the Pacific Coast, India, and Africa, as well as to missions nearer home, has this man of God been permitted to send out laborers into over-ripe harvest-fields, whence are already coming joyful tidings of many in-gathered sheaves.

This volume is not intended as a biography; but it is fitting that it should open with a brief personal sketch of this "chosen" man, this "elect" servant of God, who now for over twenty years has lived and loved and labored at the centre of this great circle of blessing.

Charles Cullis, M.D., is a native of Boston. He was born on the 7th of March, 1833, and was baptized and reared in the Episcopal Church. It does not appear that he was naturally of a religious turn of mind: but, on the contrary, his aversion to Bible-study in the Sunday school to which he was sent, and where memorizing texts of Scripture was one of the chief exercises required, was such that he determined to quit the school as soon as he was old enough to have his own way ; and this he actually did.

From the first, he was a frail and delicate child. School made him sick ; he broke down in an attempt at mercantile life ; and before he was twenty years of age, he had grown so weak that he was able to speak only in a whisper. The Doctor's compact frame and robust health, under the pressure of a double load of cares, — a physician in large practice, and the head of a system of faith-homes, chapels, and missions, amounting to a good-sized diocese — is ample proof that God gives his servants strength according to the burdens he lays upon them, and that they who wait upon the Lord shall not want any good thing.

It was during these days of enforced idleness, that a physician of his acquaintance proposed to him the study of medicine ; and, in spite of various obstacles, he finished his preliminary reading, graduated from the medical department of the University of Vermont in his twenty-fourth year, returned to his native city, and in a very short time had acquired a large and profitable practice.

During the course of study, the young man became the subject of religious convictions ; which he temporarily silenced by going forward in confirmation in the Episcopal Church, and attending to the outward duties of a Christian. Life now seemed most hopefully begun. He had married a lovely wife, had a good income from his profession in company with his brother-in-law, was at rest in his mind; and he and his bride seemed to have good reason to look forward to many years of peace and plenty. But, after a brief married life, the idol of his heart was taken away; and over the dead form of his young wife he gave up the world, and vowed to devote his entire income, over and above his personal expenses, to works of charity and religion. This vow he faithfully kept, scattering gifts with a free hand, but always doing it as a duty, and, perhaps, in part also as a means of relief from his sorrow, and a way of saving his soul.

But now a new trouble came upon him. He began to be dissatisfied with his condition before God. His life of self-enforced devotion was not enough to satisfy him. He was working and giving as a duty, and mere duty never yet satisfied a soul that was longing for holiness and for deep communion with God. In his own heart he still observed some evidences of an unsanctified nature, all of which he wished to be rid of; but he did not yet know how to believe for a clean heart and a right spirit. The methods of the charities on which he was bestowing his consecrated moneys also began to be a source of trouble to him; and, living under all these clouds, a deep despondency settled upon his mind.

It was while in this deep wretchedness of spirit, that

he was enabled to take fast hold of the Bible as the true and living word of God, wherein he soon began to see some of those spiritual mysteries which in later times he has unfolded with such light and comfort to others ; particularly the promises, of which he said, " I will take every promise in the Bible as my own, just as if my own name, Charles Cullis, were written in it."

The following account of his experience of justification, and his subsequent entrance into a state of sanctification, is from that admirable and deeply spiritual book by Rev. Dr. Boardman, entitled " Faith Work," in which he sets forth, from Dr. Cullis's own account of himself, some of the steps by which those blessed experiences were entered upon.

" One day," says Dr. Cullis — it was the 19th of August, 1862, — " I was reading in the morning the second chapter of Second Thessalonians, and came, in the thirteenth verse, to the words 'through sanctification of the Spirit ;' and they arrested my attention, and held me for some time, while I read and re-read them again and again, and prayed God to sanctify me wholly by the Spirit, and destroy all selfishness and unbelief in my heart. The longing to work for Jesus grew apace, and the yearning for purity kept even pace with it. After the Lord began to open my ears to his teachings, he led me sweetly into many things, a step at a time. Two great things must be specially mentioned. First, he unfolded clearly and fully to me the fact that he himself is my righteousness ; that in him, not in myself, I am justified ; and that in him, not in myself, I have eternal life. He caused me to see that he who believes in the Son of God hath life, — hath life already ; whilst he that believeth not in him hath not life, and maketh God a liar because he believeth not the record God hath given of his Son. This gave me full assurance of faith for present acceptance and eternal salvation ; and it was a wonderful advance, a great and glorious step out from under law into grace for salvation. For this I shall praise God for ever and ever.

"After this I found, however, that I was not saved from fret and worry and impatience. Often a hasty word would escape me, which I would willingly have given my right hand to recall. The fact is, I had not learned yet that Christ must keep me, or I could not be kept. The keeping power of Christ was the second great lesson of the two taught me by the Lord. I knew my need of being kept, but thought at first that it could be met only by a greater vigilance in self-keeping, and a greater firmness of self-reliance and de-termination ; but this failed me. Then I tried prayer for help in self-keeping, but my failures were just as frequent and grievous as ever. Finally, one day, whilst repeating the Lord's Prayer, the petition 'Keep us from evil' seemed instinct with a significance I had never before apprehended. The evil it refers to, I had always until then supposed to be that which is external to us, and which comes upon us without our choice, — accidents, diseases, losses, and the like, — but then I saw it to refer to evil in the heart, evil in the disposition, evil in the spirit. I saw, that like the petition, 'Let thy kingdom come,' it related primarily to our inner life, not to our outward circumstances. Then this new light was sealed home to me by the Spirit, in the words, 'For thine is the kingdom, and the power, and the glory for ever and ever. Amen.' I saw that the kingdom within is the Lord's, and the power to set it up and keep it up for ever and ever is his also. Not the helping power to self-keeping, but the keeping power altogether ; and when I saw this, I said with all my heart, 'Yea, Lord. Amen, so it is. Hallelujah ! Praise God, from whom all blessings flow.'

"Before this great and blessed lesson had been taught me, I thought I knew what it would be worth if I could be kept. There was no price, which could have been commanded by me, that I should have thought too great for it. Yet I must say that I knew comparatively nothing at all of its value. The power that keeps is a power that illuminates, subdues, teaches, strengthens, upholds, guides, sweetens, enlivens, gives peace and every thing else that pertains to God's kingdom within. I do not see how I ever lived without it, and I am sure that but for this I should have been poorly prepared for the dear work which the Lord has called me to do. Oh ! I bless him for it every day.

> " ' Bless the Lord, O my soul,
>   And all that is within me, bless his holy name.
>   Bless the Lord, O my soul,
>   And forget not all his benefits.'

" From that day to this, I have had daily proof of the truthfulness of the name of Jesus, for he does save his people from their sins. And I have found the prophet Isaiah's assurance verified, —

> " ' Thou wilt keep him in perfect peace
>   Whose mind is stayed on thee,
>   Because he trusteth in thee.' "

Thus was the Lord fitting his servant for the great work to which he had called him, — first a kind of legal sacrifice of his worldly goods to the cause of God ; then a desperate grasp of the Bible as his only hope in his desolation and despair; then the leading of the Holy Spirit, by means of that Word, into a clear and intelligent experience of saving grace, and afterwards into an equally clear and intelligent consecration of himself, as well as of his possessions, to the Lord, and into a perfect rest of faith, and a share in God's perfect love.

CHAPTER II.

THE CALL OF GOD.

"Show me thy way, O Lord; teach me thy paths."

IT was a still small voice that first spoke the mind of the Spirit to Dr. Cullis, concerning the special duty to which he had been appointed; and it was by slow, short steps, that he was first led on in its performance.

On the 20th of April, 1862, he makes the first record, and that even with hesitation, of the desire awakened in his heart to open a private hospital, or home, for those consumptives who were excluded from the public hospital on the ground that they were incurable. For a year and a half it was his daily prayer, that, if this were indeed the will of the Lord, the way might be opened for its accomplishment. From April, 1862, to January, 1864, he held — or was held by — this strong desire, though without the least visible encouragement. It was a time of preparation, a season of waiting on the Lord, by which his natural enthusiasm was guided and sanctified, and his faith toned up to bear the heavy strain which was to be put upon it. During all this time, his spiritual experience was growing richer and deeper day by day, and the treasures hidden in the word of God were more and more fully opened to his view.

At length — his journal says it was on the 19th of January, 1864 — the burden of the possible and yet impossible work grew so heavy that he began to pray in that alternative manner by which in after-years he has been accustomed to seek the settlement of difficult questions : "O Lord, if this thought is from thee, give me the means to realize it; and if not, I pray thee, take it out of my mind."   On the evening of that very day, a trifling sum of money was given him, unsolicited, by a friend who knew of his plan for a consumptives' home.   And this first dollar, of the more than half a million which have been intrusted to him for these works of faith and love, was received with perhaps the greatest joy of any; for it came as a token that God indeed was in the voice that had so long been whispering in his soul.

As we have already seen, his professional income was wholly consecrated to the Lord.   But it was not at all sufficient to justify such an undertaking; and, for some time after the enterprise was set on foot, the outside aid received was so very small that he says of himself, " My boldness in making the start would have been temerity and presumption, had not the Lord's will been previously so fully and satisfactorily ascertained."

Now his prayer was for a house in which to begin; for, according to the Scripture, it is "the steps of a good man," and not merely his journeys as a whole, that are "ordered by the Lord." He also prayed for a larger practice, — being now alone in business, — in order to meet the anticipated heavy drain upon his funds : nevertheless, when the day came for making the venture, he had only about three hundred dollars cash in hand with which to purchase a six-thousand-dollar house, fit it up, and lay in such stores as the case required.

At length, after long and fruitless search, he found a house on Vernon Street (afterwards re-named Willard Street), and bargained for it at a rental of five hundred dollars. But some one living opposite raised an objection to having a hospital so near, and the owner declined to carry out the agreement : he would, however, sell the place. There was a large mortgage which could remain on the property. After laying the matter before the Lord in the alternative form of prayer, "Shall I purchase, or shall I hire ?" the Doctor was led to buy ; by which arrangement a hundred dollars a year was saved off the rent, and the house came fully under his control to make such alterations in it as were required. This policy has been continued, in connection with various departments of the work ; and it has been fully justified by results. If it be objected that the institution was founded upon a debt, it is replied that the house itself was security for the amount of the mortgage, and thus the debt was really carried by the property instead of the proprietor. The only question, then, was of faith in God for money to pay the annual interest.

It was nearly two months before the place was fitted for its new uses, and during this time there was opportunity for further testing the faith of the projector of this novel enterprise. No advertising was resorted to, but of course the matter was a subject of no little interest and discussion; and from unknown sources there began to arrive various articles of furniture, so that, when the fittings were finished, the furnishing was also in such a forward state, that on the twenty-seventh day of September, 1864, this first faith-hospital on this side of the world was dedicated to the worshipful service of Almighty God, and opened for the care of such homeless and hopeless ones as he might be pleased to send. Some of the chief clergy and citizens of Boston and vicinity aided in this delightful act of consecration. The prayer of dedication was offered by the Rev. Dr. Huntington (now Bishop Huntington), and the exercises closed with a poem by B. P. Shillaber, Esq. The gifts on the occasion, in money and articles for use, amounted to a little over eighty dollars.

Both the secular and the religious press gave cordial notices of this unique dedication; and, in addition to these kind words, a circular was prepared and published by several influential friends of the enterprise, commending it to the confidence and liberality of the public. This unsolicited act was especially encouraging to Dr. Cullis. The circular is here inserted in full.

THE HOME FOR INDIGENT AND INCURABLE CONSUMPTIVES.

A hospital for the gratuitous medical treatment and tender care of cases of confirmed consumption in homeless persons, and those too poor to provide for themselves, has lately been opened at No. 4 Vernon Street, in this city.

The design originated in a simple desire to help and comfort a class of sufferers whose distresses and necessities have hitherto found no institution among us especially adapted to their relief, and thus to honor at once our common humanity and our blessed Redeemer. This institution has been founded without patronage or funds, in a humble but confident reliance upon the God of mercy and on the benevolence of his children ; in the faith that Christ, so gracious to the sick and needy when he was on earth, would move the hearts and open the hands of his people to carry the work forward. Nor has this confidence been disappointed. A house has been obtained, and for the most part furnished, and attendants have been procured. Ever since the enterprise became informally known to the public, in August, a steady stream of free offerings has flowed in upon it, gathered from widely different sources. To sustain the undertaking, it is plain that gifts must be constantly coming in. The founder, a homœopathic physician, proposes to give his time, professional services, superintendence, and property. Bedding, bed-clothing, garments for invalids, articles of food of all kinds both for patients and nurses, groceries, meats and fruits, cordials and jellies, fuel, and a considerable amount of money from week to week, will be required. This substantial assistance is sought in the name of helpless sufferers, and in the name of the Lord Jesus. It is believed that there are many in this community who will consider it a privilege to contribute to a charity conducted on this principle. Whatever is offered will be expended or used with economy and care. The hospital is open to the inspection of all its friends. No distinction as to age, sex, nationality, or religion will be made in admitting or treating inmates. Every thing that is possible will be done to soothe pain, to sustain the spirits, and to console the last hours of those appointed to die.

Further information may be had from Dr. Charles Cullis, No. 21 Bowdoin Street, between the hours of 2 and 4 P. M.; or at the hospital, on Vernon Street, during the hour from 9 to 10 in the morning.

Reference is made to

> REV. F. D HUNTINGTON, D.D.
> REV. E. N. KIRK, D.D.
> REV. WILLIAM HAGUE, D.D.
> REV. S. K. LOTHROP, D.D.
> REV. A. A. MINER, D.D.
> HON. ALEXANDER H. RICE.
> HON. JACOB SLEEPER.
> HON. E. S. TOBEY.

From the first, as this document shows, Dr. Cullis has had the confidence and co-operation of wise and large-hearted Christian men and women; among whom may be mentioned the late Vice-President of the United States, the Hon. Henry Wilson, who was one of the earliest friends of, and an annual contributor to, the work. But, on the other hand, many very religious people, as well as worldly ones, have always opposed the idea of supporting such a charity by faith in God. Indeed, the chief opposers of the enterprise have been from within the Church, rather than from without; and even after a trial of twenty years, during which the growth of the work has been constant, and the blessing of Heaven most conspicuous, there are not wanting those, professing to be Christian believers, who complain of the Doctor for believing too much. Facts weigh little against their doubts and theories. Beholding the man that was healed standing by, these modern Scribes and Pharisees *are* able to say something against it. Nevertheless the shower of blessing still falls, and, from among the incurables received, numbers of happy souls still rise; whereby the faith of God's servant in that day of heavy trials and of small beginnings has been fully justified, both before the Church and the world.

And now, the house being in readiness, the Doctor began to pray the Lord to send him suitable persons for nurses to the sick; which need was speedily met in the volunteering of two Christian women, who wished to render this service to the Lord as a free-will offering, one of whom became the first matron of the Home. From that time, most of the matrons, nurses, and other principal workers have been volunteers, who have consecrated themselves to a religious life, and who, without any stipulated salary, have labored "heartily, as unto the Lord;" who, in return for their work of faith and labor of love, has given them rare and abundant blessing. The more common and laborious service has, of course, been rendered chiefly for regular wages ; but even here there have been bright examples of consecrated lives.

Next the Lord was inquired of to send those persons, and those only, for whose care and comfort he had caused the Home to be opened ; and it was not long before the house was filled with "homeless and hopeless" ones, each case having some sad and touching interest. One poor man in the last stages of consumption came to the Doctor's door, and begged to know where he could go to die, saying he had not where to lay his head. A woman was received, who had been found wasting away on a heap of straw in a dismal attic. A poor German woman from Dorchester was admitted, who shortly afterwards died hoping in Christ, — the first representative in the Lord's immediate presence of the work of blessing he had so recently caused to be begun on earth. This was on Nov. 13, 1864.

On Thanksgiving Day, Nov. 26, the Home having now been in operation since Oct. 7, — on which day the first patient was received, — the Doctor makes the following record in his journal : —

"Nov. 26. To-day is Thanksgiving. I trust I am thankful to the Lord for all his blessings to me and mine during the year past. I daily pray for a heart wholly wedded to Christ, that I may live entirely to his glory. When I review all that the Lord has done for the hospital, I cannot but exclaim, ' What hath God wrought ! ' When the work was commenced in August, I had but little over three hundred dollars ; and out of this must come my own business and family expenses, and the hospital

to be supported.   But I knew in whom I trusted, — that I had
a rich Father, who always honors all drafts upon him.   In him
I have never been confounded.   Daily he has supplied each
need.   The hospital is established in working order; eight
patients are abundantly cared for, having all their need supplied, and many luxuries ; a matron, two nurses, two domestics,
and a man to assist, are supported, all but one (Miss K.) being
paid weekly wages ; all the expenses of the house have been
paid ; and to-day I have more money on hand than when the
work was commenced."

On the following day the second death occurred, —
of a woman who had found Christ during her brief stay
at the Home.

In a careful review of the yearly reports, one of the
most striking facts brought to notice is the almost
invariable record that those who have died here have
died in the faith of Jesus ; a large proportion of them
having been converted during their stay in the Home.
Surely this gospel mission is an investment yielding
speedy returns ; or, as it might be said, here is a
constant revival of religion going on, from whose altar
there is a rapid succession of converts actually ascending to glory.

Before the middle of December, the Home was full,
and applications had to be refused for want of room ;
whereupon Dr. Cullis began to pray for another house.
In the first three months, eleven patients had been
received, four of whom had gone safely home to
heaven.   Perhaps the word "patients" is not the best

that could be chosen, for the inmates of the Home did not come to be cured; indeed, it was only the incurables who were to be received at all, and these as a charity and not as subjects for medical experiment. They came there to die, and the treatment had far more relation to the future life than to the present. When, therefore, a patient had been brought to Christ, and had died in the triumphs of faith, that case was regarded as the largest possible success. Sometimes, contrary to all expectation, patients have recovered, and these have become bright and helpful servants of the blessed Master; but, as a rule, the "cures" wrought in the Consumptives' Home are reckoned as complete only when the feeble pulse has ceased, and a ray of the light which shines from the upper world has settled upon the calm, cold face. Such cures are full and final: they show forth the greatest skill of the Great Physician.

During the first winter there were some considerable gifts; one of five hundred dollars from a lady who was herself dying of consumption, and one of three hundred dollars from the Massachusetts Charitable Fire Society. On the 15th of March, 1865, a stranger called, and, asking, "Is this Dr. Cullis?" handed him a roll of bills which he said was for the Consumptives' Home; and departed without giving his name. Among the donors was the president of the Detroit Young Men's Christian Association, who came to explore this new development of service for Jesus, and left an order for twenty-five dollars. But the most of the gifts were in small, sometimes in trifling sums : yet each one was a proof of God's care and kindness, for it came as a voluntary offering; and, in most cases, from persons who were perfect strangers.

On the 10th of May, the Home being quite full, there were four applications for admission. This the Doctor took as an indication that it was time to act in the matter of obtaining larger accommodations, and began to make an effort to obtain an adjoining house ; praying, meanwhile, that the Lord would send him the fifteen hundred dollars which must be paid over and above the mortgage of twenty-five hundred, and also money for the fitting and furnishing. Here also it was necessary to purchase ; as the owners would not change tenants, but were intending shortly to sell the house. Still gifts were small ; but the Lord enabled the Doctor, from money of his own, to pay the sum required, — thus affording him an opportunity to act upon his pledge of giving his income, as well as his heart and hands, to the work. There was a blessed community of goods between him and the Lord ; and the frequent mention of money used for the Home, which came as professional fees, and sometimes even from the sacrifice of personal property, all goes to prove that his consecration was not only entire, but hearty and joyful. The disciple was glad to make such offerings to his

Lord. On the 31st of May, 1865, the purchase was made; and on the 27th of September, just one year from the opening of the first house, the second was dedicated with prayer and praise. Large expenses were incurred in fitting the place for its new use, but these were all met with money received in answer to prayer.

Thus, within a twelvemonth, the capacity of the Home was doubled, all bills were paid, and constant proofs were given, both temporal and spiritual, that they who really trust in the Lord shall not want any good thing. The amount of money received up to the end of the first year was $5,916.28, to which, of course, the Doctor himself was by far the largest contributor; but more than half of this amount must have been received in free-will offerings, wholly unsolicited by Dr. Cullis except in prayer to God. Besides this, there was a constant stream of little gifts of useful articles in the way of fruit, flowers, books, furniture, provisions, etc., amounting perhaps to the value of five or six hundred dollars more; all of which are carefully enumerated in the first Annual Report.

The issuing of a report of the Home has been classed by critics as an "advertisement," and "a regular system of begging;" in view whereof, the claim that the Consumptives' Home is supported wholly in answer to prayer is said to be "misleading" and "hypocritical." Such reports are issued by all benevolent societies and institutions, for the express purpose of soliciting money; why, then, should this Faith Home claim any special distinction above other charities, in the matter of answers to prayer?

To such objections, the first answer is, that no benevolent society relies upon its reports as its sole or even its chief money-raising agency: in fact, the funds received by voluntary contribution through these reports alone would, in some cases, hardly pay the expenses of the other agencies which it is found necessary to employ. Some sectarian missionary societies do indeed manage their affairs through the unpaid agency of the pastors of the denomination represented, but the amount of asking and urging required in order to keep the work alive is a matter of familiar knowledge among all church-going people. Which of these societies would venture to dispense with its well-paid secretaries, close its home and foreign offices, recall its travelling agents, cease its appeals from platform and pulpit, and rely entirely on prayer to God — and an annual report of his goodness — for the maintenance and enlargement of their operations? When any one of these societies or institutions has actually done this, and survived the crisis, it will be time enough to urge the objection against faith-missions, that *they are maintained by publishing an annual report.*

And now, concerning the value of the reports as a "business advertisement." In the first place, the larger the "business" of the Consumptives' Home, the smaller the "profits." Every thing there is free to its inmates; neither they nor their friends — if they have any — are asked to pay a penny: how, then, does "advertising," in a "business" sense, help the resources of the institution? The only "business" carried on in these wards is the business of giving something for nothing. Let the critics figure out the "profits" for themselves.

On the other hand, the value of such advertising as a means of bringing in gifts is vastly overrated. In addition to what has been said above, let it be considered that "advertisements" are supposed to tell people where they can lay out money for their own advantage, and not where they can part with it and receive absolutely nothing in return. Such advertisements are not made use of in business circles, — i.e., bad investments are not set forth in that way: but this is precisely the kind of "advertising" in the case of all genuine faith missions and charities; it is the spread of information, not concerning profitable buying or selling, but concerning an opportunity for giving money away. When any other "business" shall become profitable by merely offering to receive, and not to pay or give in return, then let the value of faith in God, as used by Cullis, Muller, and Barnardo, be carefully re-examined; but until something of that kind shall have appeared, all objections to faith-missions on the ground that they are so "well advertised" must be regarded as illogical and wholly out of order.

But there is still another feature of the first Annual Report of the Home, which has been a joy among the angels of God, as well as among his children on earth. Up to Sept. 30, 1865, the whole number of patients admitted was thirty-four, mostly incurable cases for whom there was no provision in the public hospital. They literally came to the Home to die; but the bright side of this sad picture brings out the blessed fact, that, of the thirteen who departed this life during this first year, every one died with a good hope in Christ. Of the ten who were discharged, two are reported as "cured;" two were "relieved, and able to attend to their employment;" and eight were "discharged by being provided for by friends, or other causes."

The record shows that the work was a continual occasion of spiritual growth and enjoyment, as well as of sympathy, care, and toil, to him who had thus dared to begin to walk by faith in this new and rugged path. Not once was his confidence in God suffered to waver; and not a single day passed without some token from the Lord, in the way of money or supplies.

CHAPTER III.

TRIALS AND TRIUMPHS.

"The trying of your faith worketh patience."

THE second year opened with a season of trial.
It is not the policy of our Father in heaven to keep such temporal abundance before his believing ones that the satisfying view thereof shall prevent their constant and immediate looking to him. Poverty seems to be a necessary part of the training of God's people. It is only those who have been poor without complaining, who can be rich without pride. The following notes from the Doctor's journal give an insight into his heart as well as into his affairs : —

"Oct. 2, 1865. This morning, after paying the monthly bills, I found my funds reduced to less than fifteen dollars, and this amount is all I possess in the world. With this sum the institution commences its second year. Yet I have no fear, for 'I know that my Redeemer liveth.'"

"Oct. 3. Commenced the day with a little over three dollars, the amount of yesterday having been reduced by the daily expenses. In answer to prayer, by eight o'clock three dollars was given, before noon three more.

"This afternoon, knowing the necessity of stoves for some of the upper rooms, as the weather is quite cool, I went to the

Lord in prayer, and told him of our need, praying him in some way to supply us. I then went down town to a friend, to look at stoves, and inquire the price. After deciding upon two that I thought would answer, I asked the price; when he said, 'That's all right, I shall not charge any thing,' and said he would see that they were put up. This man knew nothing of our great need: he had never visited the Home, knew but little about it, and not a word did he know of the state of my purse. Did not the Lord answer my prayer, and incline the man's heart to give the stoves? I thanked him, and thanked God for his goodness, praying that his Holy Spirit might be given to this kind friend, that he may know the preciousness of Christ's love.

"This evening a poor widow called on me, relating the following story: Her husband died two years ago, in Charleston, S.C.; afterwards, during the bombardment of that city, she lost every thing she had in the world. After great trials, she was enabled to get through the rebel lines, and come North. Before she left, she exchanged what little Confederate money she had for gold. Handing me a five-dollar gold piece, she said, 'I gave one hundred dollars Confederate money for that, and have carried it in my pocket for more than two years; but the other evening, while at the dedication of the new building, I resolved to give it to the Lord.' See how carefully the Lord kept this gold piece those two years, to be given now in our great need! 'How manifold are thy mercies!'"

"OCT. 17. But for faith in God, I should be overwhelmed. Never have I needed funds more, never have I had less. The plumbing-bill for work done in the new house is yet to come in, the furnace not yet ordered, and the winter's coal not in. I have told the Lord of all this, and I am patiently waiting. 'Rest in the Lord, and wait patiently for him.' Resting in the Lord, — oh, what comfort!"

"OCT. 21. The gifts of to-day have been two pairs woollen drawers, and shirts, but no money. I cannot but record the trial of faith in my own personal matters. I have drained my purse so low that I am unable to get in my winter coal, and am also obliged to deny myself many things necessary to my comfort. I presume many would call me foolish because I did not keep my money instead of giving it away, then I should not now be in need. Yet I have not the least regret, but wish I had thousands to return to the Lord. The promise is, 'Trust in the Lord, and do good; so shalt thou dwell in the land, and verily thou shalt be fed.' With such a promise, how can I doubt but that, if I use the means God gives me, he will supply my need in return? 'Delight thyself also in the Lord; and he shall give thee the desires of thine heart.' "

"OCT. 23. Fifty cents have been given to-day. I was asked this evening, by a friend, if I did not get discouraged in view of the large need and the small receipts. I answered, 'Not in the least. The Lord is not slack concerning his promise, but in his own time will supply all our need.' After the month's bill was paid, which was the pay of the matron and nurses, I had less than fifteen dollars for the daily expenses : yet all things needed have been as carefully provided as if there were thousands of dollars in the treasury. The matron never knows whether there is a large amount on hand, or not; for the reason, that, if she knew that funds were low, she might be tempted (and rightly too) to economize, while it is my wish that all should be bountifully dealt with, and I see that this plan is always carried out. I have not the least fear for the present or future. I feel and know that this is the Lord's work; and, with such promises as these, how can I doubt?"

"Nov. 1. The month closed yesterday, after many trials of faith; yet the Lord was gracious, and we lacked nothing. Each need was supplied, not by begging for the work, but in simple faith going and telling Jesus. Twenty dollars came in this afternoon. The month commences with but five dollars in my purse. 'Thanks be unto God, which always causeth us to triumph in Christ.' "

"Nov. 3. The Lord's name be praised! 'Because thy loving kindness is better than life, my lips shall praise thee.' 'Because thou hast been my help, therefore in the shadow of thy wings will I rejoice.' This afternoon I received a note from a friend, with one hundred and thirty-five dollars enclosed. May the Lord's blessing rest upon the donor!"

"Nov. 22. After paying for groceries needed at the Home, I find I have but sixty-five cents in the world. Dear reader, please consider for one moment: here are upwards of twenty people daily supported by the Lord. Although our funds are reduced so low, yet our heavenly Father brings home to my heart the preciousness of his promise, 'Thou wilt keep him in perfect peace, whose mind is stayed on thee, because he trusteth in thee.'"

"Nov. 23. Knowing that the wages of two of the 'help' were due this morning, I prayed the Lord to send me the amount by nine o'clock, the hour for visiting the Home. At five minutes before nine, the sum came in; after paying the wages, I have left twenty-one cents. While at the Home, a visitor gave me one dollar. Soon after, the matron asked for money to buy some flour; I handed her the dollar: thus the Lord cares for each *moment*, as well as each day."

During the last of the month some "large gifts" were received, — that is to say, large for that "day of small things, — and at its close the Doctor's cash-account shows a balance in hand of sixty-one dollars and forty-three cents; of which he writes: —

"I thank the Lord for this balance, for the expenses of last month were upwards of a hundred dollars more than receipts. The reader will please remember, that on the first day of the month after the monthly bills were paid, it left only five dollars in the treasury; yet see how bountifully the Lord has cared for us! Truly his promises are Yea and Amen."

One striking incident during this autumn is the record: "I am earnestly praying for means to purchase a furnace, for we cannot receive patients into the new house until it can be warmed." A few days later, he records with delight, that a friend, of his own accord, made inquiry as to the heating of the new house, and, finding there was no provision for it, ordered a furnace put in at his own expense, though he did not know how low were the funds in the treasury of the Home.

The matter of the Reports again and again appears in the Doctor's journal. At one time he was so troubled in mind, that he ordered the printer to stop work on them; but was re-assured by a letter proposing to make a donation, but wishing first to see a report of the work: he therefore directed the printer to proceed. When the Report was printed, he committed it especially to God; sent the first copy to his mother, who had taught him to pray, "Give us this day our daily bread;" and scattered the rest as widely as possible, fully satisfied that God approved of sending forth this account of his faithfulness and goodness. From the first, the Annual Report proved to be a very efficient piece of spiritual literature, as well as a means of promoting gifts to the Home. Here are some of the acknowledgments of the receipt of the Report, and of the blessing it brought.

DEC. 12, 1865.

DR. CULLIS.

Dear Sir, — Please accept my thanks for the Report.

I think nothing except the words of inspiration has ever more interested me than the history. It is news from near home, and so full of Christ. Indeed, it is a light shining on the narrow path leading past by the Great Rock; and though it is far ahead, it helps my feeble vision, and makes me stronger for the march. God bless you for giving it to the world !

The institution appears to me like a great fountain of good, sending out streams in every direction; and not the least of its blessings is the good it does the donors, those that give for Christ's sake. Such a fine opportunity to invest in the funds of the home government, "the land beyond the sin" !

"DEC. 23. A lady in speaking to me of the Report this afternoon said, that, owing to a severe affliction, she had lost her faith in special prayer, and had only used the Lord's Prayer until she read the Report; when the Lord blessed it to the *renewing* of her faith, and she had again commenced to take God at his word, and pray for all things."

At another time he writes : —

"Yesterday I learned that a man was brought to Christ by reading the Report; he has since made an open confession of the saving grace of the blood of Jesus. I praise God for this; and I thank him that he gave me grace to publish the book, when my heart was sinking within me for fear of man."

"JAN. 19. In the evening an old man called at my door, and, on being told that I was out, handed the attendant a dollar, saying, 'Tell the Doctor this is for the Home, from an old sailor who has read his Report.' May God bless him ! "

"JAN. 31. This morning a gentleman called to see me about the work. As I was not at home, he left word for me to call at his house, which I did this afternoon; when he told me some one had given him a Report, which he had read with great interest, saying, ' It is the most wonderful book I have ever read.' After some inquiries about the work, he handed me fifty dollars, saying he wished me to consider him an annual contributor, and requested that a Report might be sent him every year. May the Lord bless him ! Oh, how rejoiced I am, that my Father is honored by this little book ! "

" FEB. 10. I am now praying for the means to issue a second edition of the Report, as the first is nearly exhausted. A note was received from a lady in a neighboring town, from which I make the following extract : —

" ' I can see the influence of your Reports upon our praying circle of ladies ; their interest in spiritual things seems increasing, and their desires for an outpouring of God's Spirit upon us.' "

" FEB. 21. This afternoon a gentleman from the West, who is in this city collecting money for a benevolent work in his own city, called on me, saying he had seen one of the Reports at a friend's ; at the same time adding, as he handed me a little roll of bills, ' I must take some stock in your work.' I thanked him and our heavenly Father for this offering. How can I doubt the Lord's hand in this ? a man who is in this city for the purpose of raising funds for a benevolent institution hundreds of miles away, gives me twenty-five dollars out of his own purse ! "

And now comes the answer to his prayer mentioned in his entry of Feb. 10, leaving no room for doubt as to the mind of the Lord upon this point.

" FEB. 28. This morning a dear friend of mine gave me five hundred dollars. As he handed me this amount, I asked him how it should be used ; whether towards a new building, to pay for the present buildings, the general expenses, or for the printing of another edition of the Report, the first being nearly exhausted, — all of which are subjects of daily prayer. He replied, ' Use it as you please.' I replied, ' I would much rather you should designate,' when he asked which object I preferred. This I refused to answer, silently asking God to guide the decision. He replied, ' I give it for the printing of the Report.' I have been praying for many days for the means to print a new edition. See how carefully the Lord supplies all our need at the right moment! The Reports were nearly gone, the demand for them still as great as at first, with no money to print more, when the Lord inclines the heart of this dear friend to give the required sum. ' They that trust in the Lord shall be as mount Zion, which cannot be moved, but abideth forever.' "

In the light of this Divine leading, and against the dark background of temptation in respect to publishing a Report, the real object of the Lord in calling his servant into this work begins to be dimly visible. It was not merely as a charity for the relief of suffering bodies, but more as a soul-hospital, and still more as a great object-lesson of faith which should stir and stimulate the latent or sluggish faith of the Church in the practical reality of the promises of God. The fact that there are many portions of the Scriptures which are symbolic and figurative, and are to be understood in a spiritual and not in a literal sense, was crippling the power of Christians to a fearful degree. The craze for spiritualizing every thing in the word of God appears to be a cunning inspiration of the father of lies, with a view to destroying its practical value ; and so fully had it possessed the minds of the mass of so-called believers, that they actually thought it presumption to take and use the Divine promises relating to temporal things, just as they are given. Some discount must always be made; some limit must be set, to reduce the promise to lowest terms in point of time or extent of application; something must be allowed for margin all around the plainest offer of gifts and powers, — until a simple, downright, practical reliance on God to do just as he says he will had come to be regarded as extravagant and fanatical. Within the twenty years since this system of faith homes and schools and missions was first established, there has been a marked uplifting of the faith of the Church at large, not only in respect to temporal but also in respect to spiritual gifts promised by our Lord in his Gospel. And, looking back over this term of rapid progress on the line of taking God at his word, it seems as if this revival of primitive faith must have been his chief and ultimate purpose in calling the Consumptives' Home and all its associated charities into existence. In this respect, vastly more than in all the others put together, the work has been a success.

The blessing that began at the first to attend the work, in the way of bringing souls to Christ, is manifest throughout the records of all these years. Thus on March 31, 1866, Dr. Cullis writes : —

"Upon this, the last morning of the month, I would lift up my heart in thankfulness to God, for the blessings with which he has crowned our labors. During the month, six souls have found peace in Christ, while all our need has been supplied. 'I love the Lord, because he hath heard my voice and my supplications. Because he hath inclined his ear unto me, therefore will I call upon him as long as I live.'"

From the earlier records, the following cases of conversion are taken to show how the Lord used the Home as a second "holy of holies," where not the priest alone, but people of every sort, — sinners as well as saints, — might come into the immediate presence of the blessed God our Saviour.

On the 12th of March, 1866, after recording a gift from the Mount-Vernon Church Sunday school, the Doctor goes on to say, —

"I have a still greater reason to rejoice to-night, in that another soul has been born again. A poor colored man, who has been with us about five weeks, and is now near his end, has this day found Jesus a precious Saviour. Yesterday he was in agony of mind : to-day he says, 'I am so happy, I could fly.'"

"MARCH 13. How near and precious the Lord has been to-day ! Another poor sufferer is rejoicing to-night. For many weeks she has been seeking Jesus ; she would read her Bible in bed, and pray for pardon : but the faith to believe was needed, and for many days she has been groping in darkness. On asking her each morning if there was peace, she replied, 'No.' But this afternoon the Holy Spirit entered into her heart, and her countenance was radiant with joy unspeakable. Although very low, yet she wished all who were able to leave their beds to come to her. She desired even the domestics might be called ; and as they came, and stood around her bed, she told them of her happiness, and urged those unconverted to come to Christ. She told them that the Lord had stretched down his hand, and pulled her out of hell. To-night she grasped my hand, and looking up said, 'O Doctor, I am so happy! I can die now, I want to go,' and inquired how long she could live. 'Only a little while,' I replied. 'I long to go,' she said. The whole house seems alive at the great manifestation of the Holy Spirit.

"The third one of the three mentioned as unconverted asked me this morning to pray with him; said he wished to give his heart to Christ, but says, 'I am such a great sinner, God cannot forgive me.' After leaving the bedside of the woman who was so happy, I went to his room; and, on asking him how he felt, he replied, 'Most dead, Doctor.' — 'But have you found Christ?' — 'No.' — 'Why not?' — 'I am looking for some great change, but it does not come.' I told him to look for nothing, but simply to cast himself upon the mercy of his Saviour. I asked him, 'Do you repent of your sins?' — 'Yes.' — 'Have you asked God to forgive you?' — 'Yes, many times.' — 'And don't you think that he *has* forgiven you?' — 'No, I feel that I am too great a sinner to be forgiven.' — 'Then you don't believe the Lord's word, for he has promised to forgive *all* who truly come unto him. Do you realize this, that you are doubting God's word?' He looked up; and, fixing his eyes on me, his whole countenance changed, lit up with an expression that told in plainer language than his simple utterance, 'I do believe.' Oh the joy and peace of a sin-washed soul! My own heart is full to overflowing."

"MARCH 14. The poor girl who was so happy yesterday is happier to-night, she having entered the mansions prepared for those who love God. She died at six o'clock. The man who last night gave his heart to Christ died this afternoon. Some one asked him if he had found his Saviour. He could not speak, but smiled and nodded assent. This morning he said he was happy and at peace."

"APRIL 1. Sunday. I have had such a feast, and such a sense of the Lord's nearness, that to his glory I desire to record the joy that fills my soul. I found a new patient that has been with us but a short time, and who came without any hope in Christ, feeling that her sins were forgiven, and she washed clean by Jesus' blood. On going to the men's room, I spoke to one for whom I have prayed and to whom I talked for many weeks. I said to him, 'How thankful we ought to be for such a beautiful morning, the day on which our Saviour rose from the dead!' I then said, 'If you could know how anxious I am that you should give your heart to Christ, and how long and earnestly I have prayed for you, I know you would think more about it.' To my surprise, he confessed that he was a sinner, and that he had been praying for pardon. Never before would he acknowl-edge that he was a sinner or needed forgiveness.

"On the day that the dying girl requested that all in the house might come to her bedside, when she told them of her joy, and urged all to put on Christ, this young man left the room, saying, 'There is a reality in religion that I never saw before;' and from that time he became more thoughtful, though saying nothing until this morning. I asked him if he felt that the Lord had answered his prayer, and that his sins were forgiven. His eye lit up as he said. 'I *do* feel that I am forgiven.'

" I thank God for the conversion of this young man, who has so long withstood the influences of the Holy Spirit. By the grace of God, I can now make the record, that all the patients have given their hearts to Christ. There have been eight conversions in three weeks. 'What shall I render unto the Lord for all his benefits unto me?'"

" MAY 9. My heart is full of gratitude to God for his many mercies. Greater joy I could not have than to record God's goodness in bringing two more souls out of darkness into light. They are two young men who entered the Home about a week ago unconverted, but this morning both told me they had given their hearts to Christ. This did so rejoice my heart, that I could not praise God enough. 'Oh, magnify the Lord with me, and let us exalt his name together.'"

"JUNE 10. This morning, as I went from bed to bed, I talked to each of the patients of the love of Jesus. This is my frequent habit, but to-day I felt a greater need of earnestness, as we have four unconverted with us ; one a poor woman, near her end, and so hardened that she will not listen, or when she does it is only to scoff, and say she don't want to hear any thing about it. She has often promised to pray for pardon ; but when I asked her this morning if she had, she said, 'No.' I urged her not to put it off too long. It will be too late soon. Another said she wished to be a Christian, and promised she would pray for a new heart. The others say they want to be cleansed. May the Lord give to each a new heart, and put a new spirit within them ! "

"JUNE 11. The Lord's name be praised ! One of the four mentioned as unconverted told me this morning that he had given his heart to Christ."

"JUNE 15. To the glory of God I am permitted to record the conversion of another patient ; not one of the number mentioned before, but one who has since come in. Another patient entered yesterday, and she has no hope in Christ. May the Lord give her a heart to love him ! "

"JUNE 16. I have been much exercised for several days in behalf of one of the patients, who can live but a short time, and is without a comforting ray of hope to cheer her dying hour and to give her a safe entrance into the kingdom. I have often plead with her, and she has been especially prayed for ; but as yet her heart seems not in the least softened. She will not speak upon the subject, and refuses to answer my questions put to her in regard to her soul. Yesterday I found her so low, I told her she could not remain with us long, and asked if she were going to die in that manner. She replied, 'No.' — 'But you have no time to lose.' I spoke of the love of Jesus, and asked her if she would not pray for pardon, when she promised she would. On asking her this morning, if she had kept her promise, she would not reply."

"JUNE 19. 'Blessed be the Lord, who daily loadeth us with benefits, even the God of our salvation.' On going to the bedside of the poor woman mentioned yesterday, I asked her if she had prayed. No answer. I then said, 'I am more anxious for your soul than your body. Won't you pray?'—'Yes.' I then talked to her of the love of Christ, and of her nearness to eternity, and said the whole household were praying for her. Soon tears filled her eyes, and coursed down her cheeks; and she exclaimed, 'Lord, forgive me my sins for Christ's sake!' Tears continued to flow, while she told me that she did repent, and again exclaimed, 'Lord, forgive me my sins for Christ's sake!' With a heart filled with gratitude, as she grew calmer, I left her, praying that she might have 'perfect peace.'"

"JUNE 21. On going to the bedside of the patient mentioned above, she exclaimed, 'O Doctor, I am so happy! I feel now that I am ready to say, The Lord's will be done, to get well or to die; I feel that all, all my sins are forgiven.' I replied, 'I am very thankful; but why did you not give your heart to Christ before, when we have been pleading with you for so long?'—'I don't know; I was as hard as a stone.' I cannot praise the Lord enough for this woman's conversion. She is the one mentioned some days since as a scoffer."

For a period commencing in the autumn of the third year, the Rev. Dr. Boardman, in his "Faith Work," makes the following compilation from the journal of the Home:—

"'OCT. 27. It was refreshing this morning to hear one of the poor sick ones say that he felt his sins were forgiven. For two months I have prayed earnestly for this young man. Thanks be to God, we can now rejoice together.'

"'Nov. 4. "Oh, give thanks unto the Lord, for he is good, for his mercy endureth forever."'"

" 'This morning a patient near unto death told me that Jesus was her all in all. Oh the joy that filled my heart, to know that another soul was rejoicing! Blessed Jesus! His blood cleanseth from all sin.'

" 'Nov. 26. Yesterday twenty dollars were given. The Lord gave us a greater blessing than a gift of money this morning, when his Holy Spirit filled the heart of one poor sufferer, who entered the Home about a week ago without a hope in the blessed Jesus, but who now says, "I feel that the Lord has taken a great burden from my heart, and in its place given me peace through my dear Saviour." '

" At that date Dr. Cullis was able to record the fact that the Home then had in it, as patients, *not one soul unreconciled to God.* Nor was salvation confined to the patients : all who came within the sacred influence of the work were affected by it, and touched by the Spirit.

" Dec. 11, the journal says, —

" 'A young man who has been employed in the Home told me this morning he had given his heart to Christ. "Unto thee, O Lord, do I lift up my soul." '

" Others, meanwhile, having been received as patients, the journal says, —

" 'Jan. 14. The best news of yesterday was that one poor patient, who, previous to entering the Home, had been for years an intemperate man, and whose disease was probably induced by liquor, told me he had given his heart to Jesus. There are three others seeking the pearl of great price. May they cherish these strivings of the Spirit! They who seek *shall* find !'

" 'Jan. 19. One more soul is rejoicing in Jesus.'

" 'Jan. 25. Two more souls have confessed Christ, feeling that all their sins are washed away in his most precious blood.'

" 'Feb. 25. This morning a young man at the Home, who has lived without Christ in the world, told me rejoicingly that he had now the assurance of sins forgiven, *all washed in that most precious blood.*'

"'MARCH 4. Yesterday another of the patients told me that she was rejoicing in Jesus. When she entered the Home, a little more than a week ago, she had no hope; but to-day the joy that overspread her countenance, as she spoke of the blessed new birth, told more plainly than words of the perfect trust in a living Saviour. Another, lately converted, says, "It doesn't hurt so much to cough, now that Jesus is with me."'

"'MARCH 7. The best gift of yesterday was a new heart to one of our patients.'

"'MARCH 9. One patient more has confessed Christ as her living Saviour.'

"'APRIL 4. It rejoices my heart to record the witness of one more repentant soul, to the power of forgiveness and love as it is in Jesus.'

"'APRIL 17. Another patient rejoices in the new-born hope of salvation through our Lord Jesus Christ.'

"'MAY 25. Yesterday's gift was a new heart to one of our sick ones.'

"'MAY 27. A young man is rejoicing to-day in Jesus.'

"'JUNE 11. The Lord has answered prayer in the conversion of another of the inmates. His be the glory!'

"'JULY 22. One more soul rejoicing in Jesus.'

"The final record of conversions during the year occurs on the twenty-fourth day of September, the last week of the year, and three days only before the dedication day, when the Children's Home was publicly recognized as the Lord's. The Doctor's words are, 'With thanks to God, I record the conversion of two more of our sick ones.'

"In closing this remarkable record [says Dr. Boardman], the reflection comes: What if in every church and every household in Christendom there should be the same dependence upon God, the same simple trust in Jesus, and the same following of the Spirit? Would not the Lord add unto them daily such as should be saved? Would not the earth soon be full of the glory of the Lord?"

At another period, after special prayer for the out-pouring of the Spirit, Dr. Boardman collates and condenses the journal thus : —

"'OCT. 14. Precious news to-day! A soul rejoicing in Jesus, who entered about a week ago.

"'NOV. 22. The Lord has revealed his nearness to-day, in the conversion of two of our poor sufferers.

"'JAN. 16. A glorious gift to-day, — a new heart to one of the patients.

"'MARCH 27. Two.

"'MARCH 28. I rejoice to-night over another.

"'APRIL 24. Two.

"'JUNE 9. One.

"'JUNE 29. Three.

"'JULY 22. One.

"'AUG. 29. Two.

"'SEPT. 12. One.

"'SEPT. 20. One.'

"These, probably, were not all. Yet these are the recorded ones with their dates. Again, as in former years, it was true that not one died in the Home, or went out from it partially or wholly cured, without good hope in the Lord Jesus."

The second year of the record closes Sept. 27, 1866. The figures, which in this case form so small a proportion of the history of this wonderful work, are as follows : —

"Number of patients at the beginning of the year, nine.

"Admitted during the year, seventy-nine.

"Total, eighty-eight.

"Discharged by being provided for by friends, or for other causes, twenty-two.

"Relieved, thirteen.

"Cured, nine.

"Died, each with a hope in Christ, twenty-nine.

"Now remaining in the Home, fifteen.

"Whole number cared for since the opening of the Home, one hundred and thirteen.

"In answer to prayer, the Lord has given in cash, for the daily expenses, six thousand nine hundred and fifty dollars and fifty-five cents. All of this has been expended, leaving no balance in the treasury.

"There has been given towards the payment of the buildings, one thousand one hundred and ninety-four dollars and thirteen cents. With this sum, and a transfer from the cash-book, we were enabled to pay the balance of the mortgage on House No. 6. House No. 4 is still unpaid for.

"There has also been given towards the erection of a building, one hundred and fifty-eight dollars and fifty-two cents; making in all a total of eight thousand two hundred and ninety-three dollars and ten cents.

"*In answer to prayer, the Lord has given us, since the work commenced, the sum of fourteen thousand two hundred and nine dollars and thirty-eight cents.*"

The *number* of gifts during the year was very large, showing a widening of the interest taken in the Home, and giving constant proof of the good-will both of God and men: the *amount* was often far below the necessities of the case, but small gifts appear to have been received with hearty thanksgiving as well as large ones. For instance, the receipts for one day were "thirteen cents;" for another, "five cents;" for another, "one cent;" for another, "one newspaper;" for another, "a box of pins," — this last being the proceeds of a pin-fair held by some little girls, in aid of the child-patients at the Home, — but they are each recorded in the Doctor's journal as a token of love from the Lord. Even these trifling gifts serve a very important purpose; namely, keeping up the unbroken succession of daily benefactions, so that not one day passed without a tangible proof that God was mindful of his servant, and of those whom he had undertaken to provide for in his Lord's name. For the month of July, the expenses were over three hundred dollars more than the receipts; while of the month of August the Doctor writes : —

"The expenses of last month far exceeded the gifts, yet the Lord graciously cared for us so that all bills have been paid.

"I have repeatedly been asked such questions as these: How much is this a work of faith? Have not you a fund for the support of the work? Have not you means to fall back upon in case of need? I can only reply, that we have only what the Lord gives us. Whether it is donations, or whether he permits me to earn it, it is all his. We then fall back upon Him who hath so carefully supplied all our need, and tell him that all is gone that he has given ; and he never fails to answer the call."

During this year, Dr. Cullis, feeling assured of the large and long success of this work of faith, made provision for the property thereof to pass into the hands of trustees at his death. Later, as will be seen, he made over the entire establishment into the hands of an incorporated board of trust, reserving to himself, with their full consent, the sole use and control thereof during his lifetime, and the privilege of appointing his successor if he should so desire. In this way was avoided, on the one hand, the appearance of a possible personal advantage from the property; and, on the other, the embarrassments arising from a divided responsibility, by means of which so many charitable institutions have become occasions of sharp contention among their directors, and some have even been crippled and ruined.

CHAPTER IV.

STEP BY STEP.

"I have prayed for thee, that thy faith fail not."

SO narrow were the straits to which Dr. Cullis was reduced at the beginning of the third year, that an intimate friend, knowing something of the state of affairs, urged him to abandon the work; saying, "It is not your duty to suffer to take care of other people." To this he only replied, "Stand still, and see the salvation of God."

The third year opened (so his journal says) "without a dollar in the world." At another time he was unable to send a letter to England, for want of money to pay the postage. Once and again, in order to pay the wages of domestics, or meet the necessities of patients, he sold precious keepsakes, which, he says, "no money would have tempted me to part with under any other circumstances."

On the 5th of November, the inmates of the Home were thrown into consternation by the discovery that House No. 6 was on fire. A spark from a neighbor's chimney had lodged in the eave-trough, and the roof was nearly burned off before the fire was extinguished. The inmates took refuge in House No. 4, and afterwards in the house below; the Home being drenched with water, as well as unroofed by fire.   On Nov. 6 the Doctor writes:—

"The day commenced with hardly a dollar, and one house open to the sky."

And is he *now* ready to give up the work?

Not at all.   In the midst of this calamity we find him recording his purpose to open another Home,—a place where the children of poor patients might be received and cared for while their parents were under treatment, and where they might be brought up for the Lord in case the parent should die.   This is the way he talks about it:—

"Nov. 7.   'Fear thou not, for I am with thee; be not discouraged, for I am thy God; I will strengthen thee; yea, I will help thee; yea, I will uphold thee with the right hand of my righteousness.'

"How *can* I fear when God says, 'I AM WITH THEE,' 'I WILL help thee,' and 'I WILL uphold thee'?   I pray the reader to notice that all though God's holy word it is always '*I will.*' This thought has been suggested on account of the anxiety frequently expressed by friends, concerning the additional work in contemplation, viz., the home for the children; they fearing that the contributions will fail to support both institutions.   My reply is: The Lord hath commanded us, 'Open thy mouth wide, and I *will* fill it.'   Shall *I* limit *his* power? are not 'all things possible with God'?   When he says, 'Ask, and ye shall receive,' shall I question whether this means little or much?

When the promise is, 'All things whatsoever ye shall ask in prayer, *believing*, ye shall receive,' shall I doubt? God forbid !

    " ' Defend the poor and fatherless.'

    " Has not the Lord ordered me to do this, at the same time telling me to 'have faith in God'? Believing this desire to serve Him in accordance with His word is from the Holy Spirit, I *know* He will provide."

Through all these sore trials, the Doctor was true to his purpose not to ask for money of any one but God. This would have seemed, in the judgment of human sagacity, an opportune occasion for publishing special appeals for charity. But this man did not forget that the most charitable Person in the world was the One who had ordered the opening of the Home, and whose resources comprised both the heavens and the earth : therefore, being now in need of charity, he carried his case to Charity himself. And not in vain ; for He, who holdeth the hearts of all men in his hand, moved some of them to help his servant out of this peril by fire and water. The Brokers' Board of Boston sent him five hundred dollars ; a member of Congress sent him ten ; two friends in Europe sent twenty-five ; a little boy sent ten cents ; and some more little girls held another pin-fair, and sent another package of pins ; while a certain young man, hearing of the misfortune, instead of going to the opera, sent the Doctor the price of his ticket. From the manner of all these entries, it is difficult to tell which gift was received with the greatest pleasure.   Perhaps the pins and the opera-ticket-money represented quite as much love and self-denial as any of the larger benefactions which now began to flow in upon him.   In twelve days' time the scattered flock was brought home again ; money came to pay the workmen : and this deliverance from trouble gave him a new impetus towards the cherished project of still further enlarging the Consumptives' Home, as well as of opening the orphanage, both of which additions to the enterprise were pressingly required in view of applications constantly refused for want of room.

His journal (which is the basis of this volume) often mentions regretfully that such and such applications were refused "for want of room," but it does not appear that any applicant was ever turned away on account of the want of funds.   The visible treasury was often empty, but the invisible treasury was always known to be full ; drafts by faith, according to the promises, were always sure to be honored in good time if not always at sight : therefore the doors of the Home were always open to God's poor sufferers without, unless they were by necessity closed on account of the number of just such poor sufferers within.

By slow degrees the truth dawned upon the Doctor's mind, — which seldom dawns at all upon the minds of ordinary "believers," — that it does not cost the Owner of the universe any more to give his children money than to give them any thing else ; nor does he value large sums any higher than small sums, — money, indeed, being one of the very cheapest things which he has to give away. It must be that the Church has been misled, in this respect, by the common opinion of the world. Money, says the world, is the best thing to have, the hardest to get, and the easiest to lose: and the slow faith of semi-worldly Christians is apt to be hindered by the conclusion that this is also God's idea of money; that while spiritual and eternal treasures may be had for the asking, — being cheap and plenty with the Lord, — actual cash is held by him with a tighter grasp; that only by much urging can he be persuaded to give it, and then only in moderate sums to meet the sharp necessities of the saints. Pray for pardon and grace, but make or beg the money for yourself! If such institutions as the Consumptives' Home accomplish nothing else than to break down this over-estimate of the value of money as compared with the other wealth of our Father in heaven, they will have wrought incalculable good. Is God any richer for hoarding his money? What other profitable use can he make of it if he does not give it away?

The need of larger accommodations having been mentioned in the second Annual Report, and special prayer having been made therefor, gifts were occasionlly received "for the new building," "for enlargement," "for the new Home," etc., as if it were taken for granted that the new Home was about to be built;

although the donors must have known that Dr. Cullis was hard pressed for the means to maintain the work at even its present extent. On Nov. 29 (Thanksgiving Day), the sum of one hundred dollars was left at his residence, by some unknown person, with a reference to Hag. i. 8; which reads, "Go up to the mountain, and bring wood, and build a house; and I will take pleasure in it, saith the Lord." Then follow several other entries in the journal, of more than usual interest, in which appears the Doctor's sense of a Divine leading to the enlargement of the Home for Consumptives, and the founding of a new branch of the work, — the Children's Home.

"DEC. 4. This noon, a package was handed me: 'Please find enclosed eight hundred dollars to help you bear the expenses of the Consumptives' Home.' I can only thank the Lord, for the donor's name was withheld. This large gift caused no surprise; for God says, 'Open thy mouth wide, and I will fill it.' 'Be glad and rejoice, for the Lord will do great things.' Just as the above was written, a 'thanksgiving offering of one hundred dollars, twenty-five cents,' was received from members of Emmanuel Church.

"'Be glad, then, ye children of Zion, and rejoice in the Lord your God.'"

"DEC. 5. A gentleman called at the Home, bringing three barrels of potatoes, the product of a piece of ground set apart for the Home; leaving no name by which to identify a gift at once so considerate and generous."

"DEC. 6. 'I will mention the loving-kindness of the Lord and the praises of the Lord, according to all that the Lord hath bestowed on us.'

"This morning while at the Home, a gentleman called ; said he was authorized to give me some money 'from a Bostonian in London,' at the same time handing me a check for one thousand dollars. He declined giving me the donor's name, but wished me to acknowledge it in 'The Transcript.' "

"DEC. 7. 'A Friend' sends twenty dollars, with these words : 'For our blessed Saviour's sake.' By the goodness of God I have had money enough to take up the mortgage held by the former owner of House No. 4 ; there now remains thirty-five hundred to pay to the Five Cents Savings Bank."

"DEC. 10. The gift on the 8th was twenty dollars. Yesterday (Sunday) a gentleman who attended service at the Home gave me twenty dollars ; the clergyman who officiated, ten more. This morning's mail brought from a dear friend in England one hundred dollars. This noon a check was sent for twenty-five dollars, also twenty-one for the new building. This eve a gentleman called, and gave me twenty-five dollars from 'a friend.'

"I was much pleased to learn that twelve dollars, which I found in the box at the Home, a few days ago, was put there by one of the patients. It was all the money he had. He told his nurse that 'it ought to be given to the institution, for if he got well he could earn more ; if he should not recover, he would not need it.' "

"DEC. 11. The Lord sent to-day from Amherst ten dollars for the new building. From a friend, fifty.

"A young man who has been employed at the Home for several months told me this morning he had given his heart to Christ. 'Unto thee, O Lord, do I lift up my soul.' "

"DEC. 13. This noon I earnestly called upon God about the Children's Home. In less than half an hour the following note was left at my door, with thirty-eight cents : 'DR. CULLIS : Please accept this small offering as a poor sick widow's mite. It is little pieces I have had for twenty years. I know it is a small gift, but the Lord will not despise it. I have great reason to bless his holy name, that he has not cast me off forever. . . . Use this for the Children's Home.'"

"DEC. 22. The Lord's name be praised! A little girl held a fair at Dorchester a week ago, for the benefit of the work; and to-day sent me the proceeds, one hundred and fifty-seven dollars and seventy-five cents. A lady sent me this twenty-five dollars as a Christmas gift. Another, fifty dollars.

"We were obliged to refuse a poor man admittance to-day, as our male wards are full and the attics also.

"This afternoon little Eddie, who had a dollar given to him for Christmas, sent it to me. God bless him!"

"DEC. 31. The month closes with donations amounting in cash to four thousand three hundred and twenty-six dollars and nineteen cents.

"Expenses, including seventeen hundred and fifty dollars paid on the mortgage, twenty-four hundred and twenty-six dollars and forty-eight cents.

"Balance on hand, eighteen hundred and ninety-nine dollars and seventy-one cents."

"JAN. 4, 1867. It is with sorrow I am daily turning from our doors the sick who apply for admittance. God knows this, and will, I am sure, in his own good time, supply a building."

"JAN. 22. A lady called with the proceeds of a children's fair held in Dorchester two or three weeks ago, the amount two hundred and thirty-seven dollars."

"JAN. 23. To-day a lady of education and Christian culture testifies her love for Jesus by offering freely her services, as a mother to the children, as soon as our new Home shall be started. Another encouragement, and proof of our Father's continued care and leading. Following on to know his will, I still continue to use every means to obtain a house for this purpose.

"A lady of this city sends one hundred dollars to-day for the Home. From Dorchester, sixteen dollars fifty cents, further proceeds of the children's fair held in Dorchester some weeks since."

"JAN. 24. 'From a poor widow, who is desirous of doing what good she can, in the service of her Lord and Master,' sixty cents."

"JAN. 25. I received to-day, with thanksgiving, the good news that two more souls have confessed Jesus, feeling that all their sins have been washed away by his most precious blood.

"Five dollars in an envelope, directed to me, were left at my door this afternoon: this amount I have placed towards the Children's Home. I have now for that object five hundred dollars, but as yet have been unable to procure a house. I appropriate no gift for the Children's Home, unless so designated by the donor, or left to be used at my discretion. I would here request all donors, if they have a preference, to express how they wish their gifts appropriated.

"'The Burden-Bearers' of Dorchester have sent a quantity of good things for the comfort of the sick. The Home now contains twenty patients, and all are cared for by the bounty of God."

"FEB. 5. Last evening there was left at my door an envelope directed, 'For Dr. Cullis's Hospital,' which on opening I found to contain a one-hundred-dollar bill. God bless the unknown donor!"

"FEB. 7. Yesterday twenty-five dollars were sent from two persons now in Egypt."

"FEB. 26. A lady left twenty-five dollars for what I am now 'most earnestly praying for;' this is the Children's Home. A friend also gave twenty for the same object.

"My heart aches for the poor people that we are daily obliged to refuse admittance to the Home. We have now twenty-two patients, — two more than our complement; others are waiting. Will the dear reader please consider, here are upwards of thirty people, supported and bountifully cared for by a kind, loving Father, who has promised, if we 'trust in him, we shall not be confounded.' May the Lord increase and make real in every heart an ever-abounding faith! Such the gospel demands; such it promises to bless.

"A colored boy, who was 'born again' a few days since, was baptized this afternoon at his own request."

"FEB. 27. From Bridgewater, one dollar. 'Little Carrie' sends twenty-five cents of her spending-money. Three young ladies in Newton Corner got up a concert, and sent the result, — forty-five dollars. God bless them!

"I have called on parties to-day owning houses in Vernon Street, and pray God that the result may be the enlarging of the Home. At this stage of writing a gentleman calls, bringing a legacy of one hundred dollars, less government taxes, from a lady lately deceased. This is our first legacy. 'Oh that men would praise the Lord for his goodness, and for his wonderful works to the children of men!'"

"MARCH 13. This morning I asked the Lord for large gifts, that the balance on House No. 4 might be paid. Before ten o'clock, a gentleman who has been under my professional care called, and handed me a check for five hundred dollars, saying, 'Take out the amount of your bill, and give the rest to the Home.' My bill was ninety-three dollars, leaving a generous balance for the work. 'God loveth a cheerful giver.'"

"APRIL 9. A lady has manifested her kind interest and zeal for the Home, by undertaking the arduous task of arranging for a concert which is to take place at the Music Hall to-morrow evening. Her efforts have been seconded by the volunteer assistance of all the artists taking part."

"MAY 17. Several days ago I received a part of the proceeds of the concert at Music Hall. I did not record it at that time, as I hoped to obtain the whole amount in a day or two; there is still a small balance to come in. The amount thus far received is ten hundred and forty-three dollars, — the largest gift in cash I have ever received."

" From Wayland, on a piece of paper was written, 'A blind man who heard your Report read sends all he has, five cents.' "

No wonder that the Reports have been so greatly enjoyed: they are fascinating as well as profitable reading to those who are interested in the great things — and not merely in the little things — which mark the daily history of this world. Such facts as these reach away into the heavens. Why should not a story be interesting to God's children when the chief character in it is God himself?

Living by faith in temporal as well as in spiritual things, had been regarded as one of "the lost arts;" and the daily experiences here recorded caused the Reports to be read at first as if they were new editions of the "Book of Wonders." But to Dr. Cullis and his co-laborers such "wonders" have ceased to be wonderful, and have come to be regarded as the normal conditions of a fully consecrated life.

On the 6th of June, 1867, the Lord's time having apparently come for the step, a house for the Orphanage was purchased, — of which further mention will be made in a chapter by itself, — while prayer for means to enlarge the Consumptives' Home was continued with fresh impetus from the evidence afforded by this Divine leading that God was about to open his hand still wider in the bestowment of gifts upon his trusting and trusted servant.

It is not often that one feels like praising the Lord

for an empty purse, though that very emptiness is an opportunity for a fresh blessing in re-filling it ; but on the 6th of July, just a month after the purchase of the first orphanage-house, the Doctor writes thus : —

"To-night, after paying the carpenter for labor in erecting a room over our kitchen and for other repairs, I find the treasury entirely empty. For many months the Lord has blessed us with his bounty, and there has been a surplus, so that we were enabled to pay the mortgage on the building ; but at the close of this day I thank God that our funds are exhausted, for I know he will be glorified thereby."

It was not long after this, that he was obliged to break up his own home, and take his family to a board-ing-house ; his lease of the house having expired, and he having been unable either to renew it, or to find another house in that part of the city where it seemed necessary for him to reside for the sake of being near his large adopted family of invalids and orphans. In this perplexity we find him praying for submission, as if he were not yet wholly proof against the troubles of life ; but a few days later he has been enabled to master even this situation, and to thank God for this trial also, which in due time ended in his securing a larger and better home.

It was during this year that his sister died. She had loved and prayed for the work, and, in those early years of trial and trouble, had done much to strengthen his hands and heart. In this great affliction, as well as in small ones, grace was given him to look upon the heavenly side of the picture, and to say, "God be praised, she rejoices with the saints in light."

On the third anniversary of the opening of the Consumptives' Home, the first house of the Orphanage was dedicated to God, for the worshipful use of sheltering some of his homeless little ones.

The following is the summary of the Report for the third year of the work : —

"Number of patients at the beginning of the year, fifteen.

"Admitted during the year, sixty-six.

"Total, eighty-one.

"Discharged by being provided for by friends, or from other causes, twenty-three.

"Discharged as able to go to work, thirteen.

"Cured, one.

"Died, each with a hope in Christ, twenty-nine.

"Now remaining in the Home, thirteen.

"Whole number cared for since the opening of the Home, one hundred and seventy-nine.

"The Lord has given, in answer to prayer, in cash, for daily expenses, and for payment of buildings, thirteen thousand eight hundred and thirty-four dollars and two cents.

"For the building fund, five hundred and two dollars, ninety-eight cents.

"For the Children's Home, two thousand two hundred and sixty-four dollars, thirty-seven cents.

"For the tract cause, seventy-two dollars, eighty-six cents.

"*For the whole work since its commencement, thirty thousand nine hundred and eighty-three dollars, sixty-one cents.*

"Still I can record, to God's glory, that not a day since the work commenced has he failed to send a gift of some kind. 'I have chosen you, and ordained you, that ye should go and bring forth fruit, and that your fruit should remain ; that, whatsoever ye shall ask the Father in my name, He may give it you.' This precious word of the Lord answers every question concerning the work.

" Our lot at Mount Hope contains twenty-six graves. In the Lord's time we hope each grave will have a simple headstone.

" We have had unmistakable evidence that the Holy Spirit abides with us, for not one patient has died without a hope in a living Saviour. During the year there have been twenty-five conversions. Religious services continue to be held at five P.M. on the sabbath, conducted by different clergymen of the city.

" The Bible-class has been continued at noon, except through the summer."

CHAPTER V.

"At evening time it shall be light."

AMONG the first noticeable incidents of the fourth year, was the receipt of twenty-five dollars from Paris, France; a hundred and fifty dollars from Berlin, Prussia; and five hundred dollars by order of a lady residing in Rosario, Argentine Republic, South America, who had seen a notice of the Consumptives' Home in a newspaper, and thereupon directed her banker in Boston to give that sum on her account if he, on inquiry, found the object a worthy one. Thus widely do the roots of the tree of faith extend, from whose branches God drops down fruit into the lap of his chosen, trustful servants.

On the 10th of October, the Doctor speaks of praying for means to furnish the new Children's Home. During the day a dealer offered to let him have what he required, to be paid for at his convenience; but this he declined with thanks, saying, "I always buy for cash, considering it unscriptural to do otherwise; God's command being, 'Owe no man any thing.'" That very day, while at the Home, a gentleman called to examine the new premises, and handed the Doctor his check for five hundred dollars to be used in furnishing.

The purchase of houses under mortgage has been mentioned ; but the reader will not fail to remember the grounds on which that was done, namely, that the property itself was full security for the debt. But provisions, furniture, and other perishable articles do not afford such security, and, so to speak, carry the debt themselves : therefore the injunction above quoted has been faithfully obeyed in the management of the various departments of this " work of faith."

On Christmas Eve, 1867, commences an account of what, at first, seems a very strange calamity to befall a person in the position of Dr. Cullis. But God has not promised to secure even his most faithful servants against the insecurity of worldly possessions. During the last month of the year, the Doctor had accumulated, from his own professional income and from the surplus of gifts above the daily needs, over three thousand dollars; which he kept in his safe, intending soon to purchase a house in the rear of the Homes, for their still further enlargement. On Christmas Eve, when going to the safe to deposit the gifts of the day, what was his amazement to find every dollar gone !

To a faith untried, a heart only partly consecrated to God, a will not wholly yielded to the Divine will, such a calamity would have been appalling. It is, then, with glad assurance of the sustaining power of faith, that we read the workings of his mind under this sudden blow. He says, — the capitals are his own, — " I am left without a dollar except what has come in to-day. Oh, it is blessed to know and FEEL that the Lord reigns ! The money was his ; and, if he allows it to be diverted from the purposes I intended, I can only say, His will be done. Though 'thieves break through and steal,' if the work is owned of him he will provide."

Within a few days the thief was captured, but not the money. He was a poor lad whom the Doctor had employed for a few months, but had discharged some weeks before the robbery. It would appear that his record had not been good, for he was suspected of the crime. Search was made for him ; and on the 21st of January, having been arrested in New York, with a duplicate key of the safe in his possession, he was brought back to Boston for trial. The two following entries will conclude one side of this painful record : —

" FEB. 14. This morning I was detained at the court-house, by the trial of William, who robbed my safe. The verdict rendered was ' Guilty.' This evening, after paying the expenses for the day, I am entirely without funds.

" Persons who have read the former Reports frequently ask me, if, when I say that ' I am left without a dollar in the world,' it means that I have not a dollar of my own money, or if I refer merely to the Home funds. It means *that I have not a dollar, either belonging to myself or the Home.* My only income is from my profession, and that is always the Lord's. My sole hope is in God, and to him I look for all I receive ; whether it comes in the way of my profession, or as free gifts from his stewards."

"FEB. 15. This morning, knowing that five dollars would be needed to pay a bill at the Home, I asked the Lord to give me that amount before my morning visit. Just before leaving my house, a young man called, and paid five dollars on a bill he was owing. How little he knew that he was the Lord's instrument for relieving my need! Would that I could convince all that love the Lord, of the perfect freedom from anxiety he will give, when we take him at his word, and 'know' that an infinitely rich Father will never fail to supply the laborer in his vineyard! 'They that trust in the Lord shall not be confounded.'"

However wise and cunning the enemy of all righteousness may be, it is evident he does not possess foreknowledge: otherwise he would not have permitted one of his servants to steal that consecrated money. Instead of being hindered in his plans, the Doctor seems to have received a fresh inspiration and impetus of faith and courage; for he presently concluded the purchase of the house in the rear of the Home, and set about uniting it with those on Vernon Street, in such a manner as to give space for a small chapel, besides the additional wards. To make this purchase and the alterations required, would take a much larger sum than that which had been lost; yet with an empty treasury, but a full heart, this irrepressible believer in God pushed on as if he had the thousands already in hand.

And most signally did God honor that faith. Gifts large and small, from far and near, began to come in, together with words of good cheer from friends new and old. Among them was a letter from a sailor, dated at Honolulu, Sandwich Islands, containing ten dollars, and saying : —

"Those blessed Reports of the 'Consumptives' Home,' have strayed out to these Isles of the Pacific. I have been reading one ; and it has refreshed my soul to behold how wonderfully God answers prayer, and crowns with honor and blessing, simple faith. Pray for me. I am a brand plucked from the burning, but

"Yours in the Lord Jesus."

One day a load of provisions was sent, with the following note : —

" DR. CULLIS, — Noticing your recent loss, we thought a barrel of flour might be especially welcome to your Home at this time. Just as we were about putting the flour in the cart, we appealed to a few of our neighbors to increase the gift, and now have the pleasure of asking your acceptance of the following articles from 'Commercial Street.' Five barrels of flour, one barrel of Graham flour, one box corn-starch, three smoked hams, one cheese, two boxes soap, one box starch, one bag buckwheat, one bag crackers, one bundle fish, six dollars cash."

Several fairs and concerts were given in aid of the Home ; a theatrical "benefit" was tendered, and some one proposed to get up a horse-race to help on the good work : but both the race and the theatricals were declined with thanks, though the proof of good-will which they afforded must have been very acceptable.

The crowning gift was from a charity fair held at Horticultural Hall in Boston, which opened on the 24th of February, 1868, and continued a week; the proceeds of which, amounting to five thousand three hundred and ninety-three dollars and sixty cents, were placed in the Doctor's hands. At first he supposed the fair to have been projected in view of his recent heavy loss; but he afterwards learned that it had been in preparation a long time previous to the robbery, whereupon he joyfully records the promise: "And it shall come to pass, before they call I will answer."

In spite of all its distresses, this was, like the preceding ones, a year of substantial and visible growth. The Home which had already filled three houses, two on Willard Street and one on the street in the rear, was still further enlarged by uniting them in one; and on the evening of March 30, 1868, the triple house, with its chapel — which had been secured by joining the L's of the three houses — was dedicated to the service and worship of God, the prayer of consecration being offered by Bishop Eastburn. The Rev. Dr. Huntington in his address called attention to the appropriateness of the arrangements of the Home as now constituted, — wards for the sick on each side, and, in the centre of all, the place of worship, of prayer, and of praise, so that even those confined to their beds of languishing and weakness might still participate in and enjoy the privileges of social worship. "And," said he, "thus is it fitting that it should be, — the place of worship in the *heart* of the whole structure."

Still another token of God's favor marked the history of this fourth year of the work. It had been the wish of the Doctor to provide a place of worship for that part of the city in which the Home was situated, there being neither church nor chapel in the neighborhood. With this view, he purchased a house at the foot of Vernon Street (now re-named Willard Street), and fitted it for public worship ; and on the fourth anniversary. of the opening of the first little Home, Sept. 27, 1868, the Willard-street Chapel was dedicated and opened for divine service.

Thus closes a year of large loss and still larger gain. The summing-up of the Annual Report is as follows : —

"SEPT. 30, 1868. Thus closes our daily record of God's mercies for another year. 'They are new every morning : great is thy faithfulness. The Lord is my portion, saith my soul ; therefore will I hope in him.'

"Number of patients at the beginning of the year, thirteen.

"Admitted during the year, one hundred and fifty-two.

"Total, one hundred and sixty-five.

"Discharged by being provided for by friends, or other causes, sixty-seven.

"Discharged as able to go to work, fourteen.

"Cured, three.

"Died, each with hope in Christ, sixty.

"Number remaining in the Home, twenty-four.

"Whole number cared for since the opening of the Home, three hundred and thirty-one.

" The Lord has given, in answer to prayer, in cash, for daily expenses, and for purchase of two new buildings, seventeen thousand two hundred and three dollars and nineteen cents.

" For the building fund, sixty-four dollars and seventy-eight cents.

" For the Children's Home, two thousand three hundred and thirty-six dollars and ninety-three cents.

" For the tract cause, four hundred and ninety-nine dollars and sixty cents.

" For the whole work, since its commencement, *fifty thousand three hundred and twenty-seven dollars and forty-eight cents.*

"God has not allowed a day to pass, since the beginning of the work, without the assurance of his daily remembrance, in a gift of some kind. Nor has he withheld his Spirit in its quickening power, so that we are assured that every death has proved a triumphant entrance into life everlasting."

CHAPTER VI.

TRIED AND NOT FOUND WANTING.

" Though He slay me, yet will I trust in him."

IF the trial of the fourth year was severe, still more severe was that of the fifth. There was no one great calamity, but such a severe and long-continued pressure, through scarcity of funds, that even the account of it is fit to produce actual anguish of mind. Again and again the last dollar and even the last cent was reached, until it seems, from a human standpoint, that the faith of the Doctor and his little band of helpers must have failed. In view of this state of affairs, it was natural that such questions as these should arise: Have I not overstepped the limit of the promises? Is not this desperate distress a sign that God has forsaken me? Would it not be better to begin to make application to the public directly, instead of depending on God to lead people to send me money? Shall I not utterly lose my health, and perhaps my life, in carrying all these consumptives and orphans on my heart and hands, with all these houses and mortgages weighing me down? Is not this persistent poverty a proof of some error of judg-

ment on my part, respecting the doctrine and application of faith?

To all these questions, there is one common answer:
Those who have cast their burden on the Lord have
no need to carry it themselves. And so it was with
Dr. Cullis, through this year of what would seem
to ordinary believers a period of intolerable distress.
Over and over again he writes it down in his journal,
as if to re-assure himself, and to re-affirm what a casual
reader must think incredible under such circumstances:
"I am at peace;" "My soul rests in God;" "Oh, it *is*
good to trust in the Lord!" Surely this may rightly
be called "the full assurance of faith." At one time,
in his extremity, he petitions the City Government for
an abatement of the taxes on these houses of charity,
and is refused because his institution is not incorporated; at another, he says, "I have two dollars, and
I need two hundred;" at another, he mentions that
he has been obliged to take money set apart for a
building fund, to buy food for his people. In midsummer he fell sick, but rallied again. Once he was unable
to make a large payment when it became due, and was
obliged to endure the agony of a sharp dun, to which
he could only respond by begging for further patience
on the part of his creditor. Before the enlargement
was all paid for, we find him on his knees, crying to
God for money to pay the gas-bill and the water-bill
and the city-tax-bill; and at another time, with empty

treasury and an almost empty larder, he is telling the Lord that the interest on a mortgage is just coming due, and that he has not the money to pay it. There were times when he was not only brought to depend on the Lord for bread day by day, but hour by hour. Here are some of the entries in his journal : —

"JAN. 29, 1869. By the goodness of God, I was this noon enabled to pay thirty-five hundred dollars on the new house ; and to-night I am left penniless, with thirty people at the Home to be cared for, besides my own family, and one thousand dollars more to be paid on the house within a few days ; a large amount also will be needed to meet the expense of altering and connecting the houses."

"FEB. 24. It is now 8.30 A. M. I have but two cents in the world. I have asked the Lord for money to purchase the day's provisions. 'Hear, O Lord, have mercy upon me ; Lord, be thou my helper.' 2.30 P. M. Before nine o'clock A. M., four dollars were received for professional services ; this was not enough : on quitting the house, I left word, if any letters came, to have them sent directly to the Home. While at devotions there, the letters came. The contents of one were five dollars, without a word of comment ; another contained fifty cents, from Wakefield. With two cents added from the box, our dinner was purchased."

"MARCH 2. After purchasing provisions, we were again without funds. We are needing coal for all the houses, to supply seven furnaces, two ranges, and a number of stoves ; and, as we are able to buy only two or three tons at a time, the demand comes often. Being now the first of the month, pay is due the laborers. Gas-bills of one hundred dollars are also due. I can only call upon the Lord, and 'wait patiently for him.'"

"AUG. 17. 8 A. M. I have not a dollar to purchase food

for the day. God's promises are so sweet, I am kept at rest in him. While in prayer for the means needed, the blessed word came home to my soul, 'My God shall supply all your need, according to his riches in glory by Christ Jesus.'"

"AUG. 25. I have been sick for two or three days, and last night remained out of town; this morning was unable, through weakness, to come in before half-past ten. I knew there was no money on hand with which to purchase dinner; but I asked the dear Lord to supply, and was at rest. When I reached the Home, I found seventeen dollars and fifty cents had been sent from Wakefield."

"AUG. 27. By the payment of a bill, dinner was purchased. This afternoon money was needed for groceries. I had not a dollar, when the Lord reminded me to look in the box which stands on my office-table. There I found two dollars. This eve a gentleman of Winchester gave thirty dollars. From Jamaica Plain, ten dollars."

"AUG. 30. This morning I had just one cent. I asked the Lord for the means to purchase dinner. Before going to the Home, a gentleman called, and paid a bill for professional services, of nine dollars. At the Home the matron informed me that the domestics were unwilling to wait any longer for their pay; it has been many weeks now since they were paid, and my custom has been to pay them every week, but for a long time I have only been able to purchase food. I leave the whole matter with the Lord. He 'will provide.'"

"By a sale to-day I have been able to pay seventy dollars to the help. Lord, deliver us from all our indebtedness! 'Lo, this is our God; we have waited for him, and he will save us; this is the Lord; we have waited for him; we will be glad and rejoice in his salvation.'"

That "sale," be it understood, signifies parting with some of the Doctor's own portable objects of value, —

his watch, perhaps, and some furniture from his house, or it may be books from his library. But they all belonged to the Lord before, so there are no complaints made about parting with them at the call of the needs of his suffering ones.

Again he writes, near the close of this year of famine : —

"SEPT. 2. On going to the Home this morning, I had but one dollar ; fifteen cents was taken from the box ; this was all we had to purchase dinner, yet, with what was in the house, none suffered. This afternoon, two dollars have come in for professional services."

"SEPT. 4. This morning there were but fifty cents to purchase food, and to-day is Saturday. On going to the Home, I found in one of the boxes one dollar and sixty cents. It is now 2 P. M., and I am looking to the Lord for deliverance. 3.30 P. M. A friend has just given two dollars ; a friend from Baltimore, Md., fifteen dollars. 'They that trust in the Lord shall not be confounded.' "

"The question arises amid all this trial : Does the Lord mean that this work shall cease? My heart responds : It is all in Thy hands. I am only the instrument, and wait, O Lord, thy will. We have cause for rejoicing in that three souls at the Home have lately found Jesus precious.

"I would here state, that during all our perplexities the patients have been cared for as bountifully as ever, and that none in the house knew but that the treasury contained its thousands. Persons have said, 'Apply to me in your time of need ;' but such a course would conflict with the principles upon which the work was started, — to prove to the world that God would hear and answer prayer, in testimony of his own word, 'According to your faith, be it unto you.' "

The faith thus tried and not found wanting was not
only strengthened, but honored.   During the year two
important additions were made to the Lord's estate on
Willard Street, — the first, a still further expansion of
the Consumptives' Home, by the addition of a fourth
adjoining building ; and the other, the purchase of a
house to be used as a home for the " Deaconesses," as
he now began to call his female helpers, who, in the
name and faith of the Lord, had devoted themselves
to nursing the sick, training the orphans, and doing
city-missionary work, with the Willard-street Chapel
as their centre of operations.   The quadruple house,
with its enlarged chapel in the centre, was dedicated
to God on the 14th of January ; and the Deaconesses'
House, another adjoining dwelling, on the 11th of May,
1869.

Of course these facts indicate either large receipts,
or large debts.   How was the money raised ?

It was not "raised" at all: it came down from
above.   It was sent like the rain and the sunshine, and
from the self-same Hand.   No new plans were tried,
no schemes for money-making were set on foot, no
departure from the established policy of cash purchase
or self-secured investment was made ; but from unknown quarters, and from the fruits of his own professional labor, the Lord gave his servant the power
as well as the heart to keep on building this wonderful
monument, this altar of testimony to the faithfulness

of God.   There was no large gift, — except a thousand
dollars, the proceeds of a fair held by a lady at her
residence in the city, and which came in good time to
meet the mortgage on the fourth house of the Home
at maturity, — but just when the skies were darkest,
the sun broke forth, and often appeared the bow of
promise on the bosom of the passing storm.   He who
tested the faith of his friend Abraham also tested that
of his friend Dr. Cullis ; but he never weighted him
beyond what he was able to carry, as may be known
from the fact that he did not utterly break down, —
though sometimes, in reading the journal of these
days, it seems as if another feather's weight would
crush him.

Good soldiers are not made by feather-beds and
rocking-chairs, but by hard knocks, heavy marching,
and hot fighting.   Thus was this soldier of the Lord
being trained for the post of color-bearer in the advanced line of the army of the coming kingdom.

His little staff of helpers also shared in the lessons
of this school ; and the depth and sincerity of their
devotion appears in the record that some of them
not only freely gave their service without compensation, but also, in the time of sorest need, drew on
their own slender resources, and gave to the Doctor
for his people.   In the Report for the year ending
Sept. 13, 1869, a separate chapter is devoted to the
new Deaconesses' House ; but, as each of these chief

additions henceforth has a separate record, they will
be treated of, each in a chapter by itself.

During this year, also, the tract work — which was
one of the earliest forms of service for Jesus to which
the Doctor devoted himself — came into an organized
existence as "The Willard-street Tract Repository;"
and in the month of April of this year (1869) appeared
the first number of "The Times of Refreshing," a
newspaper enterprise which has been wonderfully
owned and blessed of God, and of which an account
will be given later on.

The Willard-street Chapel, near the cluster of
buildings that now comprised the Home, has also its
place in the Report for 1869; together with the doings
of the Deaconesses, who were assigned to what might
be called parochial visitation.

These five departments of the work — the Consumptives' Home, the Orphanage, the Deaconesses' House
with its training-school for nurses, the Willard-street
Tract Repository, and the Willard-street Chapel, —
may be likened to the fingers of a hand reached up
to heaven for benefactions, and then distributing them
lovingly and freely among God's friendless, neglected,
suffering children. All these works, and many more
besides, are doubtless parts of that "gospel" which the
Son of God brought down from his Father, and committed to the hands of his believing ones, that they
might give it to the poor.

"The poor," as a class, have a vested right in the gospel: if the rich, as a class, have any such right, it does not appear in the Scriptures. Hence, however pleasant it may be to preach the gospel to the rich, the surest and most abundant blessing comes upon those who, like Dr. Cullis and his fraternity, choose their parishes among the poor. Such work implies a basis of self-consecration, without which it does not appear that any professed disciple of Christ, whether priest or layman, ever attained to any knowledge of the heights and depths of the experience of saving grace. These, therefore, are the men and women who are able to teach the mysteries of the kingdom of God.

The summary of the report of the Consumptives' Home for the fifth year ending Sept. 30, 1869, is as follows:—

"Number of patients at the beginning of the year, twenty-four.

"Admitted during the year, one hundred and twenty-two.

"Total, one hundred and forty-six.

"Discharged relieved, forty.

"Discharged not relieved, twenty-one.

"Cured, three.

"Died, fifty-eight.

"Now remaining in the Home, twenty-four.

"Whole number cared for since the opening of the Home, four hundred and fifty-three.

"The Lord has given, in answer to prayer, in cash, during the year, thirteen thousand three hundred and sixty dollars and forty-five cents. *For the Home, since the commencement of the work, forty-seven thousand six hundred and twenty-seven dollars and eighty-five cents.*

" We still trust that every death has been in Christ. Regarding one case only, we cannot express ourselves with certainty ; as this patient entered in a dying state, and in about thirty-six hours passed away. During this time he was too feeble to do more than to say he would ask for pardon through the blood of Jesus.

" With thankfulness we record that God has remembered us daily with a gift of some kind, ever since the opening of the work. Religious services continue to be held in the chapel of the Home, every sabbath afternoon at 5 P.M., conducted by different clergymen.

" The Dispensary for the treatment of out-patients, under the charge of Dr. G. M. Pease, has administered three hundred and eighty prescriptions."

CHAPTER VII.

"A GOOD LAND AND A LARGE."

"For the Lord thy God bringeth thee into a good land."

FOR several years the return of the anniversary of the opening of the Consumptives' Home, which then consisted of but a single house of moderate size, was marked by the opening of some addition thereto; on which account, the 27th of September had come to be known as "Dedication Day." But on the fifth anniversary, instead of the usual feast of dedication, the Doctor. and a few of his confidential helpers held a solemn intercession with God for deliverance out of their distresses.

As the fifth year ended, so the sixth began. For a few weeks longer the trial must go on, perhaps in order to prepare his mind more fully for the great things that were in store for him. On the 6th of October he writes : —

"This noon I had but twenty cents in the world, belonging to myself or any branch of the work. Money was needed to purchase groceries for supper. I asked the Lord to send the amount in season. At three o'clock a messenger from the

Home called for the needed money. Just at the same moment, the mail arrived : the last letter opened contained a check for ten dollars from Dover, N. H. Truly 'they that trust in the Lord shall not be confounded.' "

" OCT. 8. This morning, on going to the Home, I had not a cent. As I reached the door, I lifted up my heart, and asked the Lord to send money before I should leave. Just as I had my hat in hand an hour later, a lady called whom I had not seen for a year, and who could not possibly have known of my pressing need, and gave forty dollars, to be used as I pleased. As all branches were in need, I divided the gift."

Here are two extracts, some days apart, but they may well be placed together : —

" OCT. 5. By those who read the last Report, it will be remembered that the year closed with a thousand dollars due, of the mortgage on the Children's Home. The burden of my prayer this morning was that the Lord would send this amount ; and, while in prayer, the sweet assurance, ' According to your faith be it unto you,' filled me with perfect peace, so that, every time I have thought of the matter this afternoon, there has been a flood of joy filling my soul. I knew the dear Lord was about to deliver."

" Nov. 12. During the week kind friends have held a fair at Chickering Hall, for the benefit of the Homes. To-day the treasurer paid me one thousand dollars, as a portion of the amount realized."

A few days later, a second thousand was received from the same source : the entire proceeds reaching the sum of four thousand two hundred and thirty-six dollars and forty-seven cents. With this large sum one mortgage was paid, another considerably reduced, and the Homes all put in comfortable condition. Among the articles was a magnificent Doré Bible, which was presented by the managers to Dr. Cullis ; but, in view of the pressing needs of his great household, he returned it to be sold at the fair. The amount received for it was ninety dollars.

Another blessed deliverance signalized the closing month of the year 1869. About the middle of December, the Doctor fell sick, and lay on his bed for ten days. During two days he describes himself as "critically ill ;" but on the 23d of the month he was able to resume his journal thus : —

"I would bear record to the glory of God, that, while prostrated on my sick-bed, he kept me in perfect peace, having no fear or anxiety about the work. His own word was so sweet to me ! 'Oh, fear the Lord, ye his saints, for there is no want to them that fear him.'"

On the following day he writes : —

"For the Deaconess House, from Beverly, eighty dollars to furnish a room ; also a twenty-dollar gold piece for my own use. I thank the Lord particularly for this, as a direct answer to prayer ; for while on my sick-bed, knowing that I should be unfit for labor for some days to come, and also that I could only rest when away from the scene of labor, I asked the Lord, if it were his will that I should go away, that he would send the means, as I was entirely without money. In answer to my prayer came the above, and a letter from a dear friend in another State, who, on learning of my illness, enclosed fifty dollars for the express purpose that I might go away to recruit my strength. Thus, knowing nothing of my desire, did the dear Lord incline those loving hearts to come to my aid.

"I wish I could impress upon the mind of every child of God the blessedness of trusting in Jesus for *all* things. He does not limit the demand : he says, ' *Whatsoever* ye shall ask in my name, I *will* give it.' Is there any limit to this? Are we not heirs of God, and *joint* heirs with Christ? If heirs, then the inheritance is ours, for ' *all* things *are* yours.' 'Ask, and ye *shall* receive.' Remember, you have a rich Father. His promises are 'Yea and Amen.' Are you poor? Christ says, 'Blessed are the poor.' He has the storehouse ; faith is the key : you may unlock, and take from the treasury, for ' the Lord is able to give thee much more than this.' "

Out of the fair above mentioned grew several little ones, some held by ladies, and some by children; a lecture by Rev. Dr. Stone of San Francisco yielded two hundred dollars for the Home; gifts of clothing and jewellery were sent in quite freely. Thus there was what might be called a revival of charity, wherewith the Lord refreshed the soul of his struggling servant, and placed the Homes on a sound financial basis. No longer could it be said of the Faith Hospital and Orphanage, that they had no other foundation than mortgage-debts.

With the opening of the year 1870, there were forty-four patients in the Home, and applicants were almost daily turned away for want of room. All departments of the work were now flourishing. Frequent conversions among the patients testified that the Holy Spirit was in it ; the good-will of good men had been heartily and substantially expressed. The famine was over ; and now what was there to prevent the institution from settling comfortably into the honorable position which it had attained, and, without straining the faith-theory any further, pursuing thenceforth the even tenor of its way ?

The same that prevented Israel from settling on the outward side of Jordan. God had provided still greater things for the Consumptives' Home, and its Joshua could not rest till he had entered into possession thereof. Month after month he feels the pressure of God's hand and the moving of human sorrow, till at length we find him saying, —

"The need of a new and enlarged Home is pressing upon us ; and I pray our Father to enlighten me, that I may look in the right direction for land, where every thing may favor our obtaining what we need. 'If ye abide in me, and my words abide in you, ye shall ask what ye *will*, and it shall be done unto you.'"

On the 1st of September the mind of the Lord seems to have been made known to him. He says in his journal, —

"For weeks I have been looking to the Lord for a location to build upon ; and in prayer my mind has been towards Boston Highlands, desiring a place easy of access. I asked one or two friends in that vicinity to look out for me, for either a piece of land, or old estate that might be made available ; when they both, independently of each other, mentioned one known as 'Grove Hall.' I replied to each of them, without much thought, 'It will not do.' Finally a third person said to me, 'Grove Hall is just the place.'

"An opinion so reiterated led me to consider whether it were not the Lord's will that I should ascertain more about the property. I went to see it, and found more land than I expected, there being eleven acres ; the lot favorably situated. The buildings, having been unoccupied for ten years, are quite dilapidated. The larger house could be altered and enlarged for the purposes of the Home, at a smaller cost than the erection of a new one. Another house upon the grounds could be put in suitable condition for the children. A third — a small wooden one — could be enlarged for the accommodation of the Deaconesses. The barn could probably be altered, and serve for a schoolroom and chapel, as we desire to carry the gospel wherever we go.

"At first thought, it would seem that so much land was unnecessary ; but one object in moving is that we may have sufficient space to secure fresh air, and to afford the patients and children grounds for exercise within our own enclosure. As the work expands, and we have more children, other houses will be needed ; for we believe that education on the family system has great advantages over the one of gathering large numbers together in one building. The want of a home for cancer-cases is also so frequently brought before me, that I have long prayed to God for their relief. The need seems to me as great as was that of the consumptives, and from the nature of the disease a separate building is necessary. We wait on the Lord for the means to give a resting-place to these poor sufferers.

"To-day I called upon the owner of the estate, to ascertain the price. He proposes to sell it for one hundred thousand dollars, terms to be made easy. I presume this is a fair price. The amount is large, and for a moment I felt the weight of as-

suming such a responsibility ; but *only* for a moment, when the
Spirit brought to my soul the assuring question, ' Is any thing
too hard for the Lord ?' ' And the house which I build is great ;
for great is our God above all gods.' Great peace followed, —
' *My* peace I give unto you.' I have two weeks refusal in
which to seek the Lord's will. On returning home, and laying
the matter before him, I asked, that, if it *were* his will, he
would show me by sending large gifts. In about an hour I
received a check for two hundred dollars, from a gentleman
now travelling in Europe. ' While they are yet speaking, I will
hear.' ' Whoso is wise, and will observe these things, even *they*
shall understand the loving-kindness of the Lord.' "

On the 15th of September he adds : —

" My mind is now clear, without the shadow of a doubt,
that it is the Lord's will that ' Grove Hall' should be the property of the Home. It seems the more marked, when it is known
that this estate has been unoccupied for ten years. In a conversation, two weeks ago, with the owner, he remarked that he
had already been offered one hundred and twenty-five thousand
dollars for it, but, in consideration of the work, proposed to sell
to me for one hundred thousand. My prayer this morning has
been, that he would yet reduce the price ; and this noon we
met by appointment, to decide the matter. My prayer was
answered, in that ninety thousand dollars was the price finally
agreed upon. As one hundred and twenty-five thousand was
the sum first mentioned, we can praise the Lord for inclining
the heart of Mr. K—— to make this great reduction.

" The hand of the Lord will be still more wonderfully seen
in this, when I state that we have ten years in which to pay
eighty thousand ; the other ten, in three years ; mortgages to
be given to cover the amount. No payment is to be paid
down. The Lord gave me perfect peace, although at the time
of the purchase I had not a cent in my pocket, and only a

small sum laid by that had been given from time to time towards a new building.   ' I wait for the Lord, my soul doth wait, and in his word do I hope."

The concluding entry for the year which closed Sept. 13, 1870, announces the purchase of Grove Hall.

Was it a piece of presumption?

It surely would have been, in an ordinary man, under ordinary circumstances; but for Dr. Cullis to take this step, was only to move forward into the edge of Jordan, after he had already followed the pillar of cloud and fire through the desert, and walked dry-shod through the divided sea.   But he shall speak for himself.

"SEPT. 30.   I am glad to say, as the Report is closing, that the 'Grove Hall' property is secured for the purposes of the work.   Our hearts rejoice, looking for the glory of the Lord to be revealed through this abundant gift.   As God covenanted with his people Israel, so he doth to us: 'I will rejoice over them to do them good, and I will plant them in *this land*, assuredly with my whole heart, and with my whole soul.'

"In regard to the buildings and all property belonging to the work, I would state that two gentlemen have been selected as trustees, who, at my death, will take possession of the same; they having full power to obtain an Act of Incorporation, so that the work will ever remain a public charity, for the care of the poor, sick with consumption.

"As this Report may fall into the hands of some persons who know nothing of the history or purposes of the work, it may be well to state that the Home cares for the poor, sick with consumption; and that any persons coming under the above head, of whatever nation, creed, or color, having no home or friends to provide for them, are *freely* received in the name of the Lord, and cared for as long as there is room.

"Our sole trust for the entire support of the work is not in man, but in the living God, and has been such since the beginning, when, with but three hundred dollars, the first building was opened ; receiving one patient, then another, and so on, as the Lord supplied means ; and to his own glory be it said, that he never sent the poor applicant without the needed means to sustain the increased care. Many persons say, 'Oh, yes ! it is very well to pray for money ; but you must work too.' I do not hesitate to say here, that the man who prays in faith is the most earnest and active in the vineyard of the Lord. As God's children, we are called to follow him, even to the forsaking of all ; and those who *watch* can say now, as did the Psalmist, ' I have been young, and now am old ; yet have I not seen the righteous forsaken, nor his seed begging bread.' ' *Surely* shall one say, *In the Lord have I righteousness and strength ; even to him shall men come.*' The Lord commands us to '*prove*' him, to see if he ' will not *pour* out a blessing, that there shall not be room enough to receive it.' What fulness in these assurances of God, that we may be won to trust him !

"Consider how we believe in the promises of our fellow-men, and venture the money, which is often, perhaps, our all of earthly treasure, on these promises, elated with the hope of large returns. Let me tell what returns the *Lord* has given to the trust given him. In six years, the three hundred dollars invested in his treasury has yielded upwards of eighty-six thousand dollars.

"This is only the *moneyed* interest : who shall estimate the treasures laid up in heaven ? How many come under the shelter of this Home, who, through protracted sickness, have spent all their store, and others being so blinded by poverty, ignorance, and sin, as to have scarce known of the heavenly inheritance ; while some, whose advantages have been greater, have never thought of their yet greater accountability to God.

Those of this number who have entered the Home, and from thence taken their departure to the 'mansions prepared,' have gone in the assured hope of sins forgiven; the truth as it is in Jesus illuminating pathways once darkened and drear.   Among other blessings, we have great cause for gratitude that the Lord has sent, in answer to prayer, efficient and faithful laborers, in such increased numbers as we have needed.   'Now thanks be unto God, which always causeth us to triumph in Christ.'

"Number of patients at the beginning of year, twenty-four.

"Admitted during the year, a hundred and fifty-eight.

"Total, one hundred and eighty-two.

"Discharged relieved, sixty-six.

"Discharged not relieved, twenty-one.

"Cured, six.

"Died, fifty-one.

"Now remaining in the Home, thirty-eight.

"Whole number cared for since opening of the Home, six hundred and ten.

"The Lord has given in answer to prayer, during the year, to the entire work (exclusive of the Tract Department), sixteen thousand five hundred and ninety-seven dollars and sixty-two cents.   The whole amount given since the commencement, *eighty-six thousand three hundred and five dollars and forty-eight cents*.   'For all things come of Thee.'"

During this sixth year, Dr. Cullis was led to combine the several departments, not including the Tract Repository, under one head.   This was done with the view to simplifying the accounts, and thus saving time, which was becoming a matter of great importance in view of the rapid increase in the work.   Further important changes in the legal incorporation will be mentioned in their proper places.

CONSUMPTIVES' HOME.

CHAPTER VIII.

THE HOME AT GROVE HALL.

"Is any thing too hard for the Lord?"

THE interest of the record now centres in the new enterprise at Grove Hall. Will the servant of God stagger along under this tremendous burden for a time, and then break down under it, or lay it down in despair?

So questioned some of his friends who esteemed themselves wise after the manner of this world. One of them said, —

"Dr. Cullis, I hear you have purchased the Grove-Hall property, and agreed to pay ninety thousand dollars for it."

"Yes."

"Have you any thing to buy it with?"

"Nothing but the promises of God."

"Well, Doctor, you are a good man, and understand faith and prayers, and all that; but you don't know any thing about business. That piece of property is not worth what you paid, or agreed to pay; and the end of it will be disaster and ruin to you and your missions."

"But a gentleman has already offered me ten thousand dollars for my bargain."

"Take it, then, take it; and I'll give you five thousand more if you'll buy a snug little property somewhere in the city."

The Doctor thanked him, but accepted neither his money nor his advice. Thus he burned the bridge that offered a safe retreat, and pushed on with a cheery heart; following still the fire and the cloud which had never yet misled him. For more than a year he waited to see the consummation of his great hope, the re-establishment of the Consumptives' Home under the magnificent elms and among the fresh green fields at Grove Hall; where, within easy reach of the city by street-cars, — a matter of importance to his visitors as well as himself, — he might give his great household of suffering ones what the city could not afford them, abundant liberty and light and air, in what would seem a second paradise to those cramped and crowded ones shut up within the narrow walls of a narrow street of a narrow city, without even a garden to themselves.

And now appears in the records the evidence of a glorious enlargement of soul wherewith the Master was pleased to bless his trusting servant.

There are those who, in their zeal to press people up into what they call "the higher life," have asserted that faith is an easy, simple, little act of the mind and will; and that by this act, in a moment of time, any truly regenerate child of God may come into possession of "the second blessing," or "the baptism of fire," or whatever other term they please to use to signify the absolute and perfect union of the soul with God, and the filling and energizing and abiding presence of the Holy Ghost. Whether such teachings belittle the blessing, in order to increase its apparent accessibility, need not here be discussed ; that topic may recur in the closing chapter of this volume, relative to the theology of the institution : certain it is, however, that Dr. Cullis passed through a long period of discipline and instruction before that Divine mystery was clearly unfolded to his faith. Step by step he climbed the hill of obedience, guided by the word of God and the Spirit of God, till at length the glorious table-land of Beulah was reached ; and we find him, at the opening of the seventh year's Report, giving this account of his entrance into the state of sanctification.

" More and more is it 'my heart's desire and prayer to God' for all his dear children, that they, in their very souls, may know that God is a living God, speaking to them, his ' chosen ' ones, day by day, and moment by moment, ' ordaining ' them for his work ; while their part is but to follow lovingly, obediently, trustfully, without care, him who ' goeth before.' Never has my own soul been so blessed, and filled with the love of God, as since I surrendered self and *all* I had to him ; and for what? *To receive Christ in all his fulness, he filling the undivided heart.* Now know I how Christ is made unto me ' wisdom, and righteousness, and sanctification, and redemption.' Now I

know fully how he can *save* me, and *keep* me ; so that, in absolute abandonment of trust, I can say with Paul, ' I know whom
I have believed, and am persuaded that he is able to keep that
which I have committed unto him, against that day.'

> 'I worship thee, sweet will of God !
>   And all thy ways adore ;
> And every day I live, I seem
>   To love thee more and more.
>
> When obstacles and trials seem
>   Like prison-walls to be,
> I do the little I can do,
>   And leave the rest to thee.
>
> I know not what it is to doubt;
>   My heart is ever gay ;
> I run no risk, for, come what will,
>   Thou always hast thy way !
>
> I have no cares, O blessed will,
>   For all my cares are thine ;
> I live in triumph, Lord, for thou
>   Hast made thy triumphs mine.' "

The day of small things was now past : henceforth
he was to open his mouth wide, that God might fill it.
And, along with the added opportunity, came the added
power and grace.   At first there was not strength in
his nature to carry such a mighty load, nor yet room
in his soul for the bountiful grace that must help him
to bear it.   Not all at once, but little by little, was this
greatness thrust upon him ; he would have grown dizzy,
had he been suddenly lifted to the height whereon we
see him standing now with steady nerve and wide-open

eye. Alas for those whose self-confident prayers for sudden greatness in the things of God are answered according to their will!

From this time the Doctor begins more distinctly to profess a larger and higher state of grace. He is now fully assured of his union with Christ, and sweetly conscious of the abiding presence of the Divine Spirit in his soul. Not long after, we find him taking up a new line of service for the Master; viz., that of a leader and instructor in the doctrine of entire sanctification. Soon there gathered round him a little circle of those who were thirsting after righteousness; then "The Times of Refreshing" became not only the organ of the life of faith, but also of the life of holiness. Meanwhile the little circle of consecrated ones grew larger and larger, till it extended over the Eastern, the Middle, and some of the Western States. But of this more at large hereafter.

The baptism of the Spirit, however, did not save him from further trials; but it did give him more power to endure them. His great household now comprised about seventy members, and yet he was sometimes obliged literally to pray for their "daily bread." But this did not alarm him; the experience was not a new one, and never once had his patients, his orphans, or his helpers come to actual want, though several times they had been in plain sight of it. That must be a state of mind greatly to be coveted, which enabled this

man, on awaking in the morning, and remembering that
his treasury had been drained of its last shilling the
night before, to hold out his hands to his Father in
heaven for the large amount of supplies needed for that
very day, without a shadow of doubt or a shiver of fear ;
to know for certain that what was required would come,
and come in time for dinner, or in time for supper if
the dinner were already on hand, — a rare and enviable
state of mind indeed ; but what a shame is it, that such
confidence should be so rare ! All that need be said
in praise of this absolute confidence in the promises of
the Infinite One is that the Doctor had come into the
normal condition of a child of God : he had taken the
human end of the Lord's yoke upon his neck ; and however heavy and galling it looked to worldly eyes, his
end of the yoke really was easy, and the burden actually was light.

There was small prospect of his being able to carry
a ninety-thousand-dollar property that was to be used
as a place for spending money instead of making it, to
say nothing of many thousands more to be expended
in reconstruction before the place would be habitable, —
so small a prospect, indeed, that the public faith, which
had none of the load to carry, actually broke down
from sympathy, or from an over-load of its own opinions ; and even the newspapers began to discuss the
error of the Doctor, and to show, that, even if he
could ever pay for it, the place itself was wholly unfit

for the uses to which he proposed to put it.   Such a
piece of fanaticism ought to fail ; indeed, it must fail,
or the popular judgment of Boston would be at fault :
therefore any one who could talk it down, or write it
down, was doubtless doing a praiseworthy thing.

One sagacious individual rushed into print to say
that the location was low ; to which some fanatical
friend of the Doctor replied with figures from the official levels of the city surveyor, showing that the site of
the house at Grove Hall was more than twenty feet
higher than that of the State House.   Another anxious
doubter aired his opinion that the cellar must be damp,
and the drainage difficult ; to which an old resident in
its immediate vicinity, quite familiar with the facts,
replied that the cellar was actually dusty, and, as for
the chance of drainage, there was a long and deep
descent of land immediately in front of the property.
Then, as to the possibility of fitting it up : where was
the money to come from ?   On all hands it was agreed
by conservative people, in the Church and out of it,
that the Doctor was going too far.

But, as a whole, the city of Boston is a good deal
given to faith.   Almost any fledgling religion, to say
nothing of some that are falling to pieces through age
and decay, can make a few converts in Boston : hence
the very strangeness of the faith of Dr. Cullis — strange
only from its close and literal following of the word of
God — began to call forth no small admiration.   This

quiet man, his steadfast courage, his stubborn trust, his unheralded charities, all at once became topics of popular interest.   The very opposition to his plans called forth defenders and helpers.   If pious prejudice reproved him, piety without prejudice stood by him ; if he were doing an unheard-of thing in the name of the Lord, Boston was just the place in which to do it. At any rate, he had gained the right of way to heaven with his prayers ; and why, in this city of all faiths, should he not also have the right of way for his opinions and his missions ?

The popular demonstration in his favor took the form of a fair.   Music Hall — that second of the two foci of the Boston ellipse, counting Faneuil Hall the first — was secured for the purpose.   Hundreds of "elect ladies," and dozens of "solid men," were, all at once, busy about "faith-work ;" and when the opening day arrived, — Feb. 27, 1871, — thousands of people thronged the spacious building, and for six days and nights loads of gifts called forth streams of money : bearing this substantial proof that the Consumptives' Home and its brave projector were held in love and honor by the people among whom he dwelt.   It was a case where that oft-mistaken proverb was true, "Vox populi, vox Dei."   It was a benediction given in the speech of Boston, but the undertone was the voice of God.

In words that hold no sense of amazement or even of surprise, — since it fitted so well into his faith and his experience, — the Doctor thus makes record of this grand rally on his behalf : —

"MARCH 21. The treasurer of the fair held in Music Hall announces to me that the net proceeds amount to upwards of twenty-one thousand dollars. My heart goes out in praise and gratitude to the living God, for this renewed evidence of his watchful love and care. The kind friends who have labored so arduously in this object pronounce the fair to have been a spiritual blessing to them. It was opened with prayer, and every day closed with singing 'Praise God from whom all blessings flow,' for six successive days. It might be called a social Christian re-union and sale, so free was it from all the objectionable features that have cast opprobrium upon the name of 'fair.' One of our religious weeklies thus speaks of it : 'No such fair was ever held before. It may be properly termed the "holy fair," its object was so good, and its origin so lofty. "Have faith in God," was the proper central motto ; others, alike devout, were scattered along the walls.'

"Thus the Lord has answered our prayer for means with which to commence the work of rebuilding Grove Hall. The architect has finished his plan ; which is, to raise the old build-ing, giving us on the lower story all needed rooms for business and domestic purposes, the two next stories to be used for patients. By the addition of a French roof, we obtain large and commodious rooms for the laborers. The chapel is to be in the centre of the L, with wards beyond for patients. This is the alteration and improvement upon the old building which has stood for many years ; when completed, we propose to move our patients into it, and then erect a new L, so that we may be able to accommodate altogether one hundred patients. We have to-day given the contract for the main building to a builder."

The exact amount realized by this "holy fair" was twenty-one thousand four hundred and sixty-seven dollars. There were also, during the season, other gifts that at the outset would have been accounted large ; so that the year of heaviest burden was the year of largest bounty. Among other receipts, was a bequest of ten thousand dollars from the Joy estate, which was at once used to reduce by that amount the mortgage on the new Home.

The cost of the rebuilding at Grove Hall was a little over twenty-two thousand dollars. It seems sad to be obliged to paint a black cloud in the sky of this bright picture ; but some mark of the enemy's presence might be expected to appear. The contractor, after drawing the full amount of his pay, left the work unfinished, so that it became necessary to fall back upon his sureties to complete it ; but, what was matter of still deeper regret, the man had failed to pay his workmen, and occasionally, for a year or two, Dr. Cullis was called upon to make good the wages which had been kept back by fraud. Such demands, though without a basis in law and justice, — as the contractor's receipts for his full claim most clearly proved, — appealed very strongly to the Doctor's generous heart ; and, after laying the case before the Lord, he felt justified in using a large amount of money in making up the losses incidentally incurred in his service.

The bequest from the Joy estate led to the incorpora-

tion of the Home, in the manner thus related by the
Doctor himself : —

"My first desire was, to have the Home incorporated while
under my own care ; but as I had been repeatedly told by my
legal adviser, that this could not be done without destroying
the principle of the work of faith, I had abandoned it, and
left the matter in trust by my will. As one of the trustees has
lately died in England, I have been brought to the Lord for
guidance and direction, and for several days have been asking
him whom I should select to fill the vacant place. My heart
was again inclined to ask him if some way could not be devised
by which the work could be incorporated, and still remain the
Lord's own, in simple dependence upon him for its support.

"On the next day, after praying thus, a lawyer of this city
called upon me, saying that he, with two other gentlemen, were
executors of an estate which was to be divided among the
charitable institutions of Boston, and requested that I would
make application, in behalf of the Home, for a portion of the
money. I thanked him for his kindness ; telling him I could
not do this, as we had never applied to any man, but to the
Lord alone, who always supplied our need. He then said, ' I
supposed you would not make application, so I came to you.'
He requested a Report, which I gave him.

"The next day he desired to see me, and stated, that, on
reading the Report, he found that the work was not incorporated ; and, while he and the other executors might have
confidence to give me an amount of money, yet, in disposing
of the estate of another, they felt bound to give it to incorporated institutions. I then explained to him, that the work
was established to carry out the principle taught in God's
Word, that ' they that trust in him shall not be confounded,'
and to prove to the world that God is a living God ; and as I
had repeatedly been informed that an Act of Incorporation
would destroy this principle, my will had been made as before

stated.   I further said, 'If you can tell me *how* the work can
be incorporated, and this principle kept inviolate, I would be
glad to act upon it.'   He said, after a moment's thought, 'I
think this can be done without any trouble.'

   " On further consideration, he found that the work could be
incorporated, and the incorporators give me a *life-lease of the
property, which would still leave in my hands the entire and
perfect control of the work, as I have had from the beginning.*
I thank the Lord for this his leading, which makes the work,
as I have ever wished it to be, a permanent one ; and that, long
after I shall have gone to be with Jesus, it shall stand as a
monument of God's faithfulness."

A petition for an Act of Incorporation, in accord-
ance with the plan stated, was presented to the Legis-
lature; and Hon. William Claflin, Rev. A. H. Vinton,
D.D., Hon. Jacob Sleeper, Messrs. Henry F. Durant,
Edward S. Rand, Abner Kingman, and Charles Cullis
were appointed trustees of the Consumptives' Home.

This year "Dedication Day," the 27th of September,
was grandly celebrated at the chapel of the new and
spacious Home at Grove Hall.   By reason of the
failure of the contractor to perform his obligation, the
building was only in partial readiness; but the orphans
already were housed in their new home, and it was
possible to use the main building for a public service
of grateful praise to God, consecrating to its mission of
charity the magnificent estate which was now to mark
God's approval of the faith of his servant.

In the Report for 1871, Dr. Cullis writes : —

"See how the supply has kept pace with the need. While last year's needs were supplied by the sum of sixteen thousand five hundred and ninety-seven dollars and forty-eight cents, this year, which commenced without our being able to see a hand's-breadth before us, but trusting in the sure word of the Lord, has been just as abundant, 'according to our need,' and our receipts have been *fifty-five thousand seven hundred and twenty-three dollars and thirty cents.*

"The whole amount given since the commencement of the work, *one hundred and forty-two thousand twenty-eight dollars and seventy-eight cents.*

"'Truly God is good to Israel, even to such as are of a clean heart.'

"As this Report may fall into the hands of some persons who know nothing of the history or purposes of the work, it may be well to state that the Home cares for the poor, sick with consumption ; and that any persons coming under the above head, of whatever nation, creed, or color, having no home or friends to provide for them, are freely received in the name of the Lord. Our sole trust for the entire support of the work is not in man, but in the living God, who has said, 'If ye shall ask any thing in my name, I will do it.'

"Number of patients at the beginning of the year, thirty-eight.

"Number admitted during the year, one hundred and forty-seven.

"Total, one hundred and eighty-five.

"Discharged relieved, fifty-three.

"Discharged not relieved, twenty-six.

"Cured, eighteen.

"Died, fifty-five.

"Now remaining in the Home, thirty-three.

"Whole number cared for since the opening of the Home, seven hundred and fifty-seven."

CHAPTER IX.

"ALL THINGS ARE YOURS."

"I the Lord do keep it; I will water it every moment: lest any hurt it, I will keep it night and day."

PASSING now the other departments of the growing work, — to be treated of, each in its complete
history, from the beginning, — the record of the Consumptives' Home, the chief and centre of all, will be
followed down to the date of this volume.

As has been noticed in the preceding chapter, the
reconstruction of the new Home was finished under
special difficulties which resulted in long delay : hence
the main edifice at Grove Hall was not ready for occupation until winter had set in. In October, the Doctor
records the fact, that, in answer to prayer, the Lord
had sent a purchaser for the Willard-street Chapel ;
and in November he makes a similar record concerning the four houses which had been combined for the
hospital : whereby he was able to pay ten thousand
dollars more on the Grove-Hall mortgage, making
twenty thousand dollars paid on that property within
thirteen months of its purchase, besides over twenty-

two thousand dollars expended in reconstruction and repairs.

On the 7th of December, 1871, the new Home was ready. The weather for some days had been very cold, — on the 6th intensely so, — and it was manifestly impossible to remove the patients with fierce winds blowing, and the thermometer hovering about zero. In this emergency, as in every other, the Doctor carried his case to the Lord, and asked that He who ruleth the winds, by whose breath the frost is given, and whose word melteth the ice and the snow, would send a favorable day in which to remove to Grove Hall. And the Lord seems to have answered this prayer; for, succeeding the "intensely cold" day, there came a morning "mild and pleasant, such as we had not known for weeks, so that scarcely an overcoat was needed:" and, on this day of the Lord, the removal was safely effected. On going to the Home to make ready for the ride, two of the patients were found in such a feeble condition that the Doctor feared they might die in the carriages: this also he made a subject of prayer; and the end of the day found the great family safely housed in their summer-like apartments, none the worse for the ride of four miles. This tempering of the wind and the cold was accepted as an omen for good. And truly it may be said, the skies have always smiled upon this restful little island of faith in the midst of a sea of doubts and tempests;

and, whatever may have been the cold and storms without, there has been almost perpetual summer within, — a summer not produced solely by the ample fires in the engine-room, but also by the smile of the Lord himself.

If ever an enterprise undertaken in the name of the Lord received full proof of his approbation, such an enterprise is the Consumptives' Home at Grove Hall.

About the middle of April, the wing at the rear of the main building of the Home was finished, and gifts of furniture for the new rooms began to be received. Also, as a further illustration of the business-like faith that was exercised in Him who knoweth our "need of all these things," the Doctor mentions that now, having a little farm of nearly eleven acres, he asked the Lord to send him one or more cows ; which prayer was presently answered by the gift of two cows, both very superior animals.

But more than all providential proofs of God's favor was the use he continually made of the Home as a means of grace to the souls within its walls. With the opening-out of the work on a larger scale, the Lord opened his hand wider in the bestowment of material gifts, and also in the larger baptisms of the Holy Ghost. There must needs be more faith now in exercise, since the wants were so much greater ; and, as souls and bodies both have come into the circuit of faith at the Home, the wider reach of prayer has brought not only wider but deeper spiritual blessing. So loving and precious are the records of conversions among these otherwise hopeless ones, that it is no wonder the Reports have been the means of leading sinners to the Saviour, and of deepening the piety of believers. There could be no better use for the remaining space of this chapter, than to reproduce some of the experiences which, all along, have made the Consumptives' Home a very Mount of Transfiguration.

In the spring of 1872, the following letter was received from a physician in a neighboring city : —

" DR. CULLIS, — I have found another poor waif on the hard world, who wants a home. Without father or mother, friends or connections, she is alone in the world, and sick. She had spent every dollar, and worked as long as she could stand. She came to my office to learn how long before death would relieve her, and rid the world of a worthless thing that was in the way. I was touched to the heart by her sad story, and have temporarily provided for her. When I told her of you, and the Home in Boston, she burst into tears, and thanked God with a fervor I shall never forget. She is about twenty-one ; bears no marks of depravity or abuse. She will die soon ; is now thoroughly prostrated from hard labor and her disease. I have told her I would write, and obtain a place with you. When can I send her along? If there ever was a case demanding sympathy, this is one. Please let me hear from you as early as convenient."

What appears to be the sequel to this letter appears in the journal eighteen days later. Under date of March 22, the Doctor writes : —

"Another patient has reached home to-night. We shall never forget how quickly and sweetly she learned to trust Jesus. Passing through the large ward one afternoon, I saw her with tears streaming down her face, and asked if she could tell me what troubled her. She said, 'Oh, I cannot sleep! When I shut my eyes, it seems as if there were something piercing my heart. I am such a sinner!' We told her that Jesus was waiting to forgive her; the blood of Jesus Christ cleanseth from all sin; and asked, 'Now, will you give yourself to him, just as you would give away any thing you did not want, and trust him to save you?'

"She said, 'Yes, I will.' The next morning she said she was happy, that she slept the last night; and her face wore an expression of peace that was new to her. One morning she said, 'Oh, I was so happy last night! I awoke myself saying the Lord's Prayer, and I finished it after I awoke; and it was so light about me. I used to think it was a dreadful thing to die; but now I am perfectly willing to go, whenever Jesus is ready to take me.' To-night he came, and she was all ready to follow him. Her history had been dark and sad. Praise to the Lamb of God, who hath made her clean in his own blood!"

"MARCH 28. Another weary soul has found its resting-place in Jesus. He is failing rapidly, and cannot have long to stay with us. To-day he said, 'I have some one with me now.'

"The nurse said, 'Jesus?'

"He answered, 'Yes; I wish I had had him before;' and afterwards whispered, 'Peace in Jesus; peace in Jesus!'

"Of one of the patients, our matron writes: —

"'Dear Lewis has left us. He said he was not a Christian when he came to the Home, and we do not know when the blessed Holy Spirit came to dwell in his heart; but we have seen the sunshine of his presence for some time. A few weeks ago he said, when he felt discouraged and blue, he went away and prayed, and Jesus took those feelings away from him. He knew he could not recover, and hoped he should go quickly. He changed very rapidly. Several members of the family noticed the great change in his looks, and remarked, " Lewis is going soon."

" ' He asked Jesus to give him an easy death ; but the last few days were filled with great suffering. He bore it with sweet patience, even cheerfulness, and said, " It is all right. Jesus wants I should show the power of religion to those around me. I am willing to have a hard death if that will glorify Jesus." The nurse remarked to him, that he was never irritable, or difficult to please. He said the reason was, that he knew his sickness was from the Lord, and it was all right. He counted every mercy, — was thankful that his relatives could come and stay with him so much ; he had not expected it ; and said, how nice that he could have *that* room and *that* bed, as he could have the air without feeling it too much ; also, that he did not dread the spasms of distress much, for Jesus was nearer to him then than at any other time.

" 'One night we went to see how he was, and found him sitting up in bed, unable to breathe lying down ; a friend stood by, fanning him. He beckoned us near, and said, " I am just as happy as I can be, singing every thing I can think of to myself." He very much enjoyed having us sing to him. When asked if we should sing any particular hymn, he said, " No ; sing any thing about Jesus."

" 'Last evening, at half-past nine, quietly and sweetly he ceased panting for breath, and went to see Jesus.'

" One of the dear laborers furnishes the following account : —

" ' About dark this evening, a new patient came. She looked pale and weary, and, as she sank into a rocking-chair, exclaimed, " Thanks to Jesus for a home again ! "

" " " Have you given yourself to Jesus ? " was asked.

" " " Yes," she replied.

" " " How long ago ? "

" " " When the Doctor talked with me about it."

" ' When did you see the Doctor?'

" ' This afternoon, about four o'clock.' After a little pause she added, ' If I hadn't been brought to this, I never should have accepted his grace.' Then she told of her early orphanage in England, of her poverty, waywardness, and wandering; but seemed glad to be brought back to the fold, even through suffering."

A striking example of the sovereign mercy of God is recorded in the journal for 1872. A man who had been an infidel, a scoffer, a gambler, and a rumseller, whose drinking-den was burned in the great Chicago fire, had been rendered destitute thereby; and, obtaining a pass from the Relief Society, had come to Boston, where he arrived about the first of November, sick with consumption, which had fastened upon him some time before, while a steamboat-hand on the Mississippi River. This sickness he believed to have been sent to check him in his career of wickedness. But let him tell his own story: —

" My first night's experience in Boston was sleeping in the station-house, where I applied for assistance. I told them that I was sick, and had been so for a long time, and that I was quite destitute. They put me in a cold cell, with nothing but a hard board to sleep upon; and, after coughing some two hours, it touched the heart of one of those tender guardians of the peace, and he interceded for me, when I was placed in a warmer cell, and had a blanket given to me. The next morning, at six o'clock, I was turned out in the cold, — you remember how cold it was at that time, — and, suffering so, it seemed that God had closed all avenues of mercy towards me.

"The next day I applied at the Boston Young Men's Christian Association, to two or three persons; but they could not help me. At night I slept again in the station-house. Next day I applied at the City Hospital, but was refused admission by the superintendent, because I was incurable. I asked him what I should do, as I was utterly destitute, having gone some thirty-six hours without food. He told me I had better go to Tewksbury; and, seeing I could scarcely crawl away from the place, he gave me a five-cent car-ticket. This is how I spent the first few days in Boston, — seven nights sleeping in the station-house. At last, being directed to Father Wells, I went and staid a week, that being the limit of shelter the institution allows.

"I went to the Boston Dispensary to get some medicine, where I was treated very kindly by Dr. Haskins. He told me to come again, which I did the next day. I told him I must be provided for in some way, as I had fully made up my mind, that, if I could not find the needed assistance in what is called the most charitable city in America, I would destroy my life, for my suffering was unendurable. He directed me to Dr. Cullis. He provided for me at once. And, while he made provision for all the needs of my body, Jesus commenced working on my soul. How could it be otherwise, with so many evidences of his love going on around me?

"After living in the Home about three weeks, I could remain passive no longer. The first Sunday at the new Home, I asked the prayers of God's people, that I might be converted, and be filled with that divine love which cometh only from Jesus. He answered the prayer, and converted my soul. And now, thanks be to God, I am trusting him, and him alone, for every spiritual and temporal blessing; and to him, with the help of God, I will look forever."

One morning a nurse heard a voice, and, on going to the bedside of the patient, found him praying thus : —

"'O Jesus, forgive my sins; it is my last wish; I ask it with my dying breath.'

"She said, 'He will forgive you,' and repeated some promises from the Bible.

"He replied, 'Yes, he will forgive; he *does* forgive me: glory to his name!' Soon he said, 'My limbs feel strangely; is this death?'

"The nurse told him that it was; to which he replied, —

"'Oh, death is nothing,' and soon passed away.

"Praise to Jesus, that another patient has been so sweetly converted! Last night, a man called the night-watcher, to tell her that he had found Jesus. She said, 'No matter what comes, then, life or death, you are safe.'

"'Yes,' he replied; 'I am safe, but I want to live to praise him.'

"This morning, when I went through the ward, I said, 'How do you do this morning?' He answered, —

"'I am happy.'

"'Now you can say, Jesus is mine.'

"'Yes,' said he. 'Oh, how wonderful, when I had been such a sinner all my life, that he should call after me! And he came so suddenly; and every thing seems so bright! Now I hope he'll keep me.'

"'He will keep you,' I said, 'just as long as you trust him.'

"'Well,' said he, 'that will be forever.'"

Another sweet testimony is that of a patient who died in midsummer. His last day was mostly passed in a state of unconsciousness. Seeing a look of returning intelligence, an attendant asked, —

"Are you thinking of Jesus to-day?" To which he replied, —

"When I am conscious, I am thinking of Jesus : when I am unconscious, Jesus is thinking of me."

This man had passed a lifetime in sin and ignorance, and only within a few weeks of his death had been brought to the knowledge of Christ as his Saviour.

Let us add to this group of experiences, from some of the later reports. Many striking cases of conversion occur ; and still from year to year the testimony holds good, that, almost without exception, those who die at the Home fall asleep in Jesus. Of course all are not recorded in the journal, but there is a book wherein their names are written. What a wonderful volume the book of life must be!

In January of the following year, one of the attendants at the Home says, —

"Oh, how quickly, how swiftly, Jesus saves ! A poor colored sailor came to us a short time ago ; he has failed rapidly, and this morning said he wanted some of the ladies to come and talk with him about Jesus. We went to him, feeling how utterly impossible it was to say any thing to help him, unless Jesus should speak through us. We told him that Jesus promised, 'Him that cometh unto me, I will no wise cast out.' 'He died for you ; now will you give yourself to him, and let Him save you?' He said he would. After we knelt and told Jesus about it, he asked us to sing. His face lighted up as we sang, —

'My sins are washed away in the blood of the Lamb.'

Brother B. came in just then, and asked if he had given himself to Jesus. He said, 'Yes.'

" ' When ? '

" ' Since I came here.'   We then sang, —

'Oh, how I love Jesus!'

He exclaimed, ' I *do* love Jesus, I *do*, I *do!* '   While we were singing, —

' Jesus is mine,' —

a beautiful light came over his face, and, though he was panting for breath, he attempted to sing with us, but could only articulate one or two words in a line.   At ten o'clock that morning he died."

" APRIL 19, 1874.   To-day another soul, saved by the blood of Jesus, has passed to his rest in heaven.   He gave us this account of himself : —

" ' I had often been conversed with, in regard to my soul's salvation, before coming to the Home ; but it did not make any lasting impression.   After coming here, the little acts of kindness, and the spirit shown, made me desire to be a Christian.   One night at chapel, the Doctor was urging them to come to Jesus : I could not stand it any longer, and rose for prayers. Since that night I have been so happy, I hardly know what to do with myself.'   His countenance to the last revealed the peace that reigned within."

" Nov. 6, 1875.   We are rejoicing to-day over the conversion of one of our workers.   She was the only one of our band previously without a hope in Christ.   Two patients also were converted this week, — not an unusual occurrence.   Week by week the Holy Spirit testifies to his gracious working ; wave after wave of blessing following in noiseless, quick succession."

" Another in the Home writes : —

" ' The Spirit of God is so evidently among us, that it is blessed to note his working on different minds.   I was awakened at midnight by the sound of singing in an adjoining room; and I soon found our colored servant Fanny was on her knees, singing, "Oh, Jesus has blessed me! Praise Jesus!"

"'I said, "Jesus has pardoned you."

"'"Oh, yes, miss, Jesus has saved me, *I asked him so hard.* Jesus is laughing at me. I've seen a great light!"

"'She continued these ejaculations until I asked her to be quiet, so as not to disturb the sick ones. She replied, "I forgot, miss, but I could but speak out." Next morning her joy came gushing out to all who met her. In describing it she said, "Jesus said, 'Arise, go in peace, and sin no more.' It was no more night. When I clapped my hands, they didn't feel like the hands I had worked with all day, and my feet didn't feel like the feet I had stood on all day." The genuineness of the work was more clearly proved soon after. Next day, "She felt dark in her mind; and when she asked Jesus he told her he had saved her, but that she must tell about the untruth she told about her age, for she heard them say we mustn't trifle with Jesus." When she had confessed, it was all clear again, and she went on her way rejoicing.'

"Almost like echoes from the eternal shores, come the triumphant sounds from departing saints in the dear Home. One says: —

"'I asked the Doctor if he thought I would go home to-night. He said, Yes; he thought I would be with Jesus. I was so happy, I wanted to jump from the bed, and felt like flying through the house, telling them, "I am going home to-night. Are you not happy too? Jesus has paid all the debt; he has done it all, and it is all love." Isn't it glorious?'

"The Lord saw fit to try her by continuing her life another day amid much suffering; but, when asked if she still trusted him, she replied, '.Oh, yes! I can trust him a month longer if he wants me to.' Her end was peace.

"Another said, 'One night the pain was so severe, I could hardly keep from screaming, and the tears would come fast; then I thought, "Shame, Annie! how much more Jesus bore for you : can't you bear this ? " I stopped crying, and felt so happy. Another time when the night seemed so long, the Lord shortened it for me ; for about three o'clock a little bird began to sing, and it sounded so sweetly. I thought, " That little bird praises God when it first wakes, and surely I ought to." ' "

This series of testimonies may be concluded with a case of the cure of the opium-habit, in answer to prayer, which occurred at the Consumptives' Home in the autumn of the year 1876. In this case, as in so many others, the horrible condition of bondage to appetite was brought on by the use of morphia prescribed by a physician.

Under date of Sept. 2, Dr. Cullis says, —

"We record the following interesting account of a patient now in the Home, whose emancipation from the fearful chains of habit testifies to the power of Him who is able to 'subdue all things to himself.'

"Mr. A., blind from birth, entered the Home Monday, Aug. 28, coming from Watertown, N.Y. He is reduced almost to a skeleton by long suffering from disease of the lungs, and incessant pain. Upon his arrival he was asked, among other questions, whether he loved the Lord Jesus. He replied with confidence that he did, and had for some time. As to the medical treatment which had been pursued, he stated that he had been kept up on morphia for the last two years, and had taken sometimes as much as sixteen grains in one day.

"Treatment having begun at the Home, his customary diet of morphia was at once entirely removed. Accordingly he soon became delirious and almost frenzied, so as to require very close attention. His pains greatly increased, and his constant and beseeching cry was for morphine. When he found that no amount of begging availed, his immediate request, and finally demand, was, to be placed on board the cars, and allowed to return home. He was told in reply, that he could go whenever his friends sent for him, and that they would be written to, and his desire stated. But he urged that he could not wait for his friends to send, but must go at once, and begged to be sent immediately to the depot. On being told that it would never answer to turn one blind and sick off alone, he still desired to have it done, saying he could not stay where he was not allowed to have morphine.

"Being then directed to look to the Lord Jesus to take away his appetite for it, and being told of other persons who had been relieved from similar trouble by so doing, he replied, ' Jesus cannot do it in my case.'

" By Thursday evening, Aug. 31, he grew very delirious, and was groaning and tossing on his bed continually, many of his exclamations being snatches of prayer for Divine help. From his entrance to the Home he had been made the subject of especial prayer by Dr. Cullis and many of the helpers ; and on the evening in question, as his distress increased, prayer was twice offered for him, by a small circle of helpers and patients, at his bedside : but it seemed almost impossible to gain his attention. The same night, watchers remained with him till morning to prevent his doing himself injury, as he was constantly starting from his bed, and threatened to throw himself out of the window. During the night he continually moaned, and occasionally cried out ; at times in his frenzy declaring he beheld serpents, and once he screamed ' Fire ! '

" During Friday and Friday night, Sept. 1, he seemed more subdued, but still begged for morphine, and complained of extreme pain. On being again urged to look to Jesus for the destruction of his appetite, he replied that he had been praying constantly, but it was of no use.

" On Saturday morning, Sept. 2, before the breakfast-hour,

Miss W., one of the nurses, had a few words and prayer with him, and found him still distressed, and affirming that he was no better. Not long after this interview with him, she was strongly impressed that it was her duty to stay away from morning prayer in the chapel, and visit his room when that hour arrived; but before the time came, the impression was removed from her mind, and she attended the chapel as usual. In the account which she subsequently received from Mr. A., soon to be narrated, Miss W. felt she could see why the strange impression came and went so suddenly.

" Soon after the breakfast-hour the same morning, Mr. A. sent to request Dr. Cullis to pray with him; and when the Doctor called, Mr. A. with much joy said that Jesus had, only a short time before, taken away all his craving for opium, and that his pains were much assuaged. He repeated the same statement to several other persons in the course of the morning, his face at such times fairly glowing with pleasure. Later in the day, he gave to Miss W. the following particulars.

" He said he now felt that he had been directly led of the Lord in coming to the Home. On his journey here, the previous Monday, he made the resolution to forsake morphine; but when afterwards he became so distressed in body and mind, he would gladly have broken the resolution. When he discovered he could not get the drug, he made up his mind that the Home and all connected with it were the worst possible. After being told that the only way for help was to look to Jesus to have the appetite destroyed, he tried to, but soon felt the Lord did not hear prayer in his behalf, and would not. On the previous (Friday) night, his sufferings became so intense, he had planned to take his own life. Accordingly, that (Saturday) morning, he had endeavored to borrow a knife of a fellow-patient, intending, if he obtained it, when the time came for prayers in the chapel, and he would be left for a few moments alone, to cut his throat. But about 8 o'clock A.M. (an hour previous to the time for prayers), an intense feeling

of the immediate need of Divine help overwhelmed him, so
that in very desperation he cried to the Lord with all his soul,
and asked that the desire for morphine might be taken away;
and it was instantly gone, and had not returned."

An event of much interest during this eighth year
of the work was the transformation of a large out-
building on the Grove-Hall estate into a chapel. This
was distinct from the private chapel in the Home,
which, of course, was not available for general use;
and "Dedication Day" was this year celebrated by
the consecration of the new chapel, in which a little
society was gathered, whose delightful history will be
found in the second part of this volume.

The year brought the usual tests of faith, and the
certain deliverances promised to those whose trust is
wholly in the Lord.

At one time the engine-room was overflowed with
water, and a steam-pump was given by the manufac-
turer. A heavy expense had to be incurred for deep
drainage, some of the way through rock; and to meet
this claim, together with the first year's interest on
the mortgage, amounting to twenty-four hundred and
fifty dollars, a bequest of five thousand dollars was
received under the will of a lady in Portsmouth,
N.H.

The first year of life and labor at the new Home
thus drew to a close under conditions calling for hearty
and joyful praise.

The summary of the record which closes Sept. 30, 1872,[1] is as follows : —

"During the past year, the Lord has sent us in cash forty-six thousand two hundred and one dollars and forty-seven cents.

"For the eight years that the work has been established, without any solicitation from man, but in answer to prayer, God has sent the amount of *one hundred and eighty-eight thousand two hundred and thirty dollars and twenty-five cents*. Also, in answer to prayer, towards building a Cancer Home, nine hundred and sixty-one dollars and seven cents; making, in addition to gifts of a previous year, one thousand and six dollars and eleven cents.

"'Call unto me, and I will answer thee, and show thee great and mighty things which thou knowest not.'

"Number of patients at the beginning of the year, thirty-three.

"Number admitted during the year, one hundred and fifteen.

"Total, one hundred and forty-eight.

"Discharged relieved, thirty-four.

"Discharged not relieved, twenty-five.

"Cured, five.

[1] With this date the admirable volume by Rev. Dr. Boardman ends. Those who read that book and this will of course find a similarity in them; as the same principal points in the Reports are likely to attract the notice of all who study them, and hence the works of two editors prepared from the same materials must in many things resemble each other. Still some matter will be found in each which is not in the other; besides, as the delightful history of Dr. Boardman was prepared at the close of the eighth year of the Home, it was found desirable, in writing the account of twelve years more, in order to give completeness to the later volume, to retrace some of the lines so well drawn in the book entitled "A Work of Faith." The same extracts from the Reports in many cases appear; but, wherever Dr. Boardman's original matter has been used, due credit has been gladly given. May the rich blessing that has attended the earlier book be extended over the later!

" Died, fifty.

" Now remaining in the Home, thirty-four.

" Whole number cared for since opening of the Home, eight hundred and seventy-two.

" Number of children in the Orphanage, fourteen.

" The reader, as he reflects on this mode of life with its continual need, may be led to think it a very trying life ; but to the glory of God I can say I never knew so much continued joy and peace filling my soul as during the past eight years. Although often tried, yet never cast down, but casting all my care upon him, I am kept in perfect peace."

CHAPTER X.

FAITH THAT WAS FIRE-PROOF.

" And the fire shall try every man's work, of what sort it is."

IN the month of November, 1872, while the Doctor was again in reduced circumstances, and obliged to be continually looking into the invisible for the supply of the daily wants of his great household, a terrible calamity befell the city of Boston.

The history of the great fire is too fresh in the minds of many of the readers of these pages to need recounting here. A conflagration on so vast a scale has never but once visited an American city; if, indeed, in any city on the globe, save in Chicago, property of so large a value has ever been consumed by fire. The capital of New England was staggered for a time by a blow so sudden and terrible ; but it did not weaken her courage, or break down her pride. When three or four square miles of the Western metropolis lay in ashes, and her people by tens of thousands were homeless, Boston, like the rest of Christendom, sent large sums of money for her relief. Now, a little more than a year later, when the great destroyer had been holding a carnival among the massive structures on her own most substantial streets, her neighbor by the Lakes, having still a large amount of money in the treasury of her Relief Society, offered to return through gratitude what she had received through pity. But Boston was herself, in spite of fire ; and the offer was declined by her mayor with rather scanty thanks. Her rich men, it was assumed, were the chief sufferers ; and they scorned to complain at losing their fortunes where they had made them, and where they expected to make other fortunes when the ruins should be rebuilt. But so great a loss to the rich failed not to reach the poor, whose homes indeed were standing, — if they had any homes to lose, — but whose means of livelihood had been wholly taken away.

This calamity was a terrible ordeal through which the faith-work and its workers were called to pass. But the Doctor was not cast down ; for he knew that his house was builded out of the Divine promises, with the Son of God himself as the chief corner-stone, and such material, on such a base, could never be swept away. On the 4th of December, Dr. Cullis writes : —

"This morning I called together the heads of the different branches of the work, that we might unitedly call upon God for help. During the eight years and a half since the commencement of the work, we have never been in greater straits ; and for all this my soul has rejoiced more and more in the Lord and in his word. Humanly speaking, we cannot expect any thing but trials for means : our city has been visited by a terrible conflagration, millions and millions worth of property destroyed. Many who have helped us from year to year are now unable to do for us. Yet, amid all this, God's word is true, ' For all things *do* work together for good to them that love God.' *My trust is not in Boston or man*, but in the living God. I believe he will abundantly supply all our need ; and my prayer is for this, that the world may know that God lives to fulfil his promises."

The spirit of heroism took possession not only of the chief, but of some of his assistants also ; for a few days later, while the cloud seemed darkest over the fortunes of the Home, two of the nurses came to him, and said that in future they desired to give their services to the Lord's work without compensation. The amount of money thus saved was not very large, but the thought of having such a staff of co-workers thrilled the Doctor's heart with delight.

And now begins a new era in his life. Up to this time, he had preached the gospel by means of printed pages, as well as by the great illustration of gospel faith afforded by the Consumptives' Home ; but now, while trembling beneath the weight of burdens under which a man of untried faith must have sunk to the earth, a new weight of responsibility was laid upon him, a new task was presented to his hand. But tasks, few or many, are all alike light to one who has learned to take hold of the strength of the Almighty.

On the 4th of January, 1873, he received a note from

the brother who had been preaching at the Grove-Hall
Chapel, saying that he was too ill to perform service
on the morrow.   This the Doctor felt to be the call of
God to him to stand up, at least this once, and speak
from his Word, in his name.   Accordingly on Sunday,
the 5th, he made his first attempt at preaching ; taking
for his subject the command of the Lord to Zacchæus,
" Make haste and come down, for to-day I must abide
at thy house."   Of this first effort he says, " I *know* the
Lord baptized me with power, and gave me the word ;
for my own soul was filled as he spoke through me by
his Spirit.   His be the praise ! Whether I shall preach
in the future, or not, I leave wholly to Him."

During the following week, he received a paper,
signed by the members of the Grove-Hall congregation, asking him to continue to be their pastor.   This
he accepted as the voice of the Lord ; and relying upon
Him who said, " I will be with thy mouth," he ventured
to add this new care and labor to the heavy burdens
he was already carrying.   And this he did just as he
began to do every other work for the Lord ; for he
says, in view of the pressure upon his strength and
time, " My preparation must come directly from Him
upon whom my soul continually feeds."   Thus, without
any human authority or professional training, this layman became a minister of the Word.   And if He who
inspires and fulfils the Word orders a man to preach
it, what man or what convocation of men shall dare

dispute the ordination or the call? From that day
forth, Dr. Cullis, without assuming any clerical title
or dignity, has continued to preach the gospel; "the
Lord working with [him], and confirming the word
with signs following. Amen."

There is another view of this new duty. Was it an
added burden? Was it not, rather, a fresh proof of
the love and approbation of the Lord, who thus opened
to him the door into another department of his blessed
ministry, and set the seal of full apostleship upon him?
He had already received the apostolic gift of "faith;"
now, "by the same Spirit," he receives the gift of "in-
terpretation." There can be no other test of apostolic
order and succession that for a moment is to be
compared with the actual possession and use of those
spiritual powers which, in all the Christian ages, mark
the apostolic person, and prove the apostolic call.
Whoever has these marks himself will recognize them
in this brother apostle, and whoever has merely the
tradition and pretence thereof is not entitled to judgment in the case.

The following brief extract from the journal about
this time will show how intimate was the communion
between the Lord and his servant, and how readily and
unquestioningly he had learned to obey.

"JAN. 16. To-day has brought a sweet surprise from my
loving Lord, proving his special care of the work committed
to him. A messenger called, at my request, to receive part of

the interest-money due on the mortgage. I had just two hundred dollars, the amount due on this mortgage, one of which was to be paid to him, the other was for necessary articles to be purchased at once. While the messenger was here, without any solicitation on his part the Spirit suggested to me, '*Pay the whole, and trust me for the needed supplies,*' which suggestion I immediately followed. Just as I had done this, and before the messenger had left, the door-bell rang, and a note was handed me from a lady in Brookline, containing one hundred dollars ! ' Before they call I will answer, and while they are yet speaking I will hear.'

The next entries in the record indicate a zeal and faith that are perfectly irrepressible ; for notwithstanding the drying-up of so many of the former sources of supply, by the great fire, and in spite of the fact that his hands were full with new as well as customary work, we find him praying to God for means to still further enlarge the Home. Here are three entries, all within a week, which afford a striking instance of prevailing prayer : —

" FEB. 27. Another poor woman refused, for want of room. I am praying especially about the enlargement."

" MARCH 1. Two more patients turned away. Feeling confident it is the Lord's will that we should enlarge, I am praying for the means to do so."

" MARCH 4. Three days ago I commenced to pray for means to enlarge the Home. To-day a dear friend called, from Providence, R.I. He remarked that he had met some one who mentioned incidentally that the Home was full to overflowing. He also added, ' I have called to-day to give you five thousand dollars towards building a new wing.' I had not seen this friend, to have any conversation with him, for weeks, and he knew nothing from me of our need. How precious, then, for me to trace in this my loving Father's hand, leading one of his dear children to be his co-worker in ministering to the sick and suffering ! "

The two entries below give a vivid picture of the situation. Truly this man, in the midst of trial, has the courage of his convictions.

"MARCH 19. To-day I have given the contract for building the new wing. The whole will cost about eight thousand dollars. I shall go on as far as the five thousand dollars will meet the demand, and then stop until the Lord sends the balance. Praise for the peace and joy that fill my soul to-day ! "

"MARCH 24. This morning not money enough to buy food for the day. On returning home I found a check for one hundred dollars, from a lady of this city. We have broken ground for the new wing."

The twentieth of May, 1873, was the day appointed by Dr. and Mrs. Boardman to sail for their home in London. Dr. Cullis being much worn with extra labor, it was thought by his friends that an ocean-voyage would benefit him. So deeply was this impressed upon the mind of Mrs. Cullis, that she began to pray for the means required, and assured her husband that the Lord was about to provide them. The mere matter of a voyage to Europe, under ordinary circumstances, would not imply any great amount of prayer on the part of a physician in good practice ; but with Dr. Cullis it was a great undertaking. In the first place, his own income would cease, from which so often the necessities of the Home had been met. Then it will be remembered that this was the spring after the great fire, whose power for evil had by no means spent itself : where, then, was the supply of the wants of half a hundred people, sick and well, to come from in the absence of the man who had so long stood before God on their behalf ? Then there was the interest on the seventy-thousand-dollar mortgage to be paid, and the new wing to be overlooked. Surely, if he ever could be spared from the work, this did not seem to be the time. But the Lord was in the voice that had bidden his dear wife to pray for this blessing on her husband ; and five days before the date for sailing, over a thousand dollars had been received for this purpose, besides other sums with which the interest on the mortgage was paid, a large amount paid the second time on the claims for wages of those who had been wronged by the contractor already mentioned, and a handsome balance left in hand with which to provide for the Home in his absence.

The voyage was delightful. The sea was calm. The Lord was on the ship with his servants, where they had the delight of seeing one soul brought into his kingdom. The reception of Dr. Cullis and his devoted wife, by those who already knew him through his Reports, was of the heartiest ; and the climax of the tour was reached when, after visiting the chief faith-institutions on the Continent, — Kaiserswerth on the Rhine, Dorothea Trudel's Faith-Cure at Mannedorf, Switzerland, and Wichern's " Rough House " at Horn, — he went down to Bristol to see that marvellous Orphanage under the charge of George Muller.

Refreshed thus in soul and body, the Doctor reached home again on the 16th of September, to enter upon still another great department of the faith-work, of which an account will be found in the second part of this volume ; viz., the prayer of faith, for the heal-ing of the sick. In the Report for this year, ending Sept. 30, 1873, there appears for the first time a record of the Divine leading which enabled Dr. Cullis to lay hold on the promise recorded in the Epistle of St. James : " Is any sick among you ? let him call for the elders of the church ; and let them pray over him, anointing him with oil in the name of the Lord : and the prayer of faith shall save the sick, and the Lord shall raise him up ; and if he have committed sins, they shall be forgiven him."

It would seem to be the most natural and consistent thing in the world, for this man, who was already trust-ing in the Lord for the means to feed and shelter the sick and the dying, to advance a step, and believe also for the power to heal in his name. But it must be recorded, pitiful as the fact may appear, that some of the Doctor's friends forsook him when he added the healing of the sick to all the other work of faith. It is not to be presumed that these persons had any objections to the sick being healed; but this was a strain which their faith was not able to stand, and it is only natural for men to denounce as "presumption" and "fanaticism" whatever exceeds their own capacity of understanding and belief. Alas for the faith which trusts in a God no larger than it can measure and understand!

From this time the name of Dr. Cullis became prominent as a healer of the sick. Though some of his old friends forsook him, new ones came to fill their places; and the outside world, who care little for the operations of faith to save men's souls, began to take an interest in one who could call down help from heaven for the saving of men's bodies: hence the defection of those who were shocked at the idea of faith-healing was more than made good by the new helpers who came to know and love the Doctor through bodily as well as spiritual blessings received in answer to his prayers.

The other departments of the work received a new impetus from this new gift of healing bestowed upon the leader. The Tuesday-afternoon meetings for consecration, in particular, rapidly increased in attendance, till the Doctor's parlor was too small for them; and a project was formed for a chapel, which, as will be seen in its proper place, culminated in the erection of the present spacious edifice in Beacon Hill Place, known

as Beacon Hill Church.   The slumbering faith of multitudes of believers was awakened.   It began to be seen
that the only reason why miracles had become so rare
in the Church was the same old one given by our
Lord, who could not do many mighty works among his
former neighbors "because of their unbelief."   Letters
containing requests for prayer began to pour in ; cases
of actual healing multiplied ; and, as a result of this
revival of an apostolic gift, this apostolic man became
the centre of a great circle of earnest Christians all
over the country, to whom he had brought health and
benediction.   There was, indeed, much opposition to
the cures, and to the man who wrought them ; the most
and worst of which came from professed believers in
the gospel, a portion whereof they thus determinedly
rejected.   Certain pastors who had been hearty and
fraternal now dropped out of the Doctor's meetings,
because of the hostility of some in their congregations
towards the faith-cures ; and it was now evident why
the Lord himself had kept his servant free from all
denominational entanglements and all official control,
for, without the most absolute power and liberty of
management, the prudence and sagacity of worldly-
wise directors would certainly have checked if not
choked the stream of blessing which God was pouring
out through this courageous, believing soul.   But of
this more at large in its place.

In spite of the fire, and the withdrawal of timid

friends from the work on account of the faith-cures, the year ending Sept. 30, 1873, was a year of plenty; the money received, besides many gifts of other valuables, amounting to over twenty-seven thousand dollars, thus swelling the aggregate for the nine years of the work, in round numbers, to *two hundred and sixteen thousand seven hundred dollars.* The number of patients admitted to the Home during the year was one hundred and forty-three.

CHAPTER XI.

ROOTED AND GROUNDED.

" They go from strength to strength."

THE projector of the work of faith at Grove Hall may now .be said to have passed his novitiate, and to have entered upon the full possession of the powers and blessings which the Lord had promised to him, at the beginning, on condition that he would "only believe." The experimental stage, as it might be called by those who looked on from the outside, was now complete : henceforth the Consumptives' Home with all its various belongings was a fact to be accepted, and to be accounted for as best it might.

On one occasion, Dr. Cullis was invited to give an address before one of the ministers' meetings of Boston, after which it was proposed to make a collection in aid of his work. This he declined with thanks ; leaving the kind and half-bewildered brethren face to face with the fact that the great reliance of all their charities and missions — to wit, public collections — formed no part of the plan of this work of faith.

At one of these meetings, the Doctor was pressed

with inquiries concerning the faith-cures, by the doubt-ing ministers; and among other questions he was asked, " Do all the people whom you pray for get well ? " To which the Doctor instantly rejoined, " Were all the sinners converted to whom you preached yesterday ? "

How strange that those who are so familiar with failures in their own use of the universally accepted means of grace should demand unvarying success of those who are put forward by the Spirit to recall and recover one of the gospel gifts so long lying dormant in the Church!

There were three notable events in this tenth year of the work : first, the completion and dedication of the Hartshorn wing of the Consumptives' Home, which was opened on the 18th of May, 1874, thus adding fourteen comfortable rooms to the capacity of the over-flowing wards ; second, the organization of a church at Grove Hall, on the basis of " JESUS ONLY ; " and, third, the purchase of a house in Beacon Hill Place, for a Faith Chapel, where the Tuesday consecration-meeting, which was still overflowing, might have space for com-fort and growth.

In February, 1875,[1] the friends of the Home held another great fair at Music Hall, for its benefit, from which was realized the sum of eleven thousand dollars. A painting by George L. Brown, valued at a thousand

[1] The remainder of the history of the Consumptives' Home must, for want of space, be given at large, and not a chapter to a year as has been done thus far.

dollars, was presented and sold ; several bequests and
other gifts in considerable sums were received from
time to time : so that although the previous year had
witnessed sore trials of faith, and this one had opened
with an empty treasury, the twelve months ending
Sept. 30, 1875, show the unprecedented receipts of
*seventy-one thousand eight hundred and fifty-one dol-
lars and fifty-three cents*, as against a little less than
twenty-three thousand for the previous year. Thus,
even in these times of financial depression in the country, did the Lord bountifully fill the basket and store
of those who were waiting upon him, in daily faith, for
daily bread.

With this grand outpouring of plenty, the annual
financial record may properly end. Such a balance-
sheet, leaving twenty-four thousand dollars in the treasury, — from which steadily increasing sums had been
drawn, and which had been emptied to the last dollar
again and again, — was evidence enough that there was
some sort of connection between it and the treasures
of Him who owns the world. From this time forth,
there was no room for doubt that the Lord himself was
the chief Treasurer of this institution, and that he
would not suffer it to fail. Rooted in the promises
and grounded in the providence of God, its foundations
still stand strong. Let it not be supposed that there
were no further periods of heavy pressure, and no calls
for self-denial on the part of those who were engaged

in the work : heavy and sore trials have continued to test and strengthen their faith throughout the entire twenty years, — none more severe, perhaps, than that of the year 1884, — but from all these the Lord has sent deliverance. For the year ending Sept. 30, 1876, the receipts fell to about sixteen thousand five hundred dollars ; but they rallied again the following year, and have maintained an average of nearly twenty-five thousand dollars. This is for the Consumptives' Home and its corporate belongings only ; that is, the Cancer Home, the two Orphanages, and the small Spinal Home, — all of which are included in the corporation known as "The Consumptives' Home." The large gifts to the other departments of the work will be noticed in their proper places.

The Spinal Home above mentioned was added to the work in 1876 ; a small house on the Grove-Hall grounds, which had been occupied by the superintendent, Mr. Bumpus, being taken for that use, and fitted up for the accommodation of four patients and their nurses. This small branch of the work has a precious history of its own, which will be given in its place.

The Report for 1875 gives an interesting case of a young man, a Roman Catholic, who, having been received into the Home, was teased away by his co-religionists, but afterwards came back, and was received a second time. The Doctor's record of the incident shows the position he was forced to take on this delicate question of religion.

"A few days ago, one of our former patients, a Roman Catholic, came to my office, requesting to return to the Home. He entered the first time in May, 1874, and remained until January, 1875 ; when, at the urgent solicitations of his friends, he left us to enter a Roman-Catholic hospital, where he remained a little over three months. I said to him, 'How is it that you wish to return to us? I thought you were at the Roman-Catholic hospital.' — 'So I am, but I cannot stay there.' — 'Why not?' With tears running down his cheeks, he replied, 'I want to go back to the Home, where I can hear the word of God and the song of praise, and I want to die there ; then I shall be happy.' I asked him if he had given himself to Jesus ; he answered, 'Yes, I did that before leaving the Home ; but I did not realize how much I should miss hearing him spoken of, and the voice of prayer, until I went away. I have not heard a word of the gospel since I left the Home.' I said, 'Your friends took you away : are they willing you should come back?' — 'Yes, they know I wish to go, and will not make any trouble about it.' I then gave him a permit to return to the Home.

"I am so glad to insert this experience of one who has been brought out of darkness into the light of the glorious gospel of the Lord Jesus. Almost from the beginning of the work, I have had to endure the attacks of the Romanists, and those who sympathize with them. When the work was first established, its doors were open to clergymen of every denomination, the Roman-Catholic priest not excluded. As the foundation of the work was centred in Christ, my desire and the prayer of my heart was for the conversion of every patient who should enter its walls. From the priests we had trouble ; and finding we could not have both, — the Lord Jesus and the priests, — it became necessary to exclude whatever would draw the heart from trusting in Jesus. After much prayer I came to the settled conviction, that, if we would have souls saved and brought to Jesus, the work must be made a Protestant work. And what has been the result? Hundreds have found Jesus, and have been washed in his own precious blood; so that, since the first year, the work has been distinctly a Protestant one. Patients on entering are asked if they are Romanists or Protestants. If they say ' Romanists,' they are told at once that the Home is a Protestant Home, and that the priest is not allowed to enter. They are also told they need not enter the Home if they do not wish to; they can leave any day they please, and can visit the priest whenever they please, but while in the Home they are in a Protestant institution. No effort whatever is made to turn a patient from Romanism. We preach and teach Jesus, and Jesus only, and that he saves his people from their sins."

The following instance of special deliverance in time of financial trouble, taken from the twelfth Report, shows that all the trials of faith did not end with the year of unusual plenty. Even yet there are days of small things; but never a day when the promises of God are not good for their face in money, as well as in any other form of benediction.

"DEC. 31, 1875. This morning I was entirely without money. My heart had been drawn out in prayer that the Lord would send deliverance to-day. The mail brought from Auburndale, ten dollars; from a little girl in Hartford, Conn., one dollar and twenty-five cents for the Children's Home. During the day I received a package, which the following note will explain : —

'SALEM, Dec. 29, 1875.

" ' DR. CULLIS.

Dear Sir, — You will find enclosed fifteen hundred dollars in United-States bonds, with the coupons for Jan. 1 attached; also, one hundred and forty dollars in bills. Please acknowledge by mail, so that I may be sure it has reached your hands safely.'

"Will the dear reader notice the wonderful hand of God in this deliverance? The donor of this large gift is an entire stranger to me, and the Lord inclines his heart to send this amount, while I have lying on my table before me the following bills to be paid : last month's coal-bill, four hundred and fifteen dollars and eighty cents ; gas-bill, one hundred dollars and eighty cents ; water-tax, one hundred and fifty-eight dollars. It also enables me to make a payment on the new Children's Home, the cost of which has been several hundred dollars more than was expected. 'Trust in the Lord, and do good ; so shalt thou dwell in the land, and verily thou shalt be fed. Delight thyself also in the Lord, and he shall give thee the desires of thine heart. Commit thy way unto the Lord ; trust also in him, and he shall bring it to pass.' "

To those who study closely the workings of God's providence in connection with the workings of his grace, it will plainly appear that higher calls and greater bestowments do not include immunity from the ordinary misfortunes of life : both the iniquities of men, and the temptations of devils, will still be able to assail even the most highly developed faith, and to make sad havoc sometimes in the worldly affairs of God's chosen saints.

On the 12th of November, 1876, the newly erected Orphan House at Grove Hall was found to be on fire. The alarm being promptly given, no very great damage was done ; but the city inspector reported that all the grates in this house, as well as in the

Deaconess House, with one exception, were unsafe. It was from a fire in a grate that the mischief was done. The Doctor, of course, brought the matter to the notice of the contractor who had placed these fire-traps in the buildings ; and that person coolly refused to make them good, though he did go so far as to promise to repair the damage to the wall which had to be chopped away in order to extinguish the flames.

But a severer lesson than any in this line was now in store for this servant of the Lord. It will be remembered, that, out of the proceeds of the last great fair at Music Hall, eleven thousand dollars had been laid aside to be paid on the mortgage of the Grove-Hall property, in case the bank which held it should be willing to receive an instalment of the money before it was due, which was in 1880. In some of the emergencies through which the Doctor passed, he was obliged to draw on this treasured sum ; an act which caused him no little pain until he received clear direction from Headquarters that the saving of money for debts not yet due was not to be allowed to prejudice the supply of the current needs of the work. Still the lesson was only learned in part ; for the most of the money was still kept on investment, instead of being used for the maintenance and enlargement of the work.

In the month of August, 1878, Boston was startled by the announcement of the defalcation of the treas-urer of the Boston Belting Company, an old and respectable concern, with undoubted credit, in whose stock Dr. Cullis had invested the eleven thousand dollars which he intended to use in reducing the Grove-Hall mortgage. The downfall of this corporation carried with it many "snug investments" of private persons who, like Dr. Cullis, had been led to buy its stock on account of the high character of the men concerned in it. After rehearsing the facts of the failure, the Doctor adds, —

"Among the losses of hundreds of thousands of dollars, of course is included the Home investment. While we mourn the loss of the money, our greatest grief is for the man who has thus fallen.

"Now, as ever, our stay is upon God. We cannot falter while we read, 'It shall be well with them that fear him.' 'I, even I, am he that comforteth you : who art thou, that thou shouldest be afraid of a man that shall die, and of the son of man which shall be made as grass?' 'So that we may boldly say, The Lord is my helper, and I will not fear what man shall do unto me.' "

A specially painful experience must this have been at this particular time; for the loss occurred shortly after the purchase of the house and grounds for the long-desired Cancer Home at Walpole, on which the sum of seven thousand eight hundred and fifty dollars had been paid in cash, and a mortgage given for the remaining two thousand five hundred, to be paid in instalments within three years.

It was but reasonable that the loss of this money,

through the effort to save it for "to-morrow," should occupy the Doctor's serious attention; the more, because there was a particular use to which a portion of it might have been put, and thus have prevented the fixing of another mortgage-debt on the Lord's consecrated property. Was this earthly trust a snare to his feet? Did the knowledge of having nine or ten thousand dollars still remaining of this investment prevent, by so much, his absolute and entire trust in God? In the theft of the three thousand dollars from his safe, he had learned how cheap a thing is money in the estimation of Him who owns it all: now he was to be taught, at a still greater cost, not to put any thing between himself and the Lord, but to go on in the management of the great interests, just as he had done in the days of their small beginnings, and trust for, and make free and ready use of, the current gifts from the hand of the Lord, knowing that with him large gifts are as easy as small ones.

By the loss of this investment, the affairs of the Home were once more set entirely on a foundation of faith; and, from that time forward, no more of the Lord's money has been laid aside for uses in the distant future. If God's people are not to lay up treasures upon earth for themselves, no more are they to do it for him.

In this connection may be stated the fact that just at this time, and for several months previous, while the

Doctor was in great trial on account of the smallness of the gifts received, considerable sums of money in the form of bequests were stuck fast in the courts, and could not find their way into the Lord's treasury on account of the contesting of wills. But, on the other hand, the journal of the Home, under date of June 11, contains the following entry : —

"This morning one of the patients handed me a bank-book, saying, 'Here are fifty dollars that I have been saving tò bury me with. I think it will do you more good than it will the ground.' I knew nothing of the fact that the patient had this money, as every one we receive is supposed to be entirely destitute. The Spirit led her to give up this money, as nothing had been said before the patients of our great need. He promises to 'bring to light the hidden things of darkness.' While in prayer this noon, the truthfulness of God's word, that if we 'ask any thing,' so overwhelmed me, that my prayer was turned into praise, and my soul rejoiced before the answer came."

During the month of June, 1878, at a time of great trial, a stranger from Australia called, and gave the Doctor a dollar ; the next day a letter from Auckland, New Zealand, brought him ten pounds sterling. A small gift had been received from the Cape of Good Hope some time before ; and a legacy of five hundred dollars came from Springfield, Ohio, from a person whom he had never known. Thus was his faith strengthened by these reminders that the ends of the earth are all the Lord's, whereof to fulfil his promises ; and that the hearts of all men are in his hands, whereby to supply the needs of those who trust in him.

By midsummer the clouds had lifted, and the sun once more shone out, whereupon the Doctor gives this note of joyful praise : —

"JULY 10. Will the reader notice how wonderfully God has fulfilled his promise, and praise his dear name with me? Since the last record, the gifts amount to fourteen hundred and eighteen dollars and ninety cents. These gifts have been sent from different parts of our own country, and one from England. 'I will mention the loving-kindnesses of the Lord, and the praises of the Lord, according to all that the Lord hath bestowed on us, and the great goodness toward the house of Israel, which he hath bestowed on them according to his mercies, and according to the multitude of his loving-kindnesses.' "

"Dedication Day," Sept. 27, was this year marked by the consecration of the new Cancer Home at Walpole. It had been a year of great privation, during which less than seventeen thousand dollars had been received for the Home ; but it closed with an important addition to its power of usefulness, and the faith which had carried the ever-increasing burden thus far without breaking down now gladly assumed the added weight of this new department of the work.[1]

During this year, also, a good deal of home mission and mission Sunday-school work was done by the Deaconesses and other helpers ; a mission for the Chinese

[1] See chapter on Cancer Home.

in Alameda, Cal., was started; and, in view of the increasing number of persons coming to Boston from a distance, for faith healing, a Faith-cure House was projected, for which offerings in considerable amount were received.

Thus hath crying unto the Lord in time of trouble trained the voice to sing a higher note of praise.

It is proper to add, that, after the affairs of the Boston Belting Company were finally settled, there were found to be assets over liabilities, which enabled it to pay a per cent of its debts: thus three thousand five hundred dollars of the money supposed to be lost was ultimately recovered for the Home.

CHAPTER XII.

LOOKING UNTO JESUS.

"The Lord God is a sun and shield."

THE fifteenth year throughout was one of sore trial, as were the closing months of the fourteenth. At one time the Doctor writes as follows : —

"OCT. 11. It is now 12 M. The only gift thus far has been from Milford, fifty cents ; and I am entirely out of money. I am not only asking for large gifts, but expecting them at every ring of the door-bell and every arrival of the mail."

" 7 P.M. Nothing has come in since morning except nine barrels of apples. I am not tired of trusting Jesus. I know this long trial God will bless to some soul who reads this account, and I am content. 'Blessed is the man that trusteth in the Lord, and whose hope the Lord is.' "

"OCT. 12. It is now after 2 P.M., and thus far the Lord has kept me waiting. At this moment I have not a cent in the world of my own, or belonging to the Home. I am at peace, for I am the Lord's, and he has promised that if we 'seek first the kingdom of God, and his righteousness, all these things shall be added.' "

Later in the same month, he makes this record; in which connection it will be remembered, by those not familiar with Boston, that the Consumptives' Home at

Grove Hall is over three miles from Beacon Hill on which Dr. Cullis resides, and that the street-car cash fares at that time were six cents instead of five as now : —

"Oct. 28.   This morning, after getting into the horse-car to go to the Home, I found in one pocket five cents, and in another one cent ; this paid my fare.   On reaching the Home, I found twenty-five cents in the box."

"Nov. 4.   Only thirteen dollars and fifty-one cents thus far this month, and we need thousands.   Never have we had such a trial of faith.   God knows, and I wait patiently for him.   On account of our straitened circumstances, we have curtailed in all possible ways, except in food.   We have needed new bedding, towels. tablecloths, and many such things.   I opened two packages this morning, which had been sent to the Home. One contained four dozen towels, a dozen pairs children's stockings, six calico dress patterns, and a piece of cotton flannel ; the other bundle contained underclothing, aprons, etc., — for all of which we bless God, as they were just what we needed."

"Nov. 20.   It is now 7 P.M., and the only gift thus far has been one dollar and a half for the Children's Home.   For three days my Bible has been open before me on my table at the fourteenth of John ; and many times each day I have placed my fingers upon the thirteenth and fourteenth verses, and claimed them, asking God, in his dear Son's name, to make the 'whatsoever' cover thousands for my need.   I have looked up and said, 'O Lord, if these words are not true, nothing is true.   My soul says they are true.'   I have bowed before God, I have stood and prayed, I have walked the floor, asking God to make these verses true."

"Nov. 21.   Only one dollar to-day : yet the promise is true, and I am in peace."

"JAN. 6, 1879. Eleven dollars to-day. Gradually we are coming up into a condition of relief from the great straits in which we have been for so many months. Bless his dear name ! Among the gifts to-day, was one dollar for the Cancer Home, from one who 'is afflicted with that disease.' "

"JAN. 7. Among the gifts to-day, one of fifty cents for the Cancer Home. An application also for a poor woman dying of cancer, no home, and very needy. The house is ready to furnish, and I am waiting upon God for the means for this branch of the work."

"MARCH 7. Bless the Lord for answered prayer to-day ! From Auckland, New Zealand, ten pounds."

Thus not only do "the ends of the earth see the salvation of God," but they unite to carry it forward.

"APRIL 4. God be praised for the comfort and peace passing 'all understanding ' ! It surely is of God, for in my present condition it would be distress and confusion but for his grace so fully given. Two days ago I paid the interest upon the mortgage on the Home, in amount $2,345, taking every penny I had, leaving me nothing, not even for current expenses. I praise him that this bill has been met ; and I praise him that I am without money to-day, for I know he will make good his word. All of yesterday and to-day, this word has been singing itself in my soul : 'Said I not unto thee, that if thou wouldst believe, thou shouldst see the glory of God?' I do believe, and the glory fills my soul now."

"APRIL 5. I think it has been such a day of quiet peace as my soul has never known. All the day I have rested in God for the fulfilment of his promise, 'Whatsoever ye shall ask in my name, that will I do.' "

It is evident that this great spiritual blessing was not to be taken as a prophecy of immediate and full deliverance from pecuniary trial, for that continued for many a long month after. In such a life of faith, the Lord seems to train the soul to prize spiritual gifts for their own sake, and not as preludes to or premonitions of mere temporal blessings. Bodily wants press so heavily and constantly, that the supply thereof comes to be regarded as the great question and the chief good. In order to help the believer to reverse this order, and set the graces of the spirit in the first and chief place, God sometimes withholds the former, and at the same time bountifully pours out the latter. Alas for the human souls absolutely saturated with the money-idea, whereby every thing is instinctively viewed from that standpoint! This year of such marvellous soul-rest was to the very end a year of privation, the aggregate receipts being a little less than fourteen thousand dollars : yet the great household never for one day lacked for a full supply of "the comforts of life."

In 1880 the mortgage of sixty-seven thousand dollars was due ; but it was not paid, and has not been at the date of this writing. Much prayer has been made to God for large gifts to remove this heavy drag on the finances of the work ; but doubtless he does not find it a drag at all, though so large a proportion of the annual receipts is swallowed up in this way. Probably this is among the " all things " that " work together for good to them that are called according to his purpose ; " and, when the possible uses of the mortgage have ceased, the money will be sent to cancel it. For years prayer has been made in this direction, but the time for this great gift is not yet come. If the Lord please, may it come quickly!

The following incident may not serve for an example, since there are few who have been driven to such lengths of temptation, under such great responsibilities: it is, however, an interesting study of the workings of a mighty faith, holding the fort against a long and close siege of the enemy. Under date of Oct. 18, 1880, the Doctor writes down his experience, and recites his resources and prospects, thus : —

"After an evening of prayer, last night I took my Bible, and copied some and cut other promises from an old portion of a Bible, and pasted them on a sheet of paper. I have taken that sheet of paper many times to-day, and reminded God that these were his promises, and that they must be fulfilled, for his word was at stake. Here they are ; and, if the reader does not rejoice over them, I can. I have rejoiced all the day long : —

"'And call upon me in the day of trouble : I will deliver thee, and thou shalt glorify me.' — *Ps.* l. 15.

"'As for me, I will call upon God ; and the Lord shall save me. Evening, and morning, and at noon, will I pray, and cry aloud : and he shall hear my voice. He hath delivered my soul in peace from the battle that was against me : for there were many with me.' — *Ps.* lv. 16–18.

"'And I will walk among you, and will be your God, and ye shall be my people.' — *Lev.* xxvi. 12.

"'Fear not, I will help thee.'

"'And all things whatsoever ye shall ask in prayer, believing, ye shall receive.' — *Matt.* xxi. 22.

" ' Call unto me, and I will answer thee, and show thee great and mighty things, which thou knowest not.' — *Jer.* xxxiii. 3.

" ' And it shall come to pass, that before they call, I will answer ; and while they are yet speaking, I will hear.' — *Isa.* lxv. 24.

" ' Open thy mouth wide, and I will fill it.' — *Ps.* lxxxi. 10.

" ' Whatsoever ye shall ask in my name, that will I do, that the Father may be glorified in the Son.' — *John* xiv. 13.

" ' What things soever ye desire, when ye pray, believe that ye receive them, and ye shall have them.' — *Mark* xi. 24.

" ' Commit thy way unto the Lord ; trust also in him, and he shall bring it to pass.' — *Ps.* xxxvii. 5.

" ' All things are yours.' — *1 Cor.* iii. 21.

" ' But seek ye first the kingdom of God, and his righteousness ; and all these things shall be added unto you.' — *Matt.* vi. 33.

" ' Be careful for nothing ; but in every thing by prayer and supplication with thanksgiving let your requests be made known unto God.' — *Phil.* iv. 6.

" ' Wherefore he is able also to save them to the uttermost that come unto God by him, seeing he ever liveth to make intercession for them.' — *Heb.* vii. 25.

" ' Blessed is he that considereth the poor : the Lord will deliver him in time of trouble.' — *Ps.* xli. 1.

" ' If ye abide in me, and my words abide in you, ye shall ask what ye will, and it shall be done unto you.' — *John* xv. 7.

" ' Whatsoever ye shall ask the Father in my name, he will give it you.' — *John* xvi. 23.

" Verily, verily, I say unto you, He that believeth on me, the works that I do shall he do also ; and greater works than these shall he do ; because I go unto my Father.' — *John* xiv. 12.

" ' If any man serve me, him will my Father honor.' — *John* xii. 26.

" ' He will regard the prayer of the destitute, and not despise their prayer.' — *Ps.* cii. 17.

" 'If ye shall ask any thing in my name, I will do it.' — *John* xiv. 14.

" 'The Lord also shall roar out of Zion, and utter his voice from Jerusalem ; and the heavens and the earth shall shake : but the Lord will be the hope of his people, and the strength of the children of Israel.' — *Joel* iii. 16.

" 'No good thing will he withhold from them that walk uprightly.' — *Ps.* lxxxiv. 11.

" 'I will make darkness light before them, and crooked things straight. These things will I do unto them, and not forsake them.' — *Isa.* xlii. 16.

" 'He is faithful that promised.' — *Heb.* x. 23.

" I feel that I have not to wait long for the answer to my cry, for God shall be glorified in making his own word true, and I would have all the world to know what a God our Lord is ! "

The Report for 1880 contains the following personal reference, which as a public man, and a teacher of the great doctrine of absolute faith in God for temporal as well as spiritual salvation, he is entitled to make, and which will be lovingly and gratefully received by those who know and appreciate the rare transparency and frankness of him who makes it : —

"OCT. 30. 10 A. M. While waiting upon God this morning in behalf of the work, such a baptism of the Holy Ghost came upon me, that I knew God not only heard me in my cry for help, but that he was about to answer. Oh the comfort of knowing Jesus, and to believe that He who has provided will provide ! The morning mail brought plenty of letters, but no money.

" That the reader of this account of God's dealings with me

may understand my own position in regard to the work which he has intrusted to my hands, I desire to say that I am a poor man, supporting my family by the income of my profession as a physician. In this connection I can say, by his grace, that not only has my family been supported during the years of my practice, but the Lord has enabled me to give each year a surplus to the work of the Lord. For the last two years, the increase of the work, and the many persons coming to me for the prayer of faith, as promised to the child of God in James v. 14, have largely deprived me of my income, so that I am not able to give as much to God's work as in former years. The Lord, knowing all this, accepts even the small offering, and promises 'an hundred-fold more in this present life, and in the world to come life everlasting.'

"I wish I might be able to tell to thousands of souls the joy unspeakable that has come into my soul since I consecrated all to God, and have trusted him in temporal as well as spiritual matters. He does not separate them, and why should we? 'The very hairs of your head are all numbered;' and, if he will care for the sparrows, will he not care for the bodies of those for whom Christ died? Besides this, I ought to say that my dear wife, who has no property, but an income during her lifetime, devotes every dollar of it to the work of the Lord."

"4 P. M. The hand of our God *is* upon all them for good that seek Him.

> "'Lord, I delight in thee,
>   And on thy care depend;
> To thee in every trouble flee,
>   My best, my only Friend.
>
> When nature's streams are dried,
>   Thy fulness is the same;
> With this will I be satisfied,
>   And glory in thy name.'"

In the introduction to the Report of the seventeenth year of the work, are these memorable words : —

"For seventeen years I have BELIEVED ! The Word has been true to me. My God faileth never. The promises stand out upon the firmament of his word as the stars in the blue above, and they shed their light as truly as the stars ; but, like them, they are only seen by those who look up. The promises are revealed to those who are '*looking unto Jesus*.'"

In this connection recurs one of those sweet glimpses into the Word, which the Lord often gives to and through this minister thereof. The duty of watchfulness was under consideration, upon which the Doctor said, —

"'Watch.' Yes, but whom shall we watch? Ourselves? No, watch Jesus. You will often get into trouble, in spite of watching yourselves ; but if you are constantly 'looking unto Jesus,' you will be kept in perfect peace and safety."

It was in January of this seventeenth year of the work (1881), that Dr. Cullis made his second visit to Europe. During the eight years since his former tour, the Lord had wrought by him wonderful works of healing ; and this, in addition to his other doings by faith, had brought him to the front in England as well as in America. On his return from the Continent, a friend at Highgate, near London, entertained the Doctor, Mrs. Cullis, and their three children, most delightfully ; thus relieving him of all cost and care, and leaving him free to preach once, twice, and sometimes thrice a day, to the great assemblies that thronged to hear the gospel in its entirety, — salvation for the body as well as for the soul. It does not appear that at this time he devoted himself to the work of healing ; but his word was blessed to the conversion of many souls, on which account he says, "I then knew why our Father sent me to England."

The continual conversion of sinners, and sanctification of believers, which go on both at the regular and special meetings under the care of this man, ought to be a sufficient answer to the objection sometimes urged against faith-healing, that "the cure of the body is likely to engross the minds of those seeking it in this way, to the exclusion of the more important matter of the salvation of the soul." In the fact just recorded, the Lord gave to his servant, before the eyes of his people in England, a glorious vindication from this charge of letting down his ministry to a mere physical level ; just as he has continually vindicated him from a similar charge in America. Healing and saving go together in the ministry of Dr. Cullis, as they did in the ministry of the apostles ; and the one assists — nay, is often essential to — the completeness of the other.

In this seventeenth year of the work, the entire amount of money received in response to simple faith in God reached and passed the sum of *half a million of dollars*. Visionary as the project seemed to certain practical saints at first, they surely will be able to recognize so very practical a fact as the receipt of five hundred and seventeen thousand dollars in direct answer to prayer. "Hitherto ye have asked nothing." Was our blessed Lord impatient to be handing out the great things that were waiting in the heavenly storehouses for the prayer of faith, which is the only call on which they will come forth? Is not God generous, as well as good? And does not true generosity delight more in giving great gifts than in giving little ones?

Under date of Feb. 5, 1882, Dr. Cullis feels called upon to explain, in a pleading rather than a boastful tone, why it is that the faith-work has come to be so large and wide. At the outset of the Report for the eighteenth year, he gives a catalogue of the various departments; which has the appearance of the missionary record of a whole synod or conference, rather than of the list of stations and charities which have grown up under the hand of one man, and he with no ecclesiastical standing or patronage whatever. Here is the list, both in form and substance, as it appears in the Report for 1882 : —

LIST OF

Institutions Belonging to the Work of Faith.

At Grove Hall, Boston Highlands.

CONSUMPTIVES' HOME.

SPINAL HOME.

TWO ORPHAN HOMES.

DEACONESS HOME.

GROVE HALL CHURCH.

FAITH CURE HOUSE.

At Walpole.

CANCER HOME.

CHURCHES AND MISSIONS.

BEACON HILL CHURCH	Boston.
COTTAGE STREET CHURCH	Dorchester.
LEWIS STREET MISSION	Boston.
FAITH TRAINING COLLEGE	Boston.
OUR COFFEE ROOM	Boston.
WORK AMONG THE FREEDMEN, BOYDTON INSTITUTE .	Boydton, Va.
" " " CHINESE IN ALAMEDA . . .	California.

FOREIGN MISSIONS.

BASIM	Central India.
BALASORE	India.

TRACT REPOSITORIES.

BOSTON.   NEW YORK.   PHILADELPHIA.

LONDON, ENGLAND.

In view of these manifold departments of service for Jesus, the Doctor makes this modest defence : —

"And just here I would be glad, by the help of God, to explain how and why the work increases, and thus to answer those who so frequently say, 'You are doing too much : why not be satisfied with the branches of work already begun, and which would be done much better if you confined yourself solely to them?'

"The work came in answer to the cry, 'Lord, what *is* my work?' Then followed a searching of heart as to how and what manner of spirit should lead in that work. As I sought out of the Scriptures the way, my soul was humbled within me, and I saw that an utter surrender of myself and all my notions and plans was the only condition by which God could work through me. 'All things would be added,' would I 'seek *first* the kingdom of God.' This condition I recognized as one of perfect yielding to God, that I might be the instrument of his will. As such a one, I saw exceeding great and precious promises given to me ; and as I read, 'Ask and receive, that your joy may be full ; ' 'If ye abide in me, and my words abide in you, ye shall ask what ye will, and it shall be done unto you ; ' 'If ye shall ask any thing in my name, I will do it ; ' 'What things soever ye desire when ye pray, believe that ye receive them, and ye shall have them,' — Satan came also ; he injected the thought that these promises were not for the present age, only for the disciples. Of course Satan knew and I knew that to thus take God at his word would stir up the Church and the world ; and God might be found true to his word, and stronger than Satan. Searching the Scriptures again, I found the rich legacy of the promises was not only for the disciples, 'but for them also which shall believe on me through their word.' But Satan did not leave me, and I became almost in despair ; until wrenching myself from his grasp, from what seemed almost like an actual struggle with flesh and blood, I seized the Bible, and declared, 'I will believe God and his word, the whole of it, whether I understand it or not.' More than conqueror through Him that loved me, I triumphed over Satan, and the doubts and fears and despair into which he had plunged me ; and never, from that time to this, have I had a doubt. Believing and acting upon the promises of God, faith rises from height to height ; visions of labors more abundant come as the direct behest of my almighty Father. 'Casting all my care upon him,' I float on the river of peace, and what would have seemed obstacles to faithlessness and unbelief are only the swelling waves bearing me on into the full tide of success and blessing. Every new enterprise for God lifts me over and beyond fear, beyond anxiety. 'All things are added,' as I have need. To be 'always abounding in the work of the Lord,' brings the fulness of the revelation of his 'power to usward who believe.' If one promise is true, then all are true, and my happiness and joy consist in proving their truth and their power."

Later in the same month the Doctor writes as follows : —

" FEB. 27. Another one says to me to-day, ' You are undertaking too much ; the Lord does not expect one man to do so much.' I say, God expects every man to do his duty, which is to put as much energy in the work of the Lord as he would for money-making, or to build up his own business ; God expects this. We are not living for this world, but for eternity. After hearing the above criticism, I 'went and told Jesus,' — told him I wished I had ten times the energy to put into work for him and for suffering humanity. Soon after this, a poor girl, an outcast, with no place to die in but the poorhouse, came to ask shelter ; and my heart thanked God that we had a home for her, where I pray she may find Jesus. And again I prayed for the work, that it might accomplish an hundred-fold more for Jesus."

Here is a record in the Report for 1882, the like of which very, very seldom appears in its pages : —

"JUNE 9. To-day I received from the —— Church of Malden fifty dollars."

In examining the accounts of gifts and their sources, one hardly ever finds the word "church." There have been several great uprisings in Boston and vicinity, for the help of these Homes in times of distress, and numbers of fairs and gatherings have been held by even the little children, who have come to love Dr. Cullis, his sick people, and his orphans ; but the churches, as such, have shown little interest in this way of doing good. This fact should not be lost sight of in studying the history of the faith-work : it shows that what has been done therein has not been done as a division of, or a diversion from, the work of the organized ecclesiastical guilds, but as an addition to the well-doing which they are carrying on in the Master's name. No agent for the Consumptives' Home attempts to reap any of the harvest in the congregations of the churches, and no pressure is brought to bear upon those who hold the Lord's money in their hands, to give here rather than there : therefore there is room and occasion for the most hearty Christian fraternity between this independent system of missions, whose only treasury is in heaven, and the more extensive organizations which sometimes think of humble workers in the same cause as unauthorized intruders. It is, under the circumstances, a rare pleasure to point out this churchly gift; it is proof that the unlimited authority given by the Lord to his disciples to "go" and to "preach" is recognized in the quarter from which this welcome token was received.

The eighteenth year closes with this joyful record : —

"Sept. 27, 1882.   Eighteen years ago to-day the first Home was dedicated to the living God.   I shall never forget that evening when, with friends of Christ, we stood together, and gave to God the small beginning of what has become so great in his hands.   The years have flown quickly; much blessing has come to my own soul during these years, as I have learned more and more to trust God.   Many trials have made Jesus even more near and precious, for he has made the promise true, ' I will not leave you comfortless.'   He has been my companion during these years; and to-night, as · I pen these lines, my soul rejoices in his love and the sweet sense of rest in him.

"During the last six weeks the Lord has poured his bounty upon us, and we have prospered.   There have been several gifts of hundreds of dollars, one of *one thousand*, and recently a friend sends a gift with the following letter : —

"Dear Doctor, — Enclosed I hand you a package of government bonds : $4,000 four and a half per cent, $1,000 four per cent, —five thousand dollars in all.   I have been holding them for some time subject to the Lord's call.   I hear the

Lord's call now. I do not know of any one that can use the Lord's money to better advantage than you, so I send it to you for your work. You can use at your discretion in the different branches of your work.

Yours very truly,

"Before closing I would add more interesting testimony from Miss French, our faithful matron. God's loving care in providing workers may be seen in the following incident : —

"'One of the nurses received a call one afternoon which compelled her to leave the Home early next morning. As her going would leave several sick with no one to care for them, we cried unto the Lord to send some one immediately to fill the place about to be made vacant. In about an hour after she left, a lady called at the door, and asked if we wanted a nurse. She said afterward that she had no thought of offering her services when she started for Grove Hall ; she came out to visit the place, but as soon as she entered the grounds she felt a desire to remain, and when the door was opened she felt impelled to inquire if we needed help. She has given us four months of faithful service.

"'A short time ago, Mr. R—— came as a patient to the Home. On the 19th his nurse asked him if he was a Christian. He replied, "Yes." She then asked if Jesus was in his heart as a comforter. The answer was, "I do not know what you mean by that." He proceeded to tell something of his history, and how his health gave way while he was studying to become a Catholic priest. Here was a cultivated intellect, but an empty heart. Words about the great love of Jesus were spoken, with the prayer that they might bring light into the heart so dark. Towards evening of the next day, as the nurse was passing his door and looked in, he beckoned her near, and said, "I want to be a Christian too : won't you tell me stories about Jesus?" As the "old, old story of the cross" was told in short sentences, he repeated some of them after her. One especially pleased him, and he said it over three or four times: "Jesus loves me, even me; and I will love Jesus too." As he said these words, his face lighted up with the gladness that comes alone from a sense of sins forgiven. After that he loved to hear the name of Jesus, and the reading of the Bible. On June 29, when we thought him dying, we asked him if he felt ready to go. He smiled, and said all was right. In the evening of that day, we trust he fell asleep in Jesus.

"'One day while making some changes, removing patients from one room to another, a woman in the long ward stretched out her hand to me, saying, "O Miss F——! I want to be a Christian; I am very sick, and I am not prepared to die: won't you pray for me?" So I knelt among the disarranged furniture, piles of clothing, bedding, etc., and prayed with her; she gave her heart to God, and was at peace. She died not long after, but not, we trust, unprepared.'"

"SEPT. 20. Three expressed a desire to be prayed for in the patients' meeting last evening; and also we found one of the domestics under conviction, who had long been desiring to be a Christian. We had a few moments' conversation with her, then knelt in a corner of the chapel, and she gave her heart to the Lord."

CHAPTER XIII.

TWENTY GLORIOUS YEARS.

"And it shall come to pass in the last days, that the mountain of the Lord's house shall be established in the top of the mountains, and shall be exalted above the hills; and all nations shall flow unto it."

THE last chapter closed with the eighteenth year of the Consumptives' Home. The chief incidents of the two remaining years will close the first part of this volume. Few indeed are those who are privileged to have so large a share in the work of the Lord as has been given to his servant Dr. Cullis. If a new volume of the Acts of the Apostles were to be written, extending down to the present time, those who have seen the working of the mighty hand of God through this chosen disciple would fully expect to find his name therein.

Twenty years ago when he tremblingly entered upon the work of faith in that small dwelling-house on the north side of the city of Boston, there was not in all America, so far as he knew, a single institution of the kind in existence. It was his lot to be the pioneer; and it has been his delight to realize that glorious promise, "The wilderness and the solitary place shall be glad for them, and the desert shall rejoice and blossom as the rose. The glory of Lebanon shall be given unto it ; the excellency of Carmel and Sharon. They shall see the glory of the Lord and the excellency of our God." The love and care bestowed upon nearly three thousand of God's homeless and hopeless sick ones may have made but a trifling impression upon the vast tides of sin and sickness which sweep over the world ; but the fact that this great charity has been carried on by faith, and has actually lived and increased and multiplied on the unsolicited gifts which the Lord himself has sent in direct answer to prayer, has made an impression on the tides of doubt and rationalism which had so nearly swamped the faith of the Church. Even now, when the Consumptives' Home is an accomplished fact, and the faith-cure can show its hundreds of successful cases, there are but comparatively few of those who profess to be Christian believers, who do not stumble, even if they do not scoff, at the exercise of powers and gifts which the Lord bestowed upon his disciples, and, through them, upon the Church ; which powers and gifts have indeed been almost wholly unused in later ages, but which have never been taken away.

At a recent ministers' meeting, in recounting the experience of the past twenty years, Dr. Cullis said, —

"I have suffered for this work as you will not have to suffer. I have been opposed and abused, and called all sorts of bad names, for venturing to believe God, and to act upon that belief. Especially from those unbelievers inside the Church, have I suffered persecution : they have called my trust in God 'fanaticism,' and the acting-out of my faith 'presumption.' But God has stood by me, and the truth is making its way."

Happy is the man against whom the only charges are that he has believed too well, and succeeded too much! It is a sore offence to worldly-wise Christian teachers and leaders, that their prophecies of failure, and of injury to the judicious and rational faith of the Church thereby, are farther from fulfilment than ever. So grandly has the Lord vindicated his believing ones, that it is no longer possible for scribes and elders to frighten them by threats of being put out of the synagogue. For, among other blessed accompaniments of this great faith-revival, is the discovery that no man, or body or bodies of men, have the ownership or control of the Church of the Lord Jesus Christ ; but that it is possible for a company of his loving followers to be a " church " wherever Jesus himself will meet them. But this opening out into the ultimate idea of Christian liberty and unity will be more fully treated of in the accounts of the churches at Grove Hall and Beacon Hill Place, as well as in the chapter entitled " The Theology of the Faith-work."

And now it remains to walk along the mountain-tops of this heaven-reaching history for the years from 1882 to 1885. There cannot be mountains without valleys,

so there cannot be triumphs without trials.   Hereafter,
in these pages, the trials will be understood if they are
not recounted.   Never has this work for long escaped
them ; even now there is need far beyond the supply.
But need is one thing, and necessity is another; and
there is no necessity which is not met from day to
day, and no essential comfort which the Lord does not
supply.   The heavy mortgage-debt still swallows up a
large amount of the annual receipts ; yet, if the interest thereon be reckoned as the rental of the premises,
the four thousand dollars thus used procure more for
these great households of God's afflicted ones, in the
direction of their present use, than three times that
amount will procure for any other class of people.
Then there are heavy taxes, — iniquitously heavy, —
for this institution is not a favorite with a city government managed by the rum-power ; yet one after
another of its unjust exactions has been paid, under
protest, until now they have measurably ceased to
trouble the heart and mind of the man who lives in
and for — but never upon — this work of God.   Those
who visit the various Homes may see with what pains-
taking and ingenuity the furnishing thereof — much of
it old to begin with, and none the better for added
years of hard service — is still made to do duty, and
even, in many cases, to appear respectable as well as to
serve its purpose.   Yet no mistress of palatial mansion
was ever so proud and happy in the midst of gorgeous

surroundings as is the matron of the Consumptives'
Home in the midst of her invalid chairs and tables and
men and women. Some of the former can be mended ;
but all of the latter are to be made over new, and
the process is visibly going on every day before her
delighted eyes.

Financially, too, the case is different from what it
used to be. Year by year the value of the magnificent
estate increases, till now it stands for three or four
times the debt upon it.

"Why not sell out, pay off the debt, and take the
balance to buy and build in a cheaper place ? "

To this question there are at least two good answers.
First, The Lord who gave direction to buy, and who
has enabled his servant to retain and improve the
estate, has not given him direction to sell. Second,
God is abundantly able to stand the expense of giving
this company of invalids and orphans a three-hundred-
thousand-dollar home. The rise in the value of city
real estate does not make him at all anxious to "realize ;" and the presence of this majestic object-lesson
in the most beautiful part of a great city is, doubtless,
worth more to him than all that could be bought with
the money saved by the most economical and sagacious
business management. Thanks be to God, there is
one place in the city of Boston where values are not
chiefly reckoned in dollars and cents !

And there is still another answer, and one not to

be lightly esteemed ; viz., the value of this grove and these grounds as a stimulus to the faith of those who dwell and labor there.   God's ancient people were constantly reminded by the beauty and the plenty of Canaan, that it was the Lord who had brought them up out of the land of Egypt and through the dreary wilderness, and who had thus surrounded them with visible proofs of his faithfulness and love.   In like manner, Dr. Cullis and his consecrated staff of workers, as well as the homeless and hopeless ones who here have found both a home and a hope, can look at the magnificent results of the faith of the past twenty years, — magnificent even from the worldly side, and infinitely glorious from the heavenly point of view, — and say to themselves, "The Lord Jehovah hath brought us up out of the Egypt of doubt, and through the wilderness of affliction ; and surely, right here in the promised land itself, he will not leave us to fall before the enemy, nor yet to perish by the way." With such a history behind it, such a foundation under it, and such promises before it, this work of faith may hope to stand until the King himself appears, and drives both sin and sickness from his world.

The nineteenth year, which closed Sept. 30, 1883, was one of prosperity in all departments.   In the Report for that year, the Doctor says, —

"The work has grown in spite of myself, in spite of the warnings of friends.   I listen to all the voices, and I wait on the Lord. And finally the Voice which I must heed before all others speaks : ' Behold, *I* have set before thee an open door, and no *man* can shut it.'

" It is only by waiting before the Lord, in the sense of perfect abandonment to his will, that I can know his voice. And then, by the opening-up of localities, by the sense of a pressing need, by the cry of one or more consecrated souls who desire a work for God, by the sending of means, or by the denial of them, thus moving us to press our suit, — in all these ways God unites to guide and lead us to a knowledge of his will. While we watch unto prayer, and without haste, with a continued willingness to be denied, the light does break, the door opens, and then '*no man can shut it.*'

"To lookers-on there may seem lack of judgment, and many signs of human frailty, and with all humility I acknowledge these, — that many might have done better in the eyes of men ; but I walk before the Lord with the sole desire to please him as far as he gives me light. I ' run in the way of his commandments.' I have seen many souls and bodies lightened, many delivered from the bondage of Satan ; the promises have been made true in supplying 'all my need ; ' a fire has been kindled for God in many dark places of earth ; many weak hands have been strengthened, and feeble knees confirmed : and all this has followed the single and earnest seeking to honor God by trusting his promises, by declaring them to be true, by subscribing to the faithful words of a faithful God. ' Heaven and earth shall pass away, but my word shall not pass away.' "

It is the same story as it was when the work had its feeble beginning nineteen years ago, — faith in God. Surely he who takes hold of the Infinite One, by means of faith in his promises, has the most substantial and reliable basis for success along the line of the Divine purpose.

It will be noticed that the Lord is the sole director in all these affairs. There is indeed a board of trustees for the Consumptives' Home, consisting now of Ex-Gov. William Claflin, Hon. Jacob Sleeper, Hon. E. S. Converse, Rev. A. J. Gordon, D.D., D. B. Hatch, Esq., Charles Cullis, M.D., and Mrs. Lucretia A. Cullis ; but in the Articles of Incorporation it is expressly provided that the entire management of the work, and of all the property which it holds or which it may acquire, shall be under the sole charge of Dr. Cullis during his lifetime, and that he may appoint his successor. In this manner has the personal management of the Lord, by means of his servant chosen for that purpose, been effectually guarded against the interference of irresponsible wisdom, or the dictation of worldly opinions when they conflict with the life of faith. The sole function of these two boards is to hold the property in trust, whereby the possibility of its becoming a matter of personal advantage is prevented, and whereby this work of faith and charity may be continued after the death of him under whose hand it has come into existence and success.

It has taken a long time and a special training to fit this man for this work ; and it evidently is not the mind of the Lord, now that he has become familiar with the voice of the Spirit, and fully in accord therewith, that he should be in any way hindered from the most prompt and perfect obedience. Such a position as God's vicegerent, in a place of so much power, has been known to produce a dictatorial spirit in good men, even to the extent of attempting to dictate in matters of duty to those who were in no way subject to their control. This snare this man has thus far escaped : for a marvel, his heart is as tender, and his mind as open to the truth, as if he were only a common sort of Christian, with a common line of duty before him. There are no signs of undue dogmatism about him, nor yet of overmuch ambition, even in the mighty work which now has almost put a line around the earth.

The following incident will show what place he has in the hearts of the patients in the Home. Under date of Nov. 30, 1883, occurs this entry in the Report : —

"This morning a roll was handed me, tied up with blue ribbon. I put it in my pocket to read on reaching home. May it speak gladness to the hearts of those who were contributors, as they read of the gratitude and love awakened in the hearts of the sick ones !

GROVE HALL, Nov. 30, 1882.

"'DEAR DR. CULLIS, — We, the undersigned, patients of the Consumptives' Home, do render a vote of thanks for our most excellent Thanksgiving dinner ; and we are not only grateful for this, but for all the blessings and privileges which we daily have in this holy and beautiful Home, which God has given into your care, where so many friendless are welcomed, fed, clothed, and where they finally learn that they are " children of a King."'

"This was signed by fifty of the patients."

In December of the same year, after mentioning that the work now requires two thousand dollars a month, he says, —

" Will the dear reader of this account remember that upwards of one hundred and fifty people are daily fed and clothed, and that no human hand has promised to support or help us, and that year after year this work goes on without care or anxiety ; the peace of God filling my heart, and he sending by the hand of his loving stewards gifts for our support? Have we not reason to bless his holy name, and to ' wait patiently for Him '? ' Hitherto the Lord hath helped us.' "

The question sometimes arises, Why does Dr. Cullis, if he really believes in the faith-cure, still continue the practice of medicine, and even give medical treatment to the patients in the Consumptives' Home ? An entry in the nineteenth Report answers this and some other questions so well that it must have a place in these pages.   The date is Dec. 26, 1883.

" While I have never relinquished my medical practice, — recognizing my knowledge in this profession as belonging to God for the benefit of such as have not faith, and using it as the legitimate means for the support of my family, — I have also declared my faith in the promises of God, and my willingness to claim the promise for healing for all such as are willing to trust God with me.   This latter course has led my friends and the public to *assume* that my profession as a physician was dropped.

" Many also assume that the Consumptives' Home and other

houses for the sick under my care, numbering, with nurses and assistants, some one hundred and fifty, are houses for faith-cure. It would answer the queries of many, for me to state here what can readily be understood, — that these sick ones form a little community of persons from every condition and walk of life, all subject to the infirmities, disabilities, and varied influences that have sway in larger communities. I cannot be conscience and faith for all, any more than for the larger world outside of us. I am free to use all my knowledge, all my faith, as it is required for each and all.

"Many, if not most, of those who come, are from the lowest walks of life; from meagre conditions, distorted mentally and morally.

"Like Paul, we must be all things to all, if by any means we may save some. If by successive steps into the light their desires broaden, their spiritual insight awakens, even to the committing all to God and receiving all by faith in him, we gladly minister thereunto.

"A small proportion have thus come to receive an answer to faith in the healing of the body, along with the spirit's release from the bondage of sin.

"All who enter as patients are friendless and homeless ones. They are suddenly taken from absolute want and distress, to the abode of sunshine, peace, and plenty; laid on beds sweet and clean; in tender ministrations their hunger is relieved, their pain alleviated, and nothing is left undone to restore and strengthen the bodies wasted by disease.

"Is it to be wondered at, that such as these often settle down into a complete satisfaction in being thus cared for; putting far from them the thought of going out again into the world from whence they came, the very remembrance of which is a horrid nightmare, a vision of awful, hopeless misery?

"To such, even a *cure* by faith would scarcely be apprehended, much less comprehended. Here God *does* supply their need; and by the supply of the earliest absolute need we endeavor to minister the true riches offered abundantly through our Lord Jesus Christ, looking for the 'early and the latter rain' to bring forth 'first the blade, then the ear, after that the full corn in the ear.'

"So, while a loyalty to God's truth in the promises for healing of body has cost me loss of business, loss of friends, and gifts to the work, I would not shrink or falter : I would simply, lovingly *trust Jesus.*

"One more word with regard to the sick ones. Many come *only* to die. Some of these are in despair on account of their sin. A young life has been shortened by the ravages of vice. Can *this* one find Jesus mighty to save? Yes ! we answer. The Fountain is still open for sin and uncleanness. And now, as with the thief on the cross, Jesus is near, to give the eternal word of assurance, 'To-day thou shalt be with me in paradise.' "

"DEC. 30. To-morrow is the last day of 1882, and it is the sabbath. I look back upon the year now closing, with thanksgiving in my heart and upon my lips. Great straits are upon us, but I can look up and not be afraid. The gifts for the last week have been small, not nearly enough for our current expenses, but God increases my joy. "My cup runneth over.' "

The Report for the twentieth year, ending Sept. 30, 1884, at the date of this writing (August, 1885) has only just appeared. It shows that the Doctor has been again called to pass through the fiery furnace ; but, as in the former year of distress, the Lord was with him, and the fire did not kindle upon him. Although frequent glimpses have been given into his state of mind under special stress and trial, one more — the sharpest twinge of all — may appropriately be recorded. The date is March 28, 1884.

"Several days ago I added up the amount needed for all present current expenses; and, opening my Bible, I read the fourteenth chapter of John, coming to the thirteenth verse, 'Whatsoever ye shall ask in my name, that will I do, that the Father may be glorified in the Son.' This promise I prayed over and over, claiming it for my need; and as the promise came at the end of the page, *I pasted the little bit of paper upon which I had been figuring, at the bottom of the page, that it might stay there as my claim upon the word of God.*

"I do not ask this money for myself, but for the work of God; and my soul rejoices that he has again called me to prove before the world that his word is true. Some may ask, 'Why this trial of faith, when you have been so long in the way, and so much has been accomplished?' I reply, Faith is not faith unless it is tested; it must be tried in the furnace, and purified; having thus passed through the fire, it is fit for the Master's use."

In March following, we find him saying, —

"For many days I have waited upon God for help in this our time of need. He says he is a very present help in time of need, and my soul waits all the day upon him. No one but God knows the greatness of this trial now resting upon us. He knows all about it; and, knowing that 'all things work together for good to those that love him,' I patiently wait for deliverance. It *must* come! It *will* come! While I do not know why this long trial has continued, I have been content to trust God, and ask no questions."

In closing the Report for 1884, the Doctor once more calls attention to the reason why, as he believes, the means for the maintenance of the work of faith and charity were for a time so painfully reduced.

"I know there are human reasons why there have been fewer donations.   As this Report is to go into the hands of my friends, I suppose I ought to mention that the one great weapon used against me declares itself thus : ' He practises faith-cure ! '

" On this ground I have met with great opposition.   Former friends have left me.   What has been to me but a taking of my stand on the promises of God, has been denominated ' fanaticism,' and by others, in their misapprehension, ' sacrilege.'   For this cause, friends who had been in the habit of giving to the work for the poor and sick have withdrawn their aid and sympathy.

" If the good people have made me feel my loss thus, I have at least lived to see the truth of, and the results of, ' the prayer of faith ' throughout the world.   Thousands upon thousands of the sick and suffering, ' to the uttermost parts of the sea,' who could not be helped by physicians, have been healed by the Lord ; and through this gift has come in a fulness unknown before, — the revelation of peace and joy in the Holy Ghost."

Consider how great are the cares and labors in conducting so large and varied an enterprise, even with a full treasury : what, then, must be the burden when for weeks together the receipts fall far below the necessary expenses, when coldness takes the place of kindness, and when one is compelled to suffer in himself because he has called down relief from Heaven for the sufferings of others !

The receipts of the Homes for the twentieth year of the work again fell off, the sum given for this department being only fourteen thousand one hundred and forty-six dollars and forty-eight cents ; a decrease of over six thousand dollars from the previous year. What a tension of nerves, what a wrenching of sensibilities, what a struggle of faith! Yet it was borne bravely, trustingly, triumphantly, as the present healthy and hopeful state of affairs most clearly shows.

In looking upon the Doctor's cheery face, even those acquainted with the inner life and the daily needs of this great house can hardly realize what a burden he must be carrying ; enough to crush a spirit not purified and tempered in the fire as his has been, but not enough to weigh him down or make him stumble for a single step. The secret of it is that he has become a true yokefellow with the Lord, and Jesus carries the heavy end. Nor does the withholding of gifts by human hands lead him to think of reducing the work : on the contrary, he reaches out to take new blessings along with new responsibilities. As for example, last year a farm was purchased in Walpole, near enough to the Cancer Home to be under the supervision of its steward, whereon to raise provisions for the households there and at Grove Hall. And still another advance. Shut out temporarily from Old Orchard camp-ground by a change of management, — Dr. Cullis purchased and opened a leafy temple of his own at Intervale, N.H., amidst the glorious scenery of the White Mountains, and there made provision for his annual midsummer convention. During the present year those grounds have been greatly enlarged and improved, and the showers of blessing which descended upon the convocation of 1885 gave proof and pledge of the continued favor of the Master upon this special work of his servant.

Of what spiritual upliftings this ascent from the sea to the mountains may be the prophecy, it is as yet too soon to speak; but in the light of the history of these twenty glorious years, — all the more glorious because of great trials and great deliverances, — this last ascending into the hill of the Lord must signify a still loftier range of power and helpfulness along which God is about to call his servant to pass. In the ripened prime of life, trained in schools which the great Teacher himself has opened for his instruction, tried in the fire, broadened by a world-wide sympathy, aided by a devoted wife, surrounded by a staff of consecrated men and women, and filled with faith and the Holy Ghost, it would seem as if, instead of having reached the climax of his career, this man of God, like Joshua of old, were just stepping into the bed of the Jordan whose waters have been divided for his march, and that before him opens out a land of promise wherein to make broad conquests in the name of the King of kings.

The first ten years of this faith-work were an astonishment; the second ten have been a vindication; the third ten, — with works like these upspringing far and wide, at the same ratio of increase, they ought to bring him in sight of the mountain of the Lord's house already established in the tops of the mountains, and all men beginning to flow unto it. Then farewell to the days of doubt and littleness and feebleness; and hail to the day of faith in God, whereby his people shall take hold upon his power, and begin to work those "greater works" which, during all these creeping ages, have waited for souls great enough to do them!

And now once more let the numbers speak. They tell a story which, to the common thought, seems far too good to be true.

The whole number of patients cared for in the Consumptives' Home during the twenty years ending with September, 1884, is *two thousand seven hundred and seven.*

The grand total of receipts is *six hundred and twenty-one thousand, nine hundred and sixty dollars, thirty-six cents.*

The value of real estate held in trust for the work at home and abroad, over and above the mortgages upon it, is not far from *three hundred thousand dollars.*

All this in answer to the prayer of faith.

There is one more blessed reckoning which figures will not set forth; viz., the hundreds of souls — almost a thousand now — who have have here found pardon and peace in the Saviour, and who have passed on into the heavens. There is on the grounds at Grove Hall a pretty little chapel for the dead, to which the wasted bodies of those who die are removed, and where is held over them the service of Christian burial.   As often as every week on an average, month by month and year by year, some "homeless and hopeless" one — homeless and hopeless till they entered this sanctuary of faith and love — ascends to the Home amid the groves of paradise.   The most of these have come with the calamity and the guilt of sin upon them, and have here learned to believe on the Lord Jesus Christ.

What a harvest from these fields!   No wonder the Great Husbandman smiles upon those who labor therein.

PART II.

—————

FAITH MISSIONS

AT HOME AND ABROAD.

CHAPTER XIV.

AN ELECT LADY.

THE "portrait edition" of this volume, for which reluctant consent has been given by Dr. Cullis (who has an unnecessary modesty about appearing in person in the history of his work), would not be complete without the picture of the devoted and accomplished lady who through all these years has stood by his side, shared his heavy trials, and joined her faith with his in the prayers which have received such glorious answers as are recorded in these pages.

If "the unbelieving husband is sanctified by the believing wife," how much more is the believing husband "sanctified" by the same precious union !

But there is a reason, over and above her great and essential service in the holy mission committed to her husband, which has led the editor of this book to desire the insertion of the portrait of Mrs. Cullis ; viz., the very large proportion of the Faith-work, both at home and abroad, which has, from the first, been performed by women. Surely, then, these sisters of the Lord ought to have a representative in the history of the work.

The honors of the Church of Christ in apostolic times, as well as its toils and sufferings, were given to believing women. Why should the translators of the New Testament have rendered the feminine *presbutera* in a manner merely suggestive of elderly females in the Church, while its masculine form, *presbuteros*, is set forth as the name of an office of power and honor? Women elders, and not merely "elder women" as in the Authorized Version of the Epistles, are recognized in the department of Christ's kingdom whose centre is Grove Hall. Women are set apart by the Doctor and his associates to the holy offices of the gospel, with the same forms as men; and why not? In this view of the case, as well as to meet the wishes of multitudes of her friends and co-laborers, it is especially fitting that the portrait of this elect lady should stand as the frontispiece of the second part of this volume, as the portrait of Dr. Cullis does for that of Part First.

The following brief personal sketch will be understood to mean a great deal more than it says. How could twenty years of such faith and love and patience and helpfulness be recorded in so small a compass?

It was several years after Dr. Cullis entered upon the life and work of faith to which, after the experiences just related, he had been called, that he became acquainted with Mrs. Lucretia (Bramhall) Reed, a lady who, like himself, had suffered deep affliction, and who had been led thereby to devote herself to a religious life.

Shortly after her first marriage, she made the voyage to India with her husband, who had business partners in that country; and five years later she again crossed the seas, bringing home his embalmed remains for burial. But there was one great comfort in this great sorrow: during her husband's sickness, which was of a lingering nature, she had the joy of seeing him brought to the Saviour, — whose loving disciple she had been even from childhood, — and of ministering to his spiritual needs, as well as to his temporal comfort, in the last days and hours of his life.

Settled once more in her former home in Boston, she began to look about for some simple and easy work for the Lord; and turning aside from the church of which her family were members, because it seemed too cold and self-sufficient in its orthodoxy, she joined a little company of believers calling themselves Christian Baptists, and for five or six years led a life of quiet usefulness among the sick and the poor. This kind of life was just the school in which to train her for the larger mission which was in store for her, and in which, as the wife of Dr. Cullis, she has become so great a blessing to so many souls. In prayer, in song, in godly counsel, and as a teacher of gospel work for women, she is the chief of all the helpers in the wide and diversified section of Christ's kingdom over which her husband has been commissioned to preside; while, as the centre of a Christian home, " her children rise up and call her blessed; her husband also, and he praiseth her."

Besides the daughter by her former marriage, — now Mrs. Mallory, wife of the pastor of Grove Hall Church, — the household of Dr. and Mrs. Cullis comprises one son and two daughters.   For the most part, health and prosperity have attended their domestic life ; the trials through which they have passed in earlier days have been blessed to their deeper spiritual experience ; while for years, as almoners of God's special bounty, they have realized the truth of the words of our Lord, " It is more blessed to give than to receive."   A modest income from the estate of her first husband, and the professional earnings of the Doctor, enable these two consecrated faith-workers to carry on this rapidly en-larging circle of charities without being themselves a burden upon the funds thereof.   And not only so, but many a time when gifts have been small, and necessities large, they have, out of their own personal store, met the needs of the work.   In spite of trials, privations, and personal sacrifices, they have substantial reasons for believing in the providence and promises of God ; and now, as always, do they hold their worldly goods as subject to the call of Him from whom they were received.

CHAPTER XV.

THE PUBLICATION AND TRACT WORK.

"Call for Simon, whose surname is Peter; who shall tell thee words, whereby thou and all thy house shall be saved."

IN the second part of this volume, an account is to be given of the numerous branches of the "Work of Faith" under the hand of Dr. Cullis ; taken, usually, in the order of their establishment.

As the work has providentially opened out in new directions, new departments have been organized ; and, in order to save the multiplicity of separate institutions, Dr. Cullis caused them to be incorporated together, under the title of "Faith Missions at Home and Abroad." The trustees under this Act of Incorporation are as follows : Rev. Daniel Steele, D.D. ; J. C. Hartshorn ; B. E. Perry, Esq. ; B. F. Redfern ; Charles Cullis, M.D. ; and Mrs. Lucretia A. Cullis. The powers and duties of this board, as in the case of the trustees of the Consumptives' Home, are limited to holding the property of the missions in trust ; the sole management thereof being vested in Dr. Cullis himself.

If the magnitude and diversity of these missions had

at the first been made known to him who now carries
them all so cheerily, and who is constantly on the out-
look for others, he would have sunk down in despair.
But the doing of each new task has brought strength
for the next ; and from all appearance, notwithstanding
the actual weight of care, the accumulating burdens
seem not to be heavier and heavier, but lighter and
lighter.   The secret of this is in the fact that the
faith of God's servant seems to increase faster than the
new uses for it appear.   Besides, there are devoted
men and women from time to time volunteering to
serve as his aids, and upon these he lays increasingly
heavy responsibilities ; leaving them sometimes to the
same kind of struggles (though vastly less in degree) as
those through which he himself has passed, thus com-
pelling them to rely more upon their own faith in God
as the channel of needed blessings, and less upon that
of their leader.   In this manner numbers of men and
women are trained and developed into efficient gospel-
workers, whose services are not only of great value at
home, but are in request abroad.

  This feature of the many-sided work of the Doctor
is worthy of special attention.   A small man might desire to concentrate as much power in and notice upon
himself as possible ; but on his part there is no such
attempt visible.   There is room here for any gifts and
graces that the Lord may please to send, and the arrangement of the work is such as to make the most and

best of every man and woman in it.   Every separate department is a training-school as well as a Christian mission.   People are supposed to learn how to do the Master's work by the actual doing of it ; a plan which has many undoubted merits, — among them, this, that it repels mere sentimental religionists who are more fond of professional dignity than of downright hard work for the Lord.

First in order of the faith-missions comes "The Publication and Tract Work," which even antedates the Consumptives' Home itself; as the distribution of tracts was the earliest form of service for Jesus to which the young physician set his hand after he had been brought to make a complete consecration of himself to God, and in this for some time he used nearly all the surplus income of his profession over and above his modest personal expenses.

Perhaps there is no department of Christian enterprise in which more noticeable improvement has been made of late years than in tract-publication.   There used to be a professional flavor about a "tract."   Much of this class of literature was poor and pious, and had the appearance of being "exceeding dry ;" on which account, the tract-work was perhaps the least popular of all the systematic benevolence of the Church.   What was wanting was the personal element which enters so largely into the preaching of the Word, — some human interest behind the printed page, to be a channel for the Holy Spirit.

But Dr. Cullis was his own Tract Society, hence it was an intensely personal affair. He selected his matter with sole reference to its efficiency for bringing sinners face to face with a personal Saviour. He gave away the tracts with a personal reason in each case, and he followed the tracts with his prayers. The results were glorious. One of these little messengers, entitled "A Saviour for You," is mentioned over and over again, in the early Reports, as having been the means of many conversions. It was also incidentally the occasion of the establishment of the Willard Tract Repository. But let the Doctor tell the story himself. In the fifteenth Annual Report, after his tract-distribution had come to be a matter of millions, he recounts the fact which led to its beginning, thus : —

"Twelve years ago the Willard Tract Repository was begun as a distinct work, on a small scale ; using a little room in the Mission Chapel, Willard Street, and from this taking its name. For many years, before the Lord gave me a special work to do for him, I had been in the habit of giving away tracts and books to the number of many thousands every year. I had no thought of establishing a tract-work until after the following occurrence.

"I applied to the American Tract Society of Boston, asking them to print a little tract which had been owned of God to the conversion of many souls, and thousands of which I had imported from England.

"After waiting two or three weeks, I called again ; when the secretary informed me that they already printed so many of that character, they thought it not worth while to add another.

"I then said, 'I will print for myself;' and with this little tract, 'A Saviour for You,' commenced a work which has extended itself widely through our own country and the civilized world."

Another step in the early progress along this road was the publication of the Annual Reports of the Consumptives' Home. This record of God's faithfulness to those who trust him became at once the most efficient of tracts; for, as if to give still further proof of his favor towards the Faith-work, the Lord made use of the Reports for the conversion of sinners, as well as for the awakening of somnolent saints. From the first, the issues of this annual record have been sent forth with special prayer that these results might be seen in those who might read them; and glad letters of testimony to these very experiences, through this very means, constitute a striking feature of the Reports from year to year.

When Dr. Cullis ventured to publish the first tract, the funds of the new Home were very low, and how to meet the printer's bill when it should come in, he was not able to see; but the Home was a work of faith, and why should not the tract-publishing be a work of faith also? At any rate, the Lord seemed to lead in that direction, and there was nothing for his disciple but to follow. To his surprise and joy, the printer, on sending home the little book, signified his wish to give

the amount of his bill to help on the good work;
and thus was the faith of this advanced believer still
further strengthened.

In the Report for 1867, he mentions the case of a
young man about to die, who was brought to Christ
through reading "A Saviour for You," given him by a
lady friend. Under date of Aug. 28, 1867, this entry
occurs in the Doctor's journal: "It is with gratitude
to God I record the conversion, in a neighboring city,
of five persons by the blessing of God upon the little
book, 'A Saviour for You,' and one by the same author,
S. M. Houghton, entitled 'Faith.'" Two days later he
received a note from the city of Providence, R.I., telling of the conversion of twelve persons, and the awakening of three others who had not attended a house of
worship for twenty years, all through God's blessing
on a package of tracts from the Doctor's hand. The
demand for the above-mentioned works becoming so
great, he resolved to venture on the expense of having
them stereotyped, which was the first little step towards
a permanent tract-publication house.

In November of the same year, a friend in Wil-
liamsport, Penn., sent fifty dollars for stereotyping
"Heaven, and how to get there," — a companion tract
to "A Saviour for You," — and to pay for a thousand
copies of the latter. Six weeks later the same friend
reports, as the result of reading "A Saviour for You,"
the conversion of a man sick unto death. The conver-

sion of an Irish Roman Catholic, by the same means, is recorded a little later ; and in March of the following year a further report comes from the town above mentioned, rejoicing over "a number of conversions" directly traceable to the agency of that package of tracts. By this time it was pretty well settled that tracts of this description would "pay."

At first the " Repository" was a room in the Doctor's modest residence ; but in the fourth year of the work, ending September, 1868, the building on Willard Street was purchased for a chapel, an office for the tract-work was fitted up therein, and thus the little establishment had both a local habitation and a name. The Doctor was averse to giving his own name to the enterprise, — as would have come about of itself, — hence the name of the street was taken ; and to this day letters are received addressed to "Mr. Willard of the Willard Tract Repository."

The Report of the Home for 1868 shows the printing of tens of thousands of tracts, and the circulation of over two hundred thousand. These were distributed gratuitously, that, as the Doctor puts it, "there may be no hinderance to the spread of the gospel." A very hopeful beginning, surely.

On the 24th of April, 1869, the first number of "The Times of Refreshing" appeared. Of this the Doctor says, —

"Almost from the beginning of the Work of Faith, there has borne heavily upon my mind the need of a paper of a revival character, that should carry good news to young converts, backsliders, believers as well as sinners; the paper to be, like the rest of the work, wholly unsectarian, its standard ' Jesus only.'

"I have prayed much over the matter, mentioning the design to no one. In answer to this prayer, I received, a few days ago, a letter from Mr. G. C. Needham, the Irish evangelist, in which he suggests the issuing of such a paper, offering to be its editor. Knowing that Mr. Needham could not possibly have been aware of my desire, I accepted *with assurance* this oneness of purpose, as being the mind of the Spirit, and hailed it with gratitude and delight."

The design of this tract-paper, which was at first published for gratuitous distribution, is thus set forth in its first editorial : —

"The object of this paper is to aid the children of God scattered abroad, by giving them crumbs of truth; to present Christ to poor sinners who are perishing without him; to give facts and incidents relative to the work of God in various places, and in various ways; and to exhort believers in the Lord Jesus Christ to be in earnest in the Master's work, and to ' occupy' till he comes.

"The character of the paper is purely unsectarian, having the glory of God as its *object;* ' Jesus only,' ' in whom dwelleth all the fulness of the Godhead bodily,' as its *theme;* the good of saints and the salvation of sinners as its *desire;* and simple trust in God as its *support.*"

In 1871, the Consumptives' Home having been moved from Willard Street to the spacious grounds and houses

at Grove Hall, the Repository was placed in larger
quarters on West Street, from which it was again removed to its present commodious rooms on Beacon
Hill Place.   On this account the word "Street" was
dropped, the title otherwise remaining as before.

From the receipts acknowledged it appears that "The
Times of Refreshing" was issued at a heavy cost to
its publisher.   But tidings were received of the conversion of souls through the reading of it, therefore it
was continued in spite of the financial loss.   And, not
satisfied with a paper for adults, the Doctor projected
one for the children also, entitled "Loving Words,"
which first showed its cheery face in December, 1870,
under the editorship of the children's evangelist, Rev.
E. P. Hammond.

Another enterprise was the publication of a Gospel
Almanac, containing a text of Scripture for every day
of the year.   The gospel "calculations" are not made
for any particular latitude or longitude, but they seem
to suit the needs of all; and "the verse for to-day," as
there marked down, is looked for more frequently than
the hours for sunrise and sunset or the ebb and flow of
the tide.

In 1872 the annual gratuitous circulation of tracts
from the Willard Tract Repository had reached the
number of half a million.   Of the financial side of
the subject, Dr. Cullis says, "For the whole year the
gifts have been two hundred and seventy-six dollars and

forty cents. Sale of books and tracts at the Repository, three thousand seven hundred and fifty-four dollars and fifty-seven cents." The gifts to this branch
of the work, for the whole six years, were a trifle over
seven thousand five hundred dollars The "sale of
tracts" was to those friends and helpers who were not
willing to take them for nothing; but the prices were
so small that the business was not profitable in money,
though it was so largely profitable in the work of saving
souls. On this point the Doctor says, —

"One can readily see that the gifts to this part of the work
are as yet in no way commensurate with the cost of printing; yet
God does not leave us in confusion. Wonderfully does he
deliver; so that it is often with surprise to my own soul, I see
every want met, in my business, in my own home, in the daily
support of a hundred men, women, and children, comprised
under the Consumptives' Home, Children's Home, and Deaconess work; the expenses of the publishing branch; and
added to all is the progress of the Chapel work, on the grounds
of the Consumptives' Home building."

The next year still another tract-paper, "The Word
of Life," was added to the list. The "Times" had
now reached a circulation of four thousand copies a
month, and about an equal number of the other papers
were distributed. This year a price was set on the
papers, but the distribution went on much the same
whether the money came or not. The mass of tracts
sent out had now become so large that the report by
number was abandoned.

This, be it remembered, was the year of the great fire in Boston, and by it the Willard Tract Repository was the loser to the amount of over five thousand dollars, in plates and printed sheets ; but God enabled his servant not only to stand the shock, but to report at the end of this year of wide-spread calamity a substantial increase in the strength of the enterprise.

The next year (1874), the first branch Repository was opened, at No. 239 Fourth Avenue, New York. Among the gifts received was a donation of a hundred dollars for sending "The Times of Refreshing" to the missionaries in foreign lands. The catalogue of tracts and leaflets — original or republished from English editions — now numbered one hundred and thirty, besides a small list of books of the most spiritual and helpful character. Chief among these were three works by the Rev. Dr. W. E. Boardman, — one entitled "Gladness in Jesus ;" another, "In the Power of the Spirit;" and the third, "Faith Work." This last is the history of the work under Dr. Cullis for the first eight years.[1]

A special feature of the Willard Tract Repository, which had now become prominent, was its publication of books on faith-healing, a subject quite neglected by the religious publishers in this country, though for years it had been somewhat prominent in Europe, not only

---

[1] Although the present volume covers the history of this Faith-work from the beginning until September, 1885, it is not intended to displace the above-mentioned volume. That book will still be carried on the list of publications, and will continue to be a sweet and clear instructor in the deep things of God.

among the Romanists, who — to their praise be it
spoken — always taught it, but also among Protestant
communities, especially in Switzerland and Prussia.
The fraudulent "miracles" of unscrupulous priests had
so far degraded the subject in the Protestant mind, that
well-attested cases of healing by the immediate exercise
of Divine power were passed by as mere unaccountable
marvels, consigned to the limbo of doubt, or denounced
as works of the Devil ; and it was the high privilege
of Dr. Cullis to be the pioneer, on this side of the
Atlantic, in publishing these wonderful works of God.
In his Report for 1874, the American edition of " Dorothea Trüdel " is first announced ; and to this have been
added, from time to time, a number of other volumes of
the same general import.

But the most startling of all these issues of the
Repository are the three modest little books by Dr.
Cullis, in which he reproduces the written testimonies
of those who have themselves been healed in answer
to his prayer of faith ; usually cases which had been
the despair of the physicians.   It is plain to see that
the Church was shocked by these publications, for with
their appearance the gifts to the Repository fell off to
a considerable extent.   But this sturdy believer in the
gospel did not abate one jot or tittle of the faith as
it was delivered to the saints ; and from that day to
this, while avoiding every extravagance, and adding no
dogmatic utterances of his own to the facts of God's

providence and the promises of God's Word, he has upheld the standard of the gospel in its fulness as the ultimate power of salvation both for body and soul.

The spread of this truth during the past twenty years is one of the marvels of our time. In spite of opposition, it has advanced until it has come to be one of the most prominent questions before the Christian world ; and, beyond all dispute, the chief visible cause for this is the good work of the Willard Tract Repository. God's blessing upon the faith of Dr. Cullis has furnished many cases of healing, and the pages of his books have furnished the means of spreading the knowledge thereof. By these means has the faith of the Church been able to recapture large areas of gospel territory which the enemy of all righteousness, and especially of the righteousness which is by faith, has been suffered to take and hold ; and so numerous and so wide-spread are the blessings of health and healing received direct from the hand of the Great Physician, that it seems impossible for faith in Jehovah the Healer ever again to decline.

The proper limits of this chapter, already too long, will not admit selections from the many letters received by Dr. Cullis, bearing testimony to the power and blessing attending his tracts, papers, and books. This one from ex-president De Motte of the Illinois Female College is a fair example of their helpfulness to candid and cultivated minds : —

DELAVAN, Wis., Dec. 27, 1875.

DEAR DR. CULLIS, — My heart guides my pen, at the expense
of good manners and propriety.   I want at some time to tell
you, if I can, the influence "Times of Refreshing" has had in
my life ; and I reasonably suppose I am only one of thousands.
It fell upon my desk among a lot of circulars, advertisements,
etc., such as sometimes annoy a business man, some four or
five years ago ; and was tossed aside with a casual glance.   But
God never lets good seed be lost.   It missed the waste-basket.
Day after day my eyes fell upon it, till once (I was president
of Illinois Female College, Jacksonville, at the time), perplexed
with some care, sitting vacantly at my desk, I began to read as
one in trouble will, listlessly, — as one guided of God will sometimes, unintentionally ; and as I came to myself, like Peter, *I
was out of the prison.*   I shall probably never know how the
angel came to me, but I shall always know it led me out of a
gloomy dark place into the light.   I have never missed a number since ; have loaned and read them to others ; have used the
matter in speaking and talking, and have no notion of how
much good it has enabled me to do.   God bless you, and
prosper you in this and all your other enterprises for his glory.

Yours,

W. H. DE M.

In 1879 a branch of the Willard Tract Repository
was established at 921 Arch Street, Philadelphia ; and
during the visit of the Doctor to England in the winter
and spring of 1881, so great an interest was manifested
in his publications that another branch was opened
in London, which is now at No. 39 Warwick Lane.
Since that time three other branches have been established : one in Bombay, India ; one in Santa Barbara,
Cal. ; and one at Los Angelos, Cal.

This year (1885), a new paper, "Service for Jesus," has been issued, intended to be the organ of the entire work under the Doctor's care; a special feature whereof will be letters from the staff of workers in home and foreign mission-fields.

In no department of the work has "the good hand of God" been more plainly visible than in the publishing department.   Funds have been scanty, but one of the peculiarities of this Repository is that it has learned how to do a great work with a little money: whatever has been received for sales has been turned directly into an increase of the volume of free circulation; and thus through all the years it has gone on from strength to strength.

Thanks be to God for his prescient care and goodness in training a man, and preparing an agency, whereby to spread abroad the knowledge of the great gifts and the mighty doings which in these last days are thrilling the faith of the Church, and confounding the wisdom of the world!

CHAPTER XVI.

THE ORPHANAGES AND THE SPINAL HOME.

"Inasmuch as ye have done it unto one of the least of these my brethren, ye have done it unto Me."

THESE two charities are corporate parts of the Consumptives' Home; but the account of them has been reserved for the second part of this volume, in order to give greater unity to Part First, and also to follow the order in which the various departments have sprung up.

The Consumptives' Home had been opened but a short time when the need of a home for the children of destitute consumptives began to be felt. In some cases it was impossible to receive a mother, because she had no place for her children. On this account, Dr. Cullis was especially moved to pray for means to open a house for these poor little ones, not only for their own sakes, but also for the sake of their suffering and dying fathers or mothers, — usually the latter, — who, if their children could be thus provided for, would themselves have a comfortable Christian home in which to prepare for death, and from which to go to the Lord.

CHILDREN'S HOME.

Under date of June 5 and 6, 1867, — being the third year after the opening of the Consumptives' Home, — the Doctor makes the following records : —

"JUNE 5. This afternoon I learned that a house on Vernon Street, nearly opposite the Home, is for sale. I have seen the agent, and made an appointment to look at it in the morning."

"JUNE 6. This morning I examined the house mentioned yesterday, and purchased it for six thousand dollars, for the Children's Home ; one thousand to be paid down, one thousand next year, another thousand the year following, the balance to remain on mortgage. The house is sadly out of repair, and, with what alterations will be needed for our use, will make a large bill of expense. The amount for this I have not yet, and shall only repair as the Lord furnishes the means. A friend said to me at noon, ' How can you take this care, and go to all this expense, when you have not the means, and are in need of a home yourself?' I replied, ' The Lord, who has taken care of us so well, will not forsake us now.' In less than an hour, a friend gave me one hundred dollars ; and, on asking her how I should use it, she replied, ' Just as you please : your judgment will be best.' I shall place it to the Children's Home. Thus the Lord proves that ' whosoever trusteth in him shall not be confounded.' "

On the 27th of September, 1867, the day signalized by two dedications in the two previous years, the first of the Children's Homes was consecrated ; the services being under the charge of the Rev. Dr. Huntington, then a friend of the Faith-work. On the 14th of the month following, a little babe only a week old was received as the first inmate, the mother being at the same time admitted into the Consumptives' Home.

During the year, fourteen children were received; eight of whom were discharged with their parents when they left the Consumptives' Home, and six remaining whose parents had died in the faith of the gospel. The next year, twenty little ones were received, seven of whom remained entire orphans. In the Report for 1869, the Orphanage has special mention; the gifts received for it, many of them from children in happy homes, are tenderly and thankfully recorded; and the entire amount of money received for the Orphans' Home since its commencement is set down at five thousand nine hundred and ten dollars and twelve cents.

On the 20th of April, 1871, the child-family was removed to its new home on the beautiful grounds at Grove Hall, where there are now two commodious houses devoted to its use.

It is not the purpose of Dr. Cullis to make this part of the work prominent before the public, for the reason that, as the children grow up, it becomes an embarrassment to them to be known as charity orphans. The houses are, of course, open to any who may properly desire to visit them; but the effort is to make these homes as near as possible like other Christian households, which strangers would not think of visiting merely to gratify even an amiable curiosity, and where the home-feeling is carefully cultivated as a precious and sacred emotion.

The second Orphanage was dedicated April 27, 1876. In the following year the first house was rebuilt, the matron and children being meanwhile sheltered in other buildings on the grounds. At this time, — May 15, 1877, — the Doctor writes : —

"This house was occupied by the children on our first removal to Grove Hall, although it was then quite old and needing repairs. We are now necessitated to almost rebuild, which will require time and quite a sum of money. In our two Children's Homes we have twenty-three little ones. I have been obliged to refuse three children within a week, and am praying daily for means to build another house. The uniform health of all the children is the cause of our deepest gratitude to God ; even when epidemics prevail, we have escaped, although most of the children attend the public schools. God blesses the quiet and uniform attention given to diet, bathing, exercise in the open air, proper clothing, early hours of retiring ; also, we believe, the habitual recognition of God's presence, a loving trust in him as the heavenly Father from whom cometh every perfect gift ; and the morning and evening prayer, and song of praise, in which each is taught to have a part, and personal responsibility. Too much stress cannot be laid upon the fact that here we have *homes*, and the hallowed influences of family life ministering to the best and truest development of every child God sends us to rear for him."

The training of homeless little ones being here only an incidental work, and not a great department thereof as in the case of the immense establishments at Bristol in England and Halle in Germany, this brief notice may be sufficient for these pages. In their small measure the Orphanages fulfil their parts in the holy work of faith, and share with the others in the love and favor of God and in the bounty of those who love and care for his little ones in his name and for his sake.

Next in order of time comes the little cottage home for helpless and hopeless cases of spinal disease. It is only large enough to hold its four patients with their two attendants, but in some respects it is one of the most interesting sections of this entire system of charities. The occasion of its existence is thus related in the Report for 1876 : —

"APRIL 3. As long ago as when the work was in Willard Street, my attention was called to the great need of a home for the care of poor persons afflicted with spinal disease, — the most helpless class of sufferers. About the same time, our sympathies were awakened by learning the history of deprivation and pain allotted to a faithful witness for Jesus. The person to whom we refer — a lady — had been stricken down by spinal disease, so that her condition was almost a helpless one. She was limited to a reclining position, could not speak, and could only use her hands to write, or to reach for what was placed in closest proximity. Scarcely at any time was she free from acute pains in head and entire body. Her home was a very simple one, with a married sister, who was unwearied and loving in her care, but whose circumstances rendered pecuniary aid necessary, to supply the needs of the suffering one. How sweetly and trustingly did she look to her Heavenly Father, and how gratefully accept whatever came to her relief! And so sparingly did she apply the gifts that God sent, that often

SPINAL HOME.

her mite was given to the Consumptives' Home and other branches of the work. To our remonstrances her unvaried reply was, ' My wants are all supplied : the Lord sends you this, and you cannot refuse him.' Or, ' I asked the Lord to give me such a sum for the Home, and he has sent just the amount I asked.'

"Whenever it was our privilege to visit the sanctuary of her home, it was to receive the benediction of one whose happy, trusting face bore witness to the communion of that inner sanctuary, that holy of holies, where the soul enters to behold His image, and to be changed from glory to glory. Recently, what she considers her deepest trial has come to our invalid. The dear sister, who for sixteen years has been her nurse and constant attendant, after a few weeks' illness is snatched from her. The home is broken up, and there is no other member of the family able to receive her. The family and acquaintances, knowing of my great interest and love for her, presumed I would take her directly into the Home ; forgetting that that is dedicated to the one object, — care for consumptives, — and continually filled with these. When I asked the poor child if there was any place for her, she wrote on her slate, ' Yes, one.' — ' Where ? ' — ' The poorhouse,' was her reply. I could promise her nothing ; but in my inmost heart I said, ' Never, never : as God lives, this shall not be.' The short visit that afforded the above conversation was closed by committing our every care to God ; and the placid smile worn by the dear wan face showed how truly, as we parted, the sweet will of God was hers.

"My heart has been sadly burdened to know what to do. Certainly the poorhouse is not the place for a lowly follower of Jesus, while there are Christian hearts awakened to the high calling of doing *as unto the Lord*. My cry is, ' Lord, what wilt thou have *me* to do ? ' Every effort has been made among the friends of her native town : her church has been told all the circumstances of her need, and she still remains unprovided with any permanent home.

"To-day a lady, without knowing any thing of my exercise of mind, gave me a dollar towards establishing a home for poor spinal cases. I accept this as God's will that such a home should be commenced."

About the middle of August following, the Doctor determined to fit up a small cottage on the grounds at Grove Hall, for a Spinal Home. On "Dedication Day," — Sept. 27, — it was given to the Lord for its sacred use; and on the day following, its first inmate — the lady above mentioned — was received.

The silent ministry of Miss Josephine Basford in her room at the Spinal Home has been a blessing to many who have visited her in her affliction : affliction it must be called, though hers is one of the happiest faces ever seen in this sorrowful world. "Couldst thou not watch with me one hour ?" What, then, must be the grace that helps a soul cheerfully to watch and wait and suffer with the Lord for more than twenty years!

"Well borne is more than well done," said a recent visitor to that silent, happy sufferer. Surely there is a divine ministry, as well as a divine mystery, in the suffering of the saints. To lie in a darkened room year after year, unable to stand up or even to sit up, unable to speak even in a whisper, enduring almost constant pain, and yet to be in perfect peace and patience and always happy in the Lord! is not this an object-lesson whereby the Saviour teaches the depth and power of his saving grace?

Some day those silent lips will speak ; some day that long and deep experience will be given to multitudes, of which little snatches are now written on a slate for the comfort of those who delight to visit this house of patient waiting, which sometimes may signify even more than "a house of prayer." Already faith is beginning to claim the promise of healing for this child of God ; and, in comparison with what has elsewhere been given of late in answer to believing prayer, the healing of this case, so utterly hopeless from a human point of view, will be no strange event, no stretch of the Great Physician's power. Surprise has often been expressed, that this soul should not be able to claim health for the body that cages it ; but when inquired of upon this point, Miss Basford will smilingly write her answer, — " My time is not yet come."

If any are perplexed that on the same estate there should be two houses for " incurables " and a house for the cure of those who can believe in the Lord for heal-ing, they must bear in mind that the first two houses were the early proof and test of the faith of God's ser-vant in the promises of God for the supply of temporal needs ; as such, these still stand : while the Faith-cure House is the outcome of a later and larger experience and faith, along another distinct and separate line of promises, viz., those that refer to the healing of the body.

CHAPTER XVII.

THE DEACONESSES.

"I commend unto you Phebe our sister, which is a servant of the church, . . . that ye receive her in the Lord, as becometh saints, and that ye assist her in whatsoever business she hath need of you."

A GREAT hospital like that at Grove Hall requires a large number of nurses and attendants, the most of whom are women.

In the first place, a quality of service is required which implies no small degree of native intelligence, as well as of special experience and training; and when to this is added the faith to lead dying sinners to Christ, and the grace to do all this work for love and not for money, it will be seen that the number of persons in common life who are fit for duty in the hospital depart-ment of the Faith-work must be exceedingly small. Let it be remembered, that in many modest households, even in time of health, the number of servants is half the number of the family, which proportion is much increased in times of sickness; and also let it be considered, that the care of the sick is a wearing, wearying kind of service, under which many persons soon break down or are driven into other fields of labor, — and in

DEACONESS' HOME.

view of all these facts it will be evident that three hospitals and two orphanages, containing half a hundred sick persons and young children, cannot be supplied with suitable voluntary service without some sort of a training-school, as well as a comfortable home close to, but not within, the precincts of disease and death.

All this Dr. Cullis plainly saw in the days when the Consumptives' Home was only a beginning, and early took measures to establish a guild of Deaconesses. The fifth Annual Report mentions the rental and opening of a House adjoining the Home on Willard Street, for the above-mentioned purpose ; and also its dedication on the 11th of May, 1869, though at that time there was only one person ready to enter the institution, nor did the house contain even the necessary furniture for its occupation. Like every thing else in this circle of charities, it was projected wholly by faith, and the providence and grace of God have fully justified the act.

Like all the rest of the work, this was a new departure. Nothing of the kind was at that time known in New England, if, indeed, on the American continent. The Roman-Catholic Church had its houses of Sisters of Charity ; but so far from being faith-institutions, supported by prayer, these homes are regularly organized agencies for the collection of money to be employed in helping on the various enterprises of that communion.

"In every Christian community [says Dr. Cullis in his fifth Annual Report] there is felt to be a great lack of well-qualified Christian women as nurses. That such women should be *educated* for their vocation, is just as imperative as that the physician should be educated for his. This important post, for the most part, has been filled by persons, who, having failed in every other employment, take to nursing as a last resort.

"My first plan in supplying this branch was to employ only Christian women; but I soon found, that, if this plan were adhered to, the sick would necessarily be turned from our doors, for want of such to care for them. After much prayer, we believe it to be indispensable for the permanent and best success of the Home, that we should offer to those women who desire to consecrate themselves to Christian service in its highest sense, and who feel that natural inclination and endowment call them to the care of the sick, an opportunity for that discipline and guidance that an established home for the sick alone can offer. Furthermore, our desire is not to limit our efforts to this one branch of Christian training, but in some respects to imitate the noble work at Kaiserswerth (Germany), where provision is made for education in every branch of Christian labor that is demanded for the furtherance of Christ's kingdom. We feel that the Home is peculiarly adapted to the training of nurses; and the chapel, employing missionaries and Bible-readers, offers a field for usefulness in that direction. The elements of growth are here, and we believe the present limits of the work will be extended until it shall embrace a large and ever-increasing band of workers united in the single aim of glorifying God in a life of loving, trusting service.

"I am convinced that there are women of culture and means, and others 'rich toward God,' who are yearning, with a true Christian devotedness of heart and purpose, for a way to be opened before them. With such, I would be glad to communicate.

"The question now arises, What *name* shall be given to

such laborers, as *some* name will naturally be attached to them? What objection is there to the all-comprehensive and scriptural one of Deaconess?"

At the dedication service, Bishop Huntington, in speaking of the service of women in the early Church, said, —

"The question may arise, What is the origin of this idea? . . . We know that as soon as there was such a thing as Christianity among men, there was a peculiar work for women to do; as is manifest from frequent allusions in the New Testament, where women whose lives were consecrated to works of charity and mercy are spoken of in terms of high praise, and were honored with the Saviour's blessing. . . . These persons, known in the early Church as Deaconesses, were missionaries, generally associated together and laboring wherever misery and suffering were to be found, and spending their time in acts of mercy and prayer. A peculiarly interesting account of one of these women has come down to us in the case of a noble Roman lady, who, having been converted, gathered together the remnants of her property, and with a few companions went to the East to Bethlehem, where she surrounded herself with as many as she could who shared in her feelings, and spent her time in deeds of charity and prayer. A sketch written about the time she lived, fifteen hundred years ago, says of her, in the quaint language of a translation made some three hundred years since : —

"'She was marvellous *debonair*, and piteous to them that were sick, and comforted them, and served them right humbly, and gave them largely to eat such as they asked; but to herself she was hard in her sickness, and severe, for she refused to eat flesh — however, she gave it to others — and also to drink wine. She was oft by them that were sick, and she laid the pillows aright and in point; and she rubbed their feet and boiled water to wash them : and it seemed to her that the less she did to the sick, in service, so much the less service did she to God, and deserved the less mercy : therefore she was to them piteous ; and nothing to herself.'

" Now, this Paula was but a single specimen of her class, and there is not a century but is bright with such instances. About the seventh century an order of Deaconesses was established in Paris, which still continues in existence ; and many traces of them are to be found in various parts of France. They founded hospitals ; and in one of those in Paris are six hundred beds, in another seven hundred, and in a third eleven hundred. In the beginning, these movements owed their origin to prayer, the dictates of Christian philanthropy, and a desire to follow Christ and imitate him. From that time forward, these organizations sprang up rapidly throughout Christendom, under different names : for example, the Order of St. Elizabeth, in Germany ; and the Order of St. Ursula, whose mission is to poor and ignorant children. These associations were generally the result of a single person's efforts ; and it is to be remarked, that nearly all institutions of this nature are the fruit of the prayers and labors, not of many, but some one earnest heart. . . . These blessed charities are not the product of the Roman-Catholic Church : they came from God's Spirit ; they were in the world and in God's Church four hundred or five hundred years before the Romish Church appeared, and having outlived their former superstitions, they are now re-appearing ; the old principles and ideas are coming back, and our tributes of praise and thanksgiving belong to God that it is so."

[The speaker then gave some account of the commencement of Pastor Fliedner's work at Kaiserswerth on the Rhine, about thirty-five years ago, which resulted in the formation of that most beneficent charity, the Deaconess Institution, the blessed influences of which are now felt nearly all over Europe.]

Three years later the number of Deaconesses had increased to seven; while to the duties inside the Home had been added a city-missionary work, to which the Lord gave wonderful tokens of his favor in the conversion of many of the apparently hopeless souls who were found in the by-streets and crowded tenement-houses at the North End.

Few and far between, like angels' visits, are the women who are able and willing to leave all, and follow the Lord in this line of service. There is nothing brilliant or romantic or conspicuous about it. These consecrated women do not even advertise their devotion by a " habit " or uniform, like the Deaconesses at Mildmay Park or the women in the Salvation Army; nor have they the elation of that *esprit du corps* which must be so great a charm in the life of those worldwide sisterhoods of the Romish Church; there is nothing "distinguished" about their appearance or their life, save that rare distinction of quiet, steady obedience to Christ in a round of daily duties which comprise the commonest as well as the loftiest ministries to the bodies and souls of his suffering children. It is no wonder, then, that this guild of Deaconesses has not yet become a very numerous one; yet, to the praise of God be it spoken, this house has not only a class of elect ladies equal to the needs of the work at home, but also several representatives abroad in mission-fields where the distinguishing blessing of God has made themselves and their work a wonder and a joy.

Not all who enter this guild remain long in it. Women come and go, attracted by the idea of "the religious life," and repelled by the downright hard work which is included in this form thereof. No effort is made to bring people into it, or to retain them when they tire of it: every one is left to follow the leading of the Spirit. Those who find here the mission to which he calls them will, of course, develop a fitness for it; and it is no misfortune, that others should either go away, or fail to come at all. It is the theory of the house, that God who lays out the work will not only send money to support it, but hands and hearts to do it; and thus far this has been realized, but nothing more.

The Deaconesses' House at Grove Hall was dedicated Sept. 27, 1875. It is a plain dwelling, large enough for its present uses, standing side by side with the little church, and conveniently near to the Home.

The Report for 1875 contains the following : —

PRINCIPLES AND RULES OF THE DEACONESS HOUSE, GROVE HALL, BOSTON HIGHLANDS.

Design of the Institution. — The design of this institution is to offer to Christian women a place of training, where they may receive such instruction as is necessary to fit them for the service of Christ in hospitals, prisons, asylums, and other public and private charities, as well as in mission-work at home and abroad.

Rules of Admission. — Any one who desires to enter upon this course of training must : —

1. On entering, present in writing, a request to be received, containing a declaration that she understands and approves the principles of this work, and is ready in all things to submit to the regulations of the House as here stated.

2. Must be more than twenty and less than thirty-five years of age.

3. Must be either unmarried or a widow.

4. Must have received, at the very least, a good common-school education.

5. Must produce satisfactory evidence of character and of personal piety, including a recommendation from the pastor of the church with which she is connected, and such additional certificates as may be deemed necessary in individual cases.

The Course of Training. — 1. The House will be placed under the charge of a lady, who will act in sympathy and cooperation with the manager.

2. The practical training will be given in connection with the Consumptives' Home, the Children's Home, Faith Training College, and other institutions connected with the Work of Faith. Such necessary experience as cannot be furnished in these will be sought in other existing institutions and missions in the city.

3. Special attention will be given, in connection with the Training College, to such a study of the Bible as is needed by those who are to use it constantly in practical work. Lectures will also be given by clergymen, missionaries, and others, on topics connected with various branches of Christian work. Facilities will also be given for the study of books on these subjects.

4. All who enter the house are expected to conform punctually to the regularly appointed order of the day, and to do

cheerfully any work which may be assigned them in connection with any of the branches of training.

5. It is understood that all that enter the House do so with the intention of remaining in it long enough to complete their course of training, — the whole time not to exceed two years; and, when there are reasons which make it necessary for any one to leave, it is expected that at least two weeks' notice will be given. The same notice will be given when it is felt by those in charge of the House that it is undesirable for any one to continue her connection with it.

6. It is not desired that those connected with this House should be marked by any peculiarity of dress, but it is expected that while engaged in their work their dress will be plain, economical, and similar.

7. This House will be simply a free association of those who are trained in the work, who may be ready to consecrate their acquired skill to the service of Christ in any branch, for such time as they may choose.

8. The lectures on Christian work will be free not only to those who are in the House, but to all Christian women who may desire to attend them; and it is hoped that the general influence of this institution may be to stimulate and educate not only those who enter the House for a full course of training, but all those women in our churches who desire to live and work for Christ.

The question may be asked, What are the advantages to be gained by the course of training here given? To what does it lead?

The answer is that this plan does not contemplate for those who follow it any worldly advantages whatever; it leads to no position of profit, either at the Home or elsewhere: but those who join this sisterhood are expected to make a present of themselves to the Lord, to depend directly upon him for every temporal need, and to be happy in him as their "all in all." When a Deaconess develops power and capacity for some particular department of the Faith-work, she is afforded an opportunity to exercise her talents in that direction, but without any wages or salary whatever. It is absolutely a work of love.

What ! Spend years of time and effort in learning a profession for the privilege of working at it for nothing ?

Even so ; that is, so far as this world is concerned. Here is a school wherein is taught the doctrine which Christ taught his disciples ; viz., that it is wise and profitable, as well as pious, for people to forsake all and follow him, — all, literally *all*. Not only do these women thus give themselves to the work of the Lord without remuneration, but some of them have given money in considerable sums in addition to the free gift of service. It was the contribution of two of the Deaconesses which enabled Dr. Cullis to fit up the old stable at Grove Hall for the uses of a church and Sunday school, as will be further mentioned in due course ; and these are not the only considerable gifts from that devoted band.

It will be understood, that this account includes all the ladies who now are, or at any time have been, volunteers in any department of the Faith-work. Not all have come to learn their duties here: some of the most competent and useful helpers have come into the work bringing with them a knowledge and ample experience of the care of the sick, as well as marked ability of management, that would command prominent and remunerative positions elsewhere. The holy office of Matron in the Consumptives' Home includes not only the general ordering of this great and trying household, but also the work, in many instances, of pointing the sick and the dying to the Saviour. The reward for such consecrated service, even in this life, is above all price: what, then, will it be in the world to come? There are few pastors of churches who have the care of so many souls, in their vital and final experience, as do the chief women in this great charity-hospital; and blessed is the record which they can give of the many sick and dying ones who have come to the Lord on their invitation. In the Faith-cure House, also, there is need of much gospel teaching, as well as of grace to entertain strangers; and the Matron, whose face is familiar to so wide a circle of guests, has not only an enviable experience of healing, — having first come to Grove Hall as a consumptive patient, to die, and having been raised up in answer to prayer, — but also a knowledge of the Scripture, and of facts that illustrate it, which enables her effectively to teach and apply the gospel doctrine of salvation, through faith in Jesus, for bodies as well as souls.

Others of this devoted sisterhood hold important posts at the Cancer Home, the Orphanage, the Institute at the South, and the Tract Repositories, etc. And there are still others who have undertaken to spread the gospel among the heathen in Central India, not only by precept but by practice; for they have devoted themselves to this work, trusting in the Lord for every thing just as they did at home. If it is matter of wonder to see people doing this in the midst of the highest Christian civilization, what shall be said of it in the midst of swarming millions of heathens? But of this at large in its place. No wonder such obedient faith has been blessed with exceptional success.

In the Report for 1880 occurs the following obituary : —

"Now we have to use our pen, for the first time, to record the death of one of our faithful Deaconesses, Miss Chapman, who had been with us some four or five years. It is not too much to say that her sweet, winning, and gentle Christian life had won all hearts who had the privilege of being near her. She was fragile when she came to us, evidently marked by hereditary disease. But her spirit was strong within her, anointed of God. She took the usual place of a beginner, and became a nurse in the Consumptives' Home.

"A troublesome but seemingly slight cough assailed her, which she said nothing about; only, as it was suggested that she should try a position in the Children's Home, she recognized it as the hand of her heavenly Father, and gladly accepted. Conscientious and faithful here, she remained about a year, and was improved in health. At this time a vacancy occurring in the Philadelphia Repository, Miss Chapman was considered

the best one to fill the place. This change was accepted by
her in the same loving spirit, recognizing again that her dear
heavenly Father was tenderly caring for her needs in transplant-
ing her to a softer climate. When our sister returned to us
after a year's absence, hopelessly ill unless God should inter-
pose his miraculous healing power, the only thought was, Would
that she had come sooner ! that watchful care might perhaps
have warded off the destroyer ; for we knew that our sister was
entirely thoughtless of herself, and even then she scarcely
seemed aware of the frail tenure she held of her life.

" After one short visit to her sister, the two remaining months
were passed at the Deaconess House, and the precious life was
yielded to Him, the Author and Finisher.

" This supreme moment seemed only a repetition of the glad
'Yes' that always formed the response of our dear sister to
every call of her Saviour. How rapid must have been her
flight, and how quick her spirit's transition to the rest in the
Everlasting Arms !

" 'Thou shalt guide me with thy counsel, and afterward receive me to glory.' "

Two years later another of this consecrated band was
called home, a lady who, like Miss Chapman, had only
a feeble life to give to the Lord, yet who was blessed
in giving even that. How much better thus to sanctify
and glorify a fragile strength and a suffering frame, than
to drag out the slow years in self-centred invalidism,
looking to be ministered unto instead of ministering !
Of her the Doctor writes : —

" One of our number (Miss Farrington), who first as a nurse
in the Consumptives' Home, and afterwards as an earnest helper
in the school at Boydton, Va., endeared herself to all, returned

to the Deaconess House last winter, having developed hereditary disease. She never had much physical health; and yet, for the years she was with us, her earnestness and devotion knew no bounds; and if her life-limit was short, the faithful service she performed who shall limit? To all of us who looked on, it was apparent that each succeeding day gave an added pallor to her countenance, and an unmistakable seal of the heavenly ownership. Her citizenship was in heaven, and God's 'day' for 'making her his jewel' was hastening. Her work was done: she entered into rest. May we not transcribe as her benediction these words of John's Revelation, 'And to her was granted that she should be arrayed in fine linen, clean and white: for the fine linen is the righteousness of saints'?"

The number of ladies now included in this chapter of Deaconesses is forty-two; to which may be added three or four others who have joined themselves to them in the foreign field, but have never been regularly trained for or admitted into the work. The distribution of this consecrated sisterhood is as follows: fifteen in the Homes, Orphanage, and Faith-cure House at Grove Hall; three in the Cancer Home at Walpole; five in charge of Tract Repositories in Boston, New York, Santa Barbara and Los Angelos, Cal.; three employed as teachers in the Boydton Institute, Virginia; one as assistant and Bible-reader in Santa Barbara; two at Oxford, N.C., in general mission-work; three at Monterey, Cal.,—thirty-two in all employed in this country. Of the foreign missionaries, three are at the Mission House and Tract Repository in Bombay; four at Basim,

Central India, and three are at present seeking out new locations for the extension of the " Faith-missions abroad."

The "handmaidens" are prophesying because the Spirit is poured out upon them, and some of them prophesy exceedingly well. The addition of an accomplished lady physician to the force in the foreign field is also worthy of special notice, in its proper place.

CHAPTER XVIII.

THE CANCER HOME.

"Though an host should encamp against me, my heart shall not fear."

THE only reason to be given for the existence of this peculiar institution is found in the Divine leadings of the mind of Dr. Cullis towards that end. It is distinctly declared in the Word of God, that the steps of a good man are ordered by the Lord : this is a case in point.

Early in the development of the Work of Faith, the Doctor became deeply interested in this class of patients, on account of having to refuse so many persons thus terribly afflicted who applied for admission to the Consumptives' Home. So fearful is the havoc which this malady sometimes makes with its victims, that they require to be separated from society ; and thus their lives become a double burden both to themselves and to their friends.

But what is to become of such as have no friends ?

It was to give a faint little answer, in the name of the Lord, to this dreadful and far-reaching question, that the Faith-work came to include a separate and comfortable house where a few of this class of sufferers might live and die. It is only a drop in the bucket, only a little ray of light thrown into a wide abyss of darkness; but to the half-dozen unhappy ones who may find shelter and care and love in these chambers of consolation, that single drop is unspeakably sweet, that single ray is a prophecy of the world of light.

The need of such a house was mentioned in the Annual Report for several years, and from time to time small gifts were received for that purpose; but it was not till the spring of 1876, in the twelfth year of the work, that the funds justified the commencement of the building. Having now upwards of six thousand dollars devoted to this object, and plenty of land on the Grove-Hall estate, the Doctor applied to the city of Boston for permission to erect a house for cancer-patients, — *which was refused.*

By an ordinance of the city, no one may erect a building within its limits without a "permit;" and some of the owners of property in the neighborhood of the eleven-acre tract of land on which it was proposed to locate the cancer-hospital entered a protest against it, partly on the ground of danger to health, but chiefly on the ground that such a hospital would reduce the value of real estate in its neighborhood. The first of these objections was fully answered; it being shown that the progress of medical science had made it possible to conduct such an institution without prejudice to the health of those living near it : but the second objection prevailed, not because of any rights that would be invaded, but because (as was confessed) of certain political influence which the objectors represented.

There was nothing to do but to submit, and to refer the case to the Lord for further orders. And these were not long in coming. An estate in the town of Walpole, about twenty miles south-west from Boston, and fifteen from Grove Hall, came to the knowledge of Dr. Cullis, which he found to be well adapted to his purpose ; comprising a fine large mansion of fifteen rooms, newly built, with steam-heating, convenient out-buildings, a fine grapery, and twenty-two acres of land, in a high, commanding location, partly covered with a young growth of oaks and pines. Its owner had recently died ; and, the estate being too large and fine to find a purchaser in that region, the whole property, which cost over thirty thousand dollars, was purchased for the Cancer Home at the moderate price of ten thousand three hundred and fifty dollars. By this time, — June 5, 1878, — gifts for this object had so accumulated, that seven thousand eight hundred and fifty dollars was paid in cash, the remainder being secured by mortgage.

On the fourteenth anniversary of the work, "Dedication Day" was again observed in the consecration of this beautiful country-house to the uses of Christian charity; and thus a far more advantageous plan was consummated than that which had been thwarted by financial greed and political iniquity.

Still another difficulty, and a special deliverance therefrom, signalized the opening of this branch of the work. The estate being on the top of a hill, the supply of water was found to be unreliable in dry seasons. Here is an account of the matter, under date of Nov. 18, 1882 : —

"A little more than a year ago, finding that the supply of water would not be sufficient for the work, after prayer I decided to dig the well deeper, and see if that would give such a supply as we would need. The old well was ninety feet deep. A tube was driven to the depth of one hundred and five feet, and then, finding a ledge, the old well was abandoned, and a small piece of land bought at the foot of the hill, a well sunk, windmill erected, and pipes laid to pump the water to the top of the hill. This summer we find that there is a quicksand, and that the sand continually fills up the well, giving much trouble. Having a friend who has given much attention to the subject of water-supplies, I wrote him a note for advice. He offered to go up, and look the matter over, and report to me. He kindly did this, and marked a place where he thought if we would dig thirty or forty feet we should find an abundance of water. So men were set at work, and dug forty-four feet, and then drove a pipe until they reached sixty-seven feet; then they gave it up, as there was not a drop of water. On talking with the man who had dug the well, and had employed a man to drive the tube, this morning, he thought it would be folly to go any deeper. I said, 'Well, do nothing more till you hear from me.'

"I prayed about it as I walked about the grounds; and,

going into the Home, I sat down by the side of one of our poor cancer-sufferers, and began to talk with her about putting her whole trust in the living Saviour. While talking, I took up a Bible lying on the table, not to read to her, but inadvertently took it up, and opening it, my eyes fell upon these verses: 'When the poor and needy seek water, and there is none, and their tongue faileth for thirst, I the Lord will hear them, I the God of Israel will not forsake them. I will open rivers in high places, and fountains in the midst of the valleys: I will make the wilderness a pool of water, and the dry land springs of water.' These verses are the more significant from the fact that we are upon one of the ' high places,' being on a hill that commands from its elevation a view for miles. I wait now to let the Lord ' open the fountain ' for us."

And this waiting was not in vain. Not far from the well at the foot of the hill, was a spring which for years had been concealed by a little swamp, where a railway-embankment had partially stopped its outflow, and thrown its waters back upon itself. The existence of this spring came to the Doctor's knowledge. After some difficult negotiations, it was purchased for him; and, by connecting this spring with the new well, an abundant supply of pure water was obtained. Money for these costly works was given, just as it was wanted, by unknown friends, one of whom sent a thousand dollars in an anonymous letter. Thus again was the good hand of the Lord made manifest in setting up the Cancer Home.

Another deliverance from a more terrible peril is recorded in the Report for 1883, as follows : —

"SEPT. 8. For three days the Home and all the buildings upon the hill have been in great danger from a forest fire. The long weeks of drought have left all vegetation in such a parched condition as to render the woods an easy prey to the dangerous sparks flying from the engines of the New-York and New-England Railroad. For three days the fires raged and spread so rapidly as to be almost beyond control. At one time we were sure the building must go ; and packing of goods was commenced, and considerations of how we should remove the patients. The neighbors, whose homes were also endangered, many of the townspeople, and railway-hands came to our assistance ; and by digging trenches and building back-fires the devastating foe was stopped, but not without a loss of seven hundred dollars' worth of wood, forming the forest which we had purchased a year ago as protection from the severity of the winds that swept over the hill.

"We praise God, who heard our cry, and saved the building with its helpless inmates. 'The angel of the Lord encampeth round about them that fear Him, and delivereth them.'

"I would add here, that all through the drought of summer our supply of water never failed."

Here is an inside view of the Home, full of touching personal interest : —

"We are in great straits in the Cancer Home. Every room is full, and there are three applicants waiting. The nature of the disease is such that almost every sufferer needs a room to herself. Let me give a description of our present inmates. One has not only had a cancer, but she is now badly deformed ; right arm almost powerless ; head propped up, as she sits in a chair, resting upon a cot ; the patient in a half-reclining position, with no power to move herself, but has to be lifted every time her position is changed, night or day. She requires a large amount of air, so that the windows of her room have been left open all winter ; and in consequence she has had to have a room to herself, as no one else could be comfortable in it. Another patient in an opposite room has been a sufferer for years, and came to us with the entire left side of her face eaten away, with one eye destroyed, and nose nearly gone. She is a great sufferer, and must be alone. Another, an old lady of eighty-three, with an internal cancer, and now very low : she is in a small room. Two others are in a large room together, but one keeps the other awake : I have been partitioning a room in the upper part of the house to receive one of these. Thus five fill our Home, and these five are more care than a dozen consumptives.

" It is a terrible disease. One of the three who are waiting to enter is a person who has been in one of our public schools as teacher for years, but for several years has been drawn out of shape, and has had no use of her hands, from rheumatism. Recently an internal cancer has been discovered. Friends who have helped support her for years have one by one grown weary, and lately she has been sent to the almshouse.

" Many persons ask the question, ' Where do you find nurses who are willing to undertake the care of those fearful cases of cancer ? ' We can truly answer, ' The love of Christ constraineth,' for money could not pay the faithful ones who have labored night and day, and ministered with self-forgetfulness and tenderness to those whose friends have failed them, and from whom the majority turn with loathing. The return, to them, has been in witnessing in so many instances the patient sweetness and the all-conquering power of Jesus evidenced in these suffering ones, turning the couch of pain into the ante-chamber of heaven.

" We add, in closing this record, the letter handed us by the patient of whom we have spoken as being formerly a teacher in one of our public schools : —

WALPOLE HOME, WALPOLE, Jan. 11, 1883.

DEAR DR. CULLIS, — As a patient in your beautiful and comfortable Home, I feel impelled to express to you my profound gratitude and lively appreciation for the daily comfort and benefit, consolation and sweet rest, I find in this retreat for the weary and afflicted. To me it is a heaven on earth.

Having passed through so many stages of suffering, and such a variety of medical treatment, such alternations of hopes and disappointments, until I began to feel that sickness of the heart which arises from hope deferred, I have learned so many lessons in this long school of affliction as fully to appreciate the comforts, the treatment, and the kindness of this haven of rest.

In unburdening my heart of its debt of gratitude to you, the attempt brings back the memory of other and more hopeful days, when I entered upon my life-work as a school-teacher. Then, in the bloom of health, life seemed like a fairy-tale untold.

I am also reminded of my great affliction, the breaking-up of our happy home, this sickness which compelled me to give up my school, and then the hard and thorny pathway through the dreary years, the promises of medical relief, the painful experiments, and the killing disappointments.

But God has never deserted me. I have been greatly blessed with kind friends, raised up from time to time. But after so many years of suffering and need, friends grew weary and discouraged, and one by one, like stars in the coming storm, gone out amid clouds and darkness ; which left me like Noah's wandering dove, with no abiding place to rest my weary feet. But now, dear friend, you have taken me in your ark of safety, haven of rest ; this sweet, sweet Home for my helpless and aching heart, where all is done for me and provided that human kindness can bestow. I shall not cease to pray for every blessing to rest upon you and yours, while I wait patiently.

"Looking unto Jesus, the author and finisher of our faith" (Heb. xii. 2).

"For he maketh sore, and bindeth up : he woundeth, and his hands make whole " (Job v. 18).

"For this God is our God for ever and ever : he will be our guide even unto death " (Ps. xlviii. 14).

Most faithfully and thankfully yours,

M. J. A. C.

With the following tender tribute to the memory of one of the faithful Deaconesses, who gave the remnant of her wasting life to bless the lives of others dying of the same disease as herself, — wherein is also included a kind and honorable mention of the grown-up girls from the Children's Home who have already learned to serve the Lord by serving his suffering ones, — this brief chapter, whose title stands for so much sorrow, pain, and devotion, may fitly be brought to a close. In the report for 1884, Dr. Cullis says, —

"With many, to go to Walpole, and minister to the sick with cancer, is a most dreaded step.   But to those who have gone, in the spirit of consecration to Christ, reckoning upon his power to keep and save, his word has been made true.

"As has been mentioned in the account of the Children's Home, some three of our children, who are already women, have assisted in the household work, and also in nursing during this year, when we could procure the services of none other. Under the direction of our most respected matron, Mrs. Bliss, the household was a happy one, in spite of the arduous work.

"Death came and took our dear friend and matron, Mrs. Bliss, a few months ago.   Strange as it may seem, she undertook the care of the Walpole Home while she knew that the very disease unto which she had come to minister there, had fastened itself upon her.   But she was too full of sympathy for others, to consider her own pains, and too entirely devoted to the Work of Faith as the work of God, to ever hesitate in giving her utmost enthusiasm and strength.   Thus her disease was kept under, while we all shared in her conviction that it would develop no further.   It seems inscrutable to us, that just at this time she was called to fulfil a promise made to a friend, when she was following her occupation as nurse, outside of the Home.

"She went, and was taxed beyond her strength, remaining for weeks beyond her engagement, feeling all this time that she must break down.   She returned to us, but was never well again.

"A brother from the Far West, and a sister, came to minister to her; and all in the Home were devoted to one who had won all their love.   She too suffered and died with the dread disease, patient and lovely to the end.   Another among the cloud of witnesses we reckon her, and take courage for our warfare, the good fight of faith. . . .

"Among those of the patients who have passed on with her, we remember many a shining face, illumined with divine hope, — one, especially, who entered the Home an unbeliever, who, after she saw Jesus as her Saviour, never ceased to praise him, always saying, 'My bodily sufferings are nothing compared to the glory in my soul.'   So that, while we do often look upon sufferings that try our feelings to the utmost, we are as often made partakers of the glory that follows, and know an unspeakable joy in the thought, 'Here too has the priceless gospel won trophies for Christ, and the wail of the sinful and sorrow-stricken has been lost in the shout of triumph and victory.'"

CHAPTER XIX.

GROVE-HALL CHURCH.

" Believe on the Lord Jesus Christ, and thou shalt be saved, and thy house."

ONE of the plants which has sprung up in this garden of the Lord is a little communion of Christian
believers who have formed themselves into a church on
a very simple plan, — a church whose membership is
small, whose income is smaller, and whose property is
smaller still.   Indeed, as an ecclesiastical body it literally owns nothing at all ; its only apparent possession
being an old stable fitted up for the worship of God, and
even this is included in the Consumptives' Home estate,
and is held by a board of trustees in whose selection
this church has no voice at all.   Still it is one of the
most prosperous as well as unpretentious of churches,
and approaches delightfully near the ideal which ·tra-
dition as well as Scripture suggests, of an apostolic
ecclesia.

One of the chief defects even of Protestant church
orders is that there is too much of them.   Not content
with the faith and doctrine to be found in God's Word,
they have contrived extensive faiths of their own, in

the defence whereof vast labor and learning and grace
have been wasted ; indeed, it is the extra-scriptural
"church" that is most prominent in the minds of men.
The few and simple elements which compose the
Church of Christ have been so loaded down or covered up with human inferences and theories, that the
original outlines are often but dimly seen.   By all rules
of art, this would be bad architecture: still more, by
all the words of Jesus, is this bad ecclesiology.

The assembly of believers worshipping in the modest
edifice known as Grove-Hall Church is peculiarly happy
in having no extra weight to carry, whether of property, or theology, or ritual, or polity.   Its motto is
"JESUS ONLY :" it has no life outside of him, no work
except for him, no faith but what is distinctly taught
by him, and no hope but that set forth by him.   After
comprehending these facts, one is prepared to learn
that this vine is very fruitful, and that this household
dwells in peace.

In the summer of 1872, the next after the removal
of the Home to Grove Hall, the Lord put it into the
hearts of some of his confidential friends to commence
public worship and to open a Sunday school on the
grounds.   For this there were two apparent reasons :
First, there was, and still is, no evangelical church
for a long distance in any direction, and only one of
any sort whatever.   Second, the increasing band of
workers in the Homes needed a place near by, where

they could assemble for worship after their hospital-duties for the day were over, and where the children of the Orphanage, in company with others, might have the advantage of public instruction in the Word of God and in singing his praise ; neither of which things could be permitted in the chapel at the Home, where quiet and repose are so essential.

One day one of the Deaconesses came to Dr. Cullis, and inquired how much it would cost to complete the Sunday-school room, for which purpose it had been determined to use a part of the stable on the estate ; and on being informed she said, " Well, finish it, and I will pay for it."

Shortly after this, another Deaconess felt herself directed by the Lord to give five hundred dollars towards fitting up the audience-room. It was a great sum for her to give, even approaching in value the " two mites " which were all the living of another of the Lord's daughters ; but it was given intelligently and heartily, and was owned and blessed of God.

And now the first donor desires to give again, as is seen by the following brief but significant entry in the Doctor's journal for 1872 : —

"SEPT. 2. To-day the Deaconess who finished the Sunday-school room comes with the request that she may be allowed to pay five hundred dollars more towards completing the chapel. She is thus constrained by the love of Jesus, as in so doing she gives her all of earthly possessions."

Here is one of God's children who has thoroughly learned the lesson, so generally scouted by the world, " It is more blessed to give than to receive."

"Dedication Day" (Sept. 27) was again honored by its traditional observance, in which Grove-Hall Church was consecrated to its holy uses, and opened as a free place of worship not only for the fraternity on the Home estate, but also for residents of the neighborhood. No sooner was this done, than tokens of Divine favor began to be seen in the gathering of a good congregation, and in the awakening and conversion of souls both in the congregation and the Sunday school.

The first pastor of this gospel assembly was Dr. Cullis himself. For several months after the chapel was opened, the pulpit was occupied by a clerical friend; but with the opening of the new year 1873 came the call of the Lord to his servant to enter upon still another line of service for him. Under date of Jan. 3 he writes : —

" For several weeks I have not been able to rid myself of the idea that the Lord is calling me to preach at Grove-Hall Chapel. An intense love for souls, and a burning desire to give Christ's message to the lost, seem a proof to me that God is leading by his Spirit."

On the following Sunday, the brother who had been kindly supplying the charge was sick, and the Doctor felt compelled to take his place; which he did, speaking upon the text, " Zacchæus, come down, for this day

I must abide at thy house." One effect of the discourse may be seen in the following note from the journal : —

"JAN. 11. Since the service of last sabbath in the chapel, I have received a paper, signed by the members of our little congregation, requesting me to continue to officiate in the capacity of pastor to them. I can only accept this as a call from my heavenly Father, relying wholly upon his word, 'I will be with thy mouth;' for, amid my many cares and active labors, my preparation must come directly from him upon whom my soul continually feeds. 'He that eateth Me, even he shall live by me.'"

For more than a year, this little community of believers and their chosen leader maintained the fellowship and work of the gospel; and then, in recognized form, — though not thereby proclaiming it as essential to their scriptural existence as a Christian Church, — a public service for organization and recognition was held, of which the following is an abridged report : —

ORGANIZATION OF GROVE-HALL CHURCH.

On Thursday, June 18, 1874, at 3.30 P.M., a propitious day brought together some two hundred Christian friends to participate in the exercises.

In the pulpit were seated Dr. Cullis, Rev. Dr. J. H. Means of Dorchester, Rev. Dr. J. O. Means and Rev. A. H. Plumb of Boston Highlands, Rev. F. A. Hand of Dorchester, Rev. E. B. Squire of Centreville, — all from the Orthodox Congregational churches, — Rev. E. Edmands of the Christian Baptists. Singularly enough, the ministers of the other denominations were

detained by engagements; all having expressed warm sympathy and interest in the movement which was to establish a
church of Christ, free from sectarian bias, founded on belief in,
and love to, the Lord Jesus Christ, and desiring to be united
thus to all who love his name.

Letters were read from the Rev. Phillips Brooks (Episcopal)
and the Rev. George F. Pentecost (Baptist), expressing, with
their inability to be present, warm words of approval and sympathy.

After singing

> "Join each heart and tongue to bless
> Christ our strength and righteousness," —

and an opening prayer by Rev. Mr. Hand, Dr. Cullis, in a few
words, stated that the chapel was opened and dedicated a year
and a half ago, to supply a place of worship for those in the
neighborhood who were separated from their own churches by
distance, also for any and all who desired to learn of a common salvation through our Lord Jesus Christ; placing over the
pulpit, for its watchword, "Jesus only." Commenced for God's
glory, depending alone upon the guidance of the Holy Spirit,
the result had already verified the sure word of promise : "My
word shall not return unto me void." The congregation had
largely increased, souls were saved, and the bond of fellowship,
already cementing heart to heart, sought for visible expression
in an organization that might enroll all who should choose to
join in blessed service to our Lord, under the "banner of love,
given to them that fear God, that it might be displayed because of the truth" (Ps. lx. 4). Rev. J. H. Means, D.D., of
Dorchester, then arose, speaking in cordial recognition of the
desires of the Christians who would thus publicly form a church
of Christ. He then read the following simple scriptural Statement of Faith : —

"We believe in God, the Father Almighty; in Jesus Christ
his Son, our Lord, in whom dwelleth all the fulness of the

Godhead bodily (Col ii. 9), and in whom we have redemption through his blood, the forgiveness of sins, according to the riches of his grace (Eph. i. 7) ; in the Holy Ghost, by whom we are convinced of sin, of righteousness, and of judgment, and who will guide into all truth (John xvi. 8–13).

"We take the Bible as our rule of life, believing that all Scripture is given by inspiration of God (2 Tim. iii. 16). By God's grace we will walk in the light, as he is in the light ; for thus we have fellowship one with another, 'and the blood of Jesus Christ his Son cleanseth us from all sin ' "(1 John i. 7).

Dr. Means then asked those who accepted the same to express their assent by rising.

Seven composed this number of newly converted ones, who thus covenanted together to walk in the faith of the Son of God, according to the teachings of his Word. Seventeen more names were received of those who will join by letters from their respective churches. Rev. Dr. Means in fervent prayer implored God to establish and increase this membership in the knowledge and love of the truth as it is in Jesus. The right hand of fellowship was then given to Charles Cullis, by Rev. Dr. Means.

.   .   .   .

Dr. Cullis thanked the ministers and all present, for the encouragement of their presence and words of loving recognition and sympathy ; himself acknowledging the hand of God more wonderfully in this movement than in any he had yet undertaken, and as giving more fulness of joy in seeing one soul after another saved by the blood of Jesus."

.   .   .   .

The letters of 'greeting referred to above, as read during the services, are as follows : —

211 WEST CANTON STREET, BOSTON, MASS.,
June 17, 1874.

I had expected to be with you to-morrow. . . . If I am not called out of the city as I expect, I shall certainly be with you.   I know no reason why the Grove-Hall Chapel should not be recognized as a church of Christ.   Any company of Christians associated together for work and worship constitute a Christian church.   It may not represent any sect, but sect features are not essential to the existence of Christ's Church, while Christian people are.   And so, on that broad yet simple principle that Grove-Hall Chapel is to be composed of Christian people, I do most heartily and sincerely give my voice for your recognition as a sister church in Christ, and in his dear name invoke the benediction of God the Father, Son, and Holy Ghost, to be and abide with, in, and upon you.

Yours in Christ,

GEORGE F. PENTECOST.

HOTEL KEMPTON, BERKELEY STREET, June 17, 1874.
DR. CHARLES CULLIS.

My Dear Sir, — I am sorry to find that it will not be possible for me to attend the opening of Grove-Hall Chapel to-morrow afternoon.   I should have been very glad to join in recognizing it as a church of Christ, and in asking for its work the blessing and favor of God.   That blessing may it have abundantly.

Believe me most sincerely yours,

PHILLIPS BROOKS.

In all this it will be observed that there is no act of ordination of Dr. Cullis to the Christian ministry, or his installation as pastor of the church.   This was not an omission, but of deliberate purpose.   In the first place, the Doctor felt that his call to this added ministry was of the same nature as his call to the other gospel ministries committed to his hands by the Head of the Church : he was already " set apart " by the hand of the

Lord, and did not feel it to be needful that any human hands should be laid upon him. In the second place, he desired to preach as an evangelist, and not as a settled clergyman, for the reason that any form of churchly consecration would, almost of necessity, give his ministry something of a sectarian appearance, and it was his wish to be in the fullest fellowship with the whole Church of Christ, which, of course, implies a fellowship with all the branches thereof; and, as the sects are now divided, the only way to secure this end is to avoid such ecclesiastical forms as imply allegiance to any one of them in particular.

The position of an independent evangelist is not a new one either in the pastorate or out of it; notable modern examples thereof being Mr. Spurgeon, Mr. Henry Varley, and Mr. D. L. Moody. In this high fraternity it had pleased God to place this apostolic man, and to give him not only an apostolic call, but also a wonderful measure of apostolic faith and power. This the Church at large fails not to recognize, and to this its truly spiritual and representative ministers assent.

As is the pastor, so is the church. It is composed of persons who have come from various folds, and on removal its members are freely accredited to any Christian communion. In the matter of the sacraments, about which Christendom finds it impossible to agree, the fullest liberty is claimed and allowed. The ordi-

nance of baptism is administered by immersion or by
sprinkling, as each candidate prefers.

Twelve days after the formal organization of "Grove-
Hall Church," — let it be observed that this is its full
style and title, — the Doctor received the ordinance of
baptism by immersion. On Sunday, June 29, at Savin
Hill, on the seashore front of the estate of the Rev.
Dr. Olmstead, he, with other candidates for baptism,
appeared in the presence of a large concourse of people,
and was re-baptized by the Rev. Edward Edmunds, a
minister of the "Christian" denomination; after which
the doubly baptized pastor proceeded to administer baptism in the same form to fourteen persons, who were
afterwards received as members of Grove-Hall Church
by that approved form, the right hand of fellowship.

The sacrament of the Lord's Supper is celebrated
according to the Episcopal and Methodist form, at the
"altar" which encloses the chancel and pulpit. Pastor
Cullis has not thought it necessary to ask permission of
any man, or body of men, to do this in remembrance
of the Lord ; having the command of the Lord himself.
Human "orders," transmitted or otherwise, are here
held to be among the non-essentials of the Church, and
therefore the largest liberty is exercised respecting
them. That rule which prevents Christians from the
enjoyment of the sacramental part of the gospel unless
there be some "regularly ordained clergyman" present
to "administer" them, having no scriptural basis, is not

respected in this church; and the same may be said of every other assumed "authority" or "government" which is not distinctly laid down in the Word of God. But, on the other hand, no objection is made to any of these forms and orders. It is not required of members, that they should abjure any of them, or that they should accept, in theory, the simple usages of this communion : all it asks is a sincere love and fellowship in Christ, and a peaceable acquiescence in the exercise of Christian liberty on the part of all with whom they are associated. This church virtually says to those who knock at its doors, "Enter, in Christ's name. Bring all your theology with you, so as you also bring the Lord. Make all the good use you can of all your religious opinions, only do not try to force them upon your brethren and sisters who have the same right to their opinions that you have to yours. Contend for the faith, but do not contend about it. If you come in this spirit of love and peace, seeking to know and do all the will of Christ, we gladly give you a place among us. If you should ever tire of our company, that fact shall not be judged against you as a crime, as the manner of some is ; but we will send you away in love and charity, even as you were in love and charity received."

Surely there is very little extra lumber in this style of ecclesiastical architecture.

The first great blessing which came upon this little communion, as has already been mentioned, was the baptism of the Holy Spirit for the conversion of souls. The second was the outbreak of the missionary spirit. Under date of Dec. 8, 1873, occurs this entry in the Doctor's journal : —

"This morning my heart was made glad by finding in the box of the chapel a five-dollar bill marked 'For foreign missions.' Some four or five years ago I recorded in my journal my desire to do something for Jesus in foreign lands, — that he would permit us to send some one from our number, who should go forth to publish a full and free salvation, in whatever field of labor He might designate. For the encouragement of those who are tempted to become weary when the blessing tarries, we record that here was the beginning of an answer we had waited years for ; and now my prayer is for more means, and the right person to go, — one baptized with the Holy Ghost.

"Calling together brother Bumpus, who has been for a long time a faithful helper in the work, and two of our Deaconesses, we knelt before God, giving him thanks for this first gift, as an earnest of a new harvest for our glorious Lord. One who has just received the sum of eight dollars, his first gift for preaching, gives it to this object. 'Honor the Lord with thy substance, and with the first fruits of all thine increase ; so shall thy barns be filled with plenty, and thy presses shall burst out with new wine.'"

From this time forward, foreign missions was a leading topic in the little church. Gifts also began to come in from friends at a distance ; and so marked did this feature become, that the Report of the church for 1875 was almost wholly devoted to this topic.

It was not long before the missionary praying and

giving led to actual missionary-work in the foreign field. Here is the account from the Report for 1875, together with a glimpse into the home-life of the society : —

"AUG. 16. God has answered the cry of our hearts, that one from among us should be called and anointed of him for labor in the harvest-fields of India. One of our beloved co-laborers, Miss Lucy R. Drake (from the Deaconesses), has decided to go forth as a missionary, quite unexpectedly to us, fully convinced that she is answering to the voice of God. Her soul is filled to overflowing, and the perishing millions of India her one absorbing theme. And now, that all things needed 'shall be added' for the long journey and outfit, we cannot doubt. 'Go ye into all the world; and lo, I am with you alway.' When God calls us to *leave all, and follow him*, it is never separated from the assurance that *with himself he freely giveth all things*.

" We have added to the members of Grove-Hall Church, during the present year, twenty-three persons; a portion by letters from other churches, the remainder on confession of faith. Our entire membership numbers fifty-four. We cannot praise God enough that he so signally blesses by the presence of the Holy Spirit in our midst, taking of the things of Christ and showing them unto us, and drawing one soul after another to his blessed Person and leadership. We, as the Bride, take the name of our heavenly Bridegroom, 'Jesus only,' and find his tender, watchful care a safeguard from every harm and danger. Together on our knees, before the blessed Lord, how sweet the leading, how tender the reproof, how searching the Spirit's power to 'know the heart,' to 'try the thoughts,' to 'see if there be any wicked way in me, and lead me in the way everlasting !' Intensely personal would we be in all our ministrations together, to know a personal Saviour, to abide in his presence, and to wear the living Word of a living God as our 'shield and buckler.' Aggressive, too, would we be upon the stronghold of sin, workers together with him in all times and seasons, beseeching the world to be reconciled to God ; in love and tenderness ministering to any needy among us ; bearing one another's burdens.

"The 1st of November is the time appointed for Miss Drake to sail for India. Little by little the means have been given towards the expenses of her journey. A most generous wardrobe has been provided, almost wholly by the liberality of one person, a lady, who, from the first moment of Miss Drake's decision, entered into heartiest co-operation and sympathy.

"And may we not pray in faith for still other willing hearts to be sent of God into this distant mission-work? Some say, 'Oh, there is enough to do at home.' True, but there are enough strong hands and hearts that work everywhere at home and abroad. Look at the freighted ships that go to foreign lands to follow the behests of trade and commerce ; look at the travellers that seek the distant shore for health and pastime : and then ask, Cannot God send the consecrated hand and heart to proclaim his gospel, and hasten, in his own harvest-fields, the hour when the kingdoms of this world shall become the kingdoms of our Lord and his Christ? Ah ! yes. 'His ear is not heavy that he cannot hear, nor his hand shortened that it cannot save.'

"The gifts for foreign missions have been three hundred and twenty-three dollars and seventy-five cents. We bespeak the prayers of all Christian friends for God's blessing upon Miss Drake, who leaves us upon her mission to India, about the first of November."

This has continued thus far to be a missionary church. Its membership now numbers only eighty-two, and yet it has eight representatives in the foreign-mission work, besides several others who have never been in actual communion but are in practical connection therewith. It might not be easy to find another church having *ten per cent of its membership "at the front."* Further account of this foreign-mission work will be found in its appropriate chapter.

The growth of the Sunday congregations at Beacon Hill, in the chapel which had been opened for the Tuesday-afternoon consecration-meeting, led to the removal of Dr. Cullis from the active pastorate at Grove Hall to that of the new organization in the city, though he still held the general direction of its affairs ; an arrangement which, in at least one instance, has saved the little communion from disaster if not from disruption. This transfer from the pulpit of the first to the second church which had grown up under his hand occurred Sept. 23, 1880; and shortly after, Rev. H. P. Welton was received as pastor at Grove Hall. In December of the same year, his pastorate ceased ; and the church was supplied with occasional preaching until it pleased God to send to them their present pastor, the Rev. E. D. Mallory, whose term of service began Dec. 8, 1882.

Pastor Mallory is a native of Canada, in which Dominion the Doctor has many and faithful friends, some of whom have taken great delight in his conventions at Old Orchard Beach and elsewhere. It was while attending one of those seaside assemblies, that this young Wesleyan minister, then stationed in Montreal, made the acquaintance of the Doctor and his family,

of which he at length became a member through his
marriage with Miss Reed, the only daughter of Mrs.
Cullis by her former marriage. In this delightful way
it pleased the Lord to send to his servant a most efficient and congenial helper, whose devout faith, kindly
manners, tender sympathy, and ready address have
endeared him to multitudes of people, who, both at
home and in faith-conventions elsewhere, have been
blessed by his gospel teaching, and cheered by his
Christian love.

The religious and theological training of Pastor Mallory has brought him into a line of thought and life
wholly in harmony with his "senior preacher," as his
father-in-law would be called under the Wesleyan circuit system ; he has also been used of the Lord in the
healing of the sick, and, in the absence of Dr. Cullis,
takes his place in that holy office.

The financial system of this church is very simple.
Like every other department of the faith-work, it is
supported by voluntary gifts. The actual requirements
of the society are not large, and there is no temptation
to descend to worldly and questionable means of raising or scraping together the money to meet its current
expenses. It is a faith-church, just as the Home is a
faith-home. It does not depend on the world for its
maintenance ; and while it does not, like some of the
most radical Christian fraternities, refuse assistance
irom all except believers, it does not depend upon the

world for support, hence the world has no voice in its counsels.

But let no money-loving soul imagine that he would find in the Grove-Hall Church a refuge from unpleasant solicitations in the name of the Lord. Such persons would indeed escape the dunning and drumming, the teasing and urging, which so often worry the worshippers in the majority of our little sanctuaries; but the demands here made upon the congregation are vastly more sweeping than the severest strain ever put upon a dedication audience, or the most exigent stress ever brought to bear on a flock to bring up the heavy arrears in the salary of its shepherd. Nothing less than the absolute gift of one's entire being and belongings will meet the claims of the Lord, as here set forth; and when one has reached that state of grace, the gift of money to the Lord is a very simple and easy matter. Nor do its members shrink from the grip of this rightful demand. The most of them have accepted their duty of giving all to Christ. If they hold any of this world's goods, it is as his stewards, as occupants and not proprietors; and to this absolute and entire consecration they are continually held by the teachings of the minister and the spirit of the membership. A penurious Christian — or apology for one — would find here a place of absolute torment, unless his soul were calloused by hypocrisy and steeped in self-conceit.

In a word, the gospel is here preached just as it

stands; its commands are not toned down to suit
human prejudice or convenience, and an honest effort
at full obedience is constantly being made. In view of
these facts, no one will be surprised to learn that this
is not a fashionable place of worship, and that its altar
is not thronged with persons who would like to divide
their hearts between the church and the world; but on
the other hand, it will be seen by those whose spiritual
sight is clear, that this is one of the sanctuaries where
those who seek the Lord "with a humble, lowly, peni-
tent, and obedient heart" are very likely to find him.

The Sunday school is after the same manner and
spirit as the church, — a gospel school, the object
whereof is not "to keep our children in our communion," but to teach Jesus Christ to young and old as the
Lord, the Saviour, and the Governor of men.

In conclusion, it may be a matter of interest to state
that the church has no other arrangements for eating
and drinking than those which appertain to the holy
Eucharist. It has no dining-room or kitchen, no con-
veniences for cooking oysters or making coffee, no
tables for the spread of baked beans or "New-England
boiled dinners," no ice-cream parlor, no stage for Sunday-school theatricals, no place for strawberry-festivals
or fancy fairs. This sort of apparatus for "social religion" will be missed by those who come here from
churches which boast of possessing "all the modern
improvements;" but perhaps the fellowship of feeding

may be spared when there is such sweet, glad, loving fellowship of faith.

During the first year of Pastor Mallory's labors (1883), he was blessed with a gracious revival of religion, in which, after some weeks of successful labor, he was assisted by the beloved evangelist F. W. Mc-Kenney of Portland, Me. In his annual church Report, the pastor says, "Brother McKenney labored with us for some weeks, and almost daily abundant fruit was manifest. Sinners were converted, believers made perfect in love, and many hearts were baptized with the Holy Ghost. With a joy and power before unknown they have been laboring for the Master with increasing fruitfulness."

Of his own experience he writes thus: "It is such a glorious privilege to be a worker not only *for* but *with* Jesus! Once I worked *for* Jesus, taking all the care and responsibility upon myself. While I saw but little fruit, I was nearly crushed with the burden. There was so much anxiety and worry that my life was nearly all prayer, and, as I thought, few occasions for praise. Now working *with* Jesus, the victory is always his, and always sure; and so my heart is filled with praise all the day long."

May the Lord multiply such churches and pastors a thousand-fold!

CHAPTER XX.

" The very God of peace sanctify you wholly."

PERHAPS there is no feature of all the Faith-work that is more familiar to the Christian public than "the consecration-meeting" as it is called, which for the past sixteen years has been held on Tuesday of every week, first at four and afterwards at three o'clock in the afternoon. Its present location is Beacon-Hill Church, which edifice was, indeed, erected chiefly for its accommodation ; and here one may find, summer and winter, year after year, a gathering of earnest, devout men and women, — chiefly the latter, — who from far and near come together to seek and to teach the higher experiences of the life of faith.

In the year 1869, a man who had realized in his own experience some of the deep things of divine grace, while on a visit to his friend Dr. Cullis, was invited to hold a meeting in his parlor for the purpose of helping those who were seeking a more complete salvation ; and in that meeting, which has continued ever since, the one truth studied was the completeness of the gospel,

NEW BEACON HILL CHURCH
AND WILLARD TRACT REPOSITORY.

THE CONSECRATION-MEETING.

which provides for the pardon, sanctifying, and glorifying of those who are willing to take Jesus Christ on his own terms as a present and perfect Saviour.

Week by week the little band increased, till the meeting overflowed the parlor into the hall and stairway ; and when there was not even standing-room for the people inside the door, the question of a larger room began to be raised. The removal of the Doctor to his present residence, 16 Somerset Street, on Beacon Hill, gave the meeting ampler quarters, the large drawing-room being able to accommodate two hundred persons; but this capacity was outgrown in a single season, and the necessity for a hall or chapel began to appear. Two of the brethren opened a subscription by voluntary offerings of five hundred dollars each ; and at every weekly gathering the increase of the little fund was reported, until by March, 1872, the sum of sixteen hundred dollars had accumulated, and it became a settled thing that the Tuesday prayer-meeting was to have a chapel of its own, — quite a novelty in the way of houses of worship, which are always supposed to be built for the service of God on Sunday. The following extracts from the Report for 1872–73 and 1873–74 show the progress of the enterprise : —

"OCT. 15. A crowded meeting at my house."
"NOV. 19. The meetings are more and more owned of God. Crowds come to the house ; many are obliged to go away, unable to get in. Eight dollars and twenty cents given toward the new chapel."

"DEC. 13. One of the Deaconesses, twenty-five dollars for the chapel; a lady of this city, a gold chain for the same object."

"DEC. 31. Meetings crowded. Fifteen dollars and eighty cents given for the chapel."

"JAN. 7, 1873. God is blessing more and more the crowds that fill the meeting. To-day twelve dollars were given."

"FEB. 25. A packed house this afternoon; many went away, unable to get in. I am daily asking God to give us a larger place for the meetings, and to give all the means for the training-college. At the close of the meeting to-day, a dear brother who had already given five hundred dollars said, 'I will give another five hundred to build a chapel.'"

"MARCH 4. This afternoon a friend called to say that he had engaged 'Pilgrim Hall,' in the Congregational House, for the use of our Tuesday meetings. The hall holds upwards of five hundred persons, so that we shall have an abundance of room. This friend holds himself responsible for the rent."

"MARCH 11. To-day we held our first meeting in Pilgrim Hall. Although a stormy day, there must have been three hundred persons present. Six dollars and sixty cents were given for Faith Chapel."

"MARCH 18. Full meeting."

"SEPT. 30. During the summer, in my absence, the chapel receipts amounted to about sixty dollars; making in all two thousand six hundred and seventy-eight dollars, eighteen cents."

"OCT. 14. To-day we have rented Freeman-Place Chapel. Many were prevented from attending the Tuesday meetings in the Congregational Building, the hall being four flights from the street. While we obviate this one difficulty, others render our present place of meeting unsuitable and inconvenient, and incite us to earnest prayer for the new building."

"MARCH 4, 1874. From a gentleman of this city, one hundred and fourteen dollars toward the new chapel. Yesterday at the regular Tuesday meeting ten dollars were given. So, little by little each week, the regular attendants help to swell the sum needed for the new chapel and college work.   Each week, also, the dear Lord is with us, by his presence and power, delivering souls from the bondage of sin, and bringing many a hungry and thirsty one into the liberty of the gospel as it is in Jesus."

"MAY 7. For many months I have been asking God to direct my steps to a suitable building for the meetings, and for the chapel and college work. Last week my attention was called to the fact that the house of the late Deacon Daniel Safford, on Beacon-Hill Place, was to be sold by auction. The location seemed most admirable, — quiet, yet central. I went to see it, and found it to be roomy, with opportunity to build in the rear, so making a chapel that would accommodate our usual number. The first floor could be made suitable for the tract-work. I prayed much about the house. A kind friend made all needed inquiries for me regarding terms of sale, which I found were to be one-third cash and two-thirds on mortgage. I knew I had not sufficient money to meet the terms, having but little over three thousand dollars on hand. That I might know the perfect will of the Lord in the matter, I prayed him to indicate and assure me, by the sending of a large gift directly for this branch of the work before the day of sale. My prayer was on Monday : the sale was to be two days later. The next day, at the Tuesday meeting, I did not mention the matter. Only three dollars and seventy-nine cents were put in the box, — a smaller sum than usual. I thought, 'If the Lord does not want the house, I do not : it is for his glory, and not man's.' At nine o'clock in the evening (the sale was to be on the next day at noon), a dear friend, a clergyman, the only person who knew any thing about my desires, and had made the needed inquiries about the house for me, called to say that, in mentioning the matter to a friend of his, he at once said, 'If the Doctor wishes to purchase the house, I will give him one thousand dollars towards it.' Thus my prayer was answered.

Yesterday, the day of sale, I bid off the house at twenty-two thousand one hundred dollars, one thousand down, the balance of the cash payment to be made by the 16th. By that time three thousand dollars will be needed to complete the purchase. 'Who knoweth not in all these, that the hand of the Lord hath wrought this?'"

"MAY 12. To-day, at the regular Tuesday meeting, an announcement was made of the purchase of the house."

The following note gives an interesting fact relative to the purchased house to be made into the Faith Chapel : —

CAMBRIDGE, May 13, 1874.

DEAR DOCTOR, — Enclosed please find seven dollars for the new chapel. I feel a wee bit ashamed to send so little, but it is all the dear Lord gives me now, and will show you that I feel much for you. I am *sure* our Father will give you all you need. The house in Beacon-Hill Place I know well; it has been for many years a consecrated place.

Yours in Christ,

S. M. M.

"MAY 16. From Woburn, five dollars; Norwich, Conn., one hundred dollars; a clergyman of this city, one hundred dollars; a lady, twenty-five dollars. By mail the following : —

MAY 15, 1874.

DR. CULLIS, — *Dear Sir*, — The enclosed sum, one hundred dollars, was sent to me in direct answer to prayer, for Faith Chapel. Please do not mention my name in acknowledging it.

Yours most truly,

E. P."

"SEPT. 19. Two thousand two hundred dollars have been promised towards the alteration of the purchased building into a chapel. On consulting a builder, I find that the cost of alterations and additions will be about seven thousand three hundred dollars, exclusive of heating and seating. Having an opportunity to obtain five thousand dollars to be secured by mortgage, I have availed myself of it, and, with the two thousand two hundred dollars previously mentioned, have made a contract for the work, looking to the Lord for the further funds needed to make the house complete with heating and seating, and also to pay the one thousand three hundred and fifty dollars due on the purchase; this balance, as before mentioned, was one thousand seven hundred and fifty dollars, and I have been enabled to pay four hundred dollars of it."

"SEPT. 25. The entire gifts for Faith Chapel and Training-College have been six thousand two hundred dollars and forty-one cents. 'O Lord of hosts, blessed is the man that trusteth in thee.'"

The project of a "college" for the training of Christian workers is repeatedly mentioned in the Reports, in connection with the new prayer-chapel, which would give an additional reason and use for the room. Of this a further account will be duly given, since it well deserves a record by itself.

On the 16th of March, 1875, the alterations were completed; and with the gift of two thousand two hundred dollars by a modest and generous friend, whose face and name are still familiar at the consecration-meetings, the Doctor was able to pay the contractors, but a mortgage of five thousand dollars was left on the property. Having now a great, empty, unfurnished room on his hands, the next question was, how to furnish it. The following extract from the Report for 1875 will show how this want was met : —

" MARCH 30. For many weeks I have been asking the dear Lord for the means to complete the seating of the chapel, for which slight sums have already been given. Last week, having about one hundred and sixty dollars, I ordered seats to that amount. To-day being the regular day for the Tuesday meeting, just before the hour some one called and said that the people could not get into Freeman-Place Chapel, where we had customarily met. A crowd were waiting outside. I soon learned that a new sexton had been engaged, and, after preparing the chapel, had gone off with the key in his pocket, closing the door behind him. Not knowing where to find him, I suggested that we repair to our new chapel, holding the meeting as best we could. By carrying up settees and chairs, we were enabled to seat about one hundred and fifty, and had a delightful meeting. Utterances were joyous and spontaneous, stirred by the signal manner in which the Lord had given us the first use of the chapel. Gifts came as freely towards supplying the needed seats, so that in a few moments one hundred and twenty-seven dollars and sixty-six cents were handed to the desk."

At the next meeting, April 7, a hundred and fifteen dollars was added to the furnishing fund. During the week a lady gave a clock, a brother carpeted the platform, another gave a handsome seat for it, another sent a marble table for a pulpit, and a lady gave a pulpit-Bible. Thus the finishing touches were put to the work by joyful hearts and loving hands, and now the consecration-meeting had a habitation of its own.

On the 24th of April, Mr. Henry Varley, the chief of the English evangelists who have visited America, gave a Bible-reading in the new hall; and on the 12th of May it was publicly dedicated to the worship and service of God. In this service the college idea completely covered up the consecration-meeting, for which the most of the gifts had actually been made; and in the Report the event is set down as the "Dedication of Faith Training College." Ordinarily a college is a bigger thing than a prayer-meeting, and so by courtesy is entitled to take the precedence; but in this instance it may be doubted whether the greater did not give place to the less.

In this doubly consecrated place,[1] the Willard Tract Repository also found a new and permanent home. The little "Place," that only extended across the front of the chapel and the two handsome dwellings between which it was sandwiched in, at once took on a religious air; for the long Gothic windows of the hall, and, more than these, the signs, "BEACON HILL CHURCH," "WILLARD TRACT REPOSITORY," and "FAITH TRAINING COLLEGE," gave evidence of the fact that here was a nook in the great, noisy, hurrying, worrying city, where one might find a trysting-place with the Lord Jesus, and for a little season talk with him in peace and silence,

---

[1] It is said that in the foundation of this building are the identical stones which, a hundred years ago, supported the lofty "beacon," with its signal-fires, from which the hill received its name. The Safford mansion on this spot was also a centre of missionary interest, and a place for missionary counsels.

or praise him in a sweet and quiet assembly of those who really did, or ardently wished to, love him with all their hearts.

Having now a room for public worship, a Sunday service was a most natural suggestion. Besides, there were precious memories still cherished in certain souls, of the first little chapel, down in Willard Street, where the Lord had wrought so much salvation; which place had been long deserted by the removal of the Consumptives' Home to Grove Hall. It did seem, indeed, as if there were churches enough in that locality; nevertheless, without the thought of drawing upon them for the benefit of a new conventicle, a little company of congenial spirits joined themselves in churchly fellowship for sabbath worship and instruction, taking the name of " Beacon-Hill Church."

On the 11th of October, 1875, the first Sunday service was held, Dr. Cullis preaching the opening sermon. The Rev. Samuel Cutler and Rev. P. C. Headley were present, assisting in the services. A Sunday school was opened in the afternoon; followed by a prayer-meeting in the evening, conducted by Rev. W. E. Boardman, whose very presence is a benediction.

Nov. 4, the gift of a communion-service is mentioned; and on the 8th of November a church was organized in due form, of which the following records were made : —

" Yesterday a church was organized from among the friends who have met regularly since Faith Chapel was opened for sabbath services. Nine persons were received as members. Rev. Edmund Squire, a brother from England, and Rev. P. C. Headley assisted. We were deeply conscious of the dear Lord's presence, hallowing and sanctifying the scene. Rev. E. Squire is to be the pastor; one who in the purest sense has 'counted all things loss for the excellency of the knowledge of Christ Jesus my Lord: for whom' he has 'suffered the loss of all things.'

"This church is called 'Beacon-Hill Church' from its locality. The chapel in Beacon-Hill Place, opened first for the Tuesday meetings, afterwards for the needs of Faith College, could scarcely remain closed one-seventh of the week, when hungry souls were to be fed, and when one of the consecrated professors of the college was burning to proclaim the message of salvation. Thus the sabbath service was commenced; and earnest ones enough gathered immediately to form another church, which, like Grove-Hall Church, drops all denominational name, and stands upon the Scripture foundation of 'Jesus only.' 'For in him dwelleth all the fulness of the God-head bodily.' 'For there is none other name under heaven *given among men*, whereby we must be saved.' 'And he is the head of the body, the church.'

"God gives us faith and patience to count our success not by wealth or numbers as a congregation, but by the actual winning of souls, and by the going-out from among us of those who are inflamed with love for Jesus, fed by the undying principle of loyalty to him who 'was slain, and hath redeemed us to God by his blood, out of every kindred, and tongue, and people, and nation.' The tiniest seed cannot perish, placed in the garden of the Well-Beloved, whose word is pledged, 'I will water it every moment.'

"A bookseller has given about fifty dollars' worth of books for the Sunday-school library. Another friend gives twenty-five dollars for the same purpose.

" Our brother Rev. E. Squire gives us a brief item concerning Beacon-Hill Church : —

"'The truth that is preached in this church, and in its mother church at Grove Hall, can be expressed by no other word than " Jesus." Christ is literally our All, and therefore we cannot truthfully be called by any other name. This church was organized in October last. Of course its number is small. Such a church will not rapidly increase; but we are a united little band, happy in each other and in the Lord, well assured that in his own time " the little one will become a thousand." We know that we have the truth, and so we wait on the Lord. Candidates are admitted to this church after private examination, on the public confession that they do accept the Lord Jesus Christ, the second person in the Godhead, as their atonement, their sanctification, their All; and that they will be called by his name alone. The Lord provides for its ministry through the voluntary offerings of believers, who are exhorted to make them as to the Lord, and not to man.' "

For four years this little vine continued to live, — it could not be said either to grow or flourish, — its chief fruit being in the way of edification; for sinners did not know of the place, and if they had known would scarcely have cared to enter it, there being no other attraction than the plain and simple preaching of the gospel, and the fellowship of a very small company of saints. On the 23d of September, 1880, Dr. Cullis assumed the personal charge of the congregation, which during the previous year had somewhat increased; and with the assistance of Mr. Frank D. Sandford, a young evangelist who had been converted from a life of wickedness, and was fully saved at one of the Framingham Faith Conventions, the usual ordinances of religion were maintained for more than a year, with no special event to mark the quiet on-flow of its peaceful life. Then the skies began to brighten ; and under dates of Jan. 5 and 8, 1882, the pastor mentions the manifest presence of the Spirit's power in the Sunday services, and the addition of nine new members to the Beacon-Hill Church. Still its numbers were less than thirty.

But the Tuesday meeting continued rapidly to grow and thrive. Within the time above mentioned, the new hall became too strait for it, and again the question of larger accommodations was raised. Of this period the Doctor writes, in the Report for 1882–83 : —

"For two or more years I have been praying for the next building, which makes the corner on Bowdoin Street. With the addition of this building we could obtain more room, light, and ventilation, and gain rooms for the college and other work for the Master. The building until recently has been occupied, but it is now vacant and for sale. I do not talk about it, but am praying the Lord, if it please him, to give us this building, also the means to purchase and alter, making the two into one. For this purpose it will cost many thousands of dollars : yet my Father is rich, and I can trust him for it all if it is the good purpose of his will."

"I do not talk about it." Here is a matter of personal confidence between the Lord and his servant. It is a great matter, one implying "many thousands of dollars ; " yet the thing is not set forth before men who might be supposed to have those many thousands to give, but only before the Lord who is the sole proprietor of the earth and the fulness thereof.

There is a faith which leads the soul to ask great things of God, and there is still a larger faith which enables the soul to keep still about it in all other company.

At length the Doctor reached the point where he felt free to open his mind to one of his earthly friends, who at once promised a thousand dollars towards the purchase of the adjoining house on the Bowdoin-Street side, with the conditional pledge of four thousand more in case a certain business enterprise should prove a success. With this thousand dollars the Doctor set out to find the agent, and purchase the house; asking time to meet the remaining payments, and relying on the Lord to give their mutual friend the "success" in question, in which case he would have all except five hundred dollars of the money required, the property being already under a mortgage of ten thousand dollars.

The next day he received a note saying that the owner had bought for cash, and must sell for cash; and thus this coveted morsel seemed almost taken out of his mouth. He did not grieve over it, — having long ago learned that his way was not always the Lord's way, — but still kept on with his praying. The rest of the story is best told in the Doctor's own words : —

"This morning, while coming in from the Home, as I sat in the horse-car I prayed again about it, and what I should say to the brother who had promised the thousand dollars, and whether I should write him to-day that, humanly speaking, there was no prospect of the purchase being made, as the owner had declined to take one thousand dollars. When near home I looked at my watch, and thought, 'I will get off here, and run into Dr. Earle's meeting at Tremont Temple for a few moments.' Just as my feet touched the sidewalk, there, coming towards me, was the brother who had promised to give the thousand dollars. Was not this all of the Lord? At once he asked, 'What about the house?' I then told him the story, when he replied, 'I want you to have that house. I will advance the other four thousand, and if my business is successful, as I feel it will be, I will give it. If not — well, I guess you will get it anyway.' I thanked him, and going to the broker I told him I was ready to pay the five thousand five hundred dollars if he could find some one who would take the mortgage for ten thousand dollars. He thought he could do that, and there the matter rests. I was just in time, as other parties had the keys, and were looking then at the house. I can only stand in awe before the King of kings, who hears and answers prayer. In any possible way this whole matter is looked upon, there can be only one answer, and that is that God is in it. The brother who gave the money does not live in this State : I did not know of his being in the city : and just after I had prayed, I left the horse-car to meet him face to face."

The sequel of the story is most remarkable. On Feb. 13, 1883, the purchase of the adjoining house, as above indicated, was joyfully announced at the Tuesday meeting ; and shortly after, at brief intervals, the following entries occur in the journal : —

"FEB. 16. To-day the friend who promised me the five thousand dollars sends a check for five thousand five hundred dollars. May the Lord bless the dear donor!"

"FEB. 19. At noon to-day I paid five thousand five hundred dollars on the new house, giving a mortgage for the other ten thousand dollars at five per cent per annum."

"FEB. 26. Under date of the 9th there will be found recorded the account of the purchase of the new building, and that the donor who gave the one thousand dollars, and would give four thousand dollars more if a business project were successful, and who then advanced the whole amount, five thousand five hundred dollars, writes me to-day that the entire amount is now an out-and-out gift, without waiting for the success of the business enterprise.

"'Bless the Lord, O my soul, and all that is within me bless his holy name.'

"My prayer is for the means to alter and annex the new building to the former one, thereby giving us a large and commodious audience-room."

"Requesting the architect [who had examined the premises with a view to making plans for the alterations] to give me his price for plans and specifications, his answer was, 'Five hundred dollars.'

"I told him I must thank him for his kindness in looking over the property, but that I did not feel warranted to pay such a price. On reaching home I received in less than one hour a note from another architect, which read as follows: —

BOSTON, March 23, 1883.

MY DEAR DR. CULLIS, — If at any time I could be useful to you professionally, in any thing connected with your Faith-work, I should think it a privilege, and I would most gladly give you free and unlimited use of my services.

Yours very faithfully,

H. P. K.

"Truly, the Lord is my helper."

"APRIL 17. The friend who so generously gave the money towards the purchase of the new building told me to-day that he would give five thousand dollars towards the alterations. Praise the Lord!"

"JUNE 12. There seems no end to the work of the Spirit upon the heart of the dear brother who has already given so much for the new building. He now proposes that he make his gift ten thousand dollars towards the alterations."

"JULY 16. The contract for altering and uniting the two buildings has been given to a builder, and work commenced to-day. The whole cost will be five or six thousand dollars more than my friend's gift, fifteen or sixteen thousand dollars in all; but I shall only give the contract for as far as my money will carry, and wait upon God for the rest.

" 'This is the confidence that we have in him, that if we ask any thing according to his will he heareth us : and if we know that he hear us, whatsoever we ask, we know that we have the petitions that we desired of him.' "

"JULY 17. The brother who has so generously given for this branch of the work proposes to put a memorial window in the church in memory of his wife who has recently gone to be with Jesus. I hope at no distant day all the church-windows may become mementos to loved ones gone before."

"As the year closes [Sept. 30, 1883], the work upon the church is more than half completed. I hope, God helping, that we may occupy the building by the first of November. I ask the prayers of God's people everywhere, that this house of God may be filled with his glory, and that every year within its walls may go up the song of praise for the many souls converted and sanctified to God."

The dedication of the prayer-room, which from a moderate-sized parlor had grown to be a spacious and attractive church-edifice, occurred on the 9th of December, 1883. The preacher of the morning was the Rev. Hugh Johnston, one of the two or three chief Methodist clergy of Canada, and an old-time friend of the Doctor and his work. In the afternoon addresses were given by Rev. A. J. Gordon, D.D., Rev. William McDonald, Rev. S. L. Gracey, and Dr. Cullis. The audience-room has pews for about six hundred people. At the inner end is a spacious chancel with the communion-rail, reading-desk, and organ; while below, opening upon Bowdoin Street, are the two lecture-rooms for the various uses of the church, Sunday school, and college. The meetings held in this consecrated place are at present as follows : —

Public worship on Sunday morning and evening.

Sunday school immediately following morning service.

Prayer-meeting every week-day, from twelve to one o'clock.

The Tuesday-afternoon consecration-meeting, at three o'clock ; the principal meeting of the week.

The meeting for faith-healing, on Thursday morning, at eleven o'clock ; for the sick only.

The Thursday-evening church prayer-meeting.

The lectures of the Faith Training College, three evenings in the week, from October to April.

And, last and largest of all, the annual Midwinter Faith Convention, which tests the full capacity of the house, and brings together an assemblage of advanced believers only rivalled in numbers (and quite unrivalled in interest) by the great summer Faith-assemblies at Old Orchard Beach and Intervale Park.

Here Dr. Cullis has his office where he ministers to the souls and bodies of the sick, both by natural and supernatural means ; and here also are the rooms of the Willard Tract Repository, including the publishing-office of "Service for Jesus," and "Times of Refreshing." This, then, is at least one churchly building whose constant and varied uses in the Lord's name and work amply justify its existence, and where daily evidence is to be found of the saving power of the gospel.

The noonday prayer-meeting furnishes an hour of very lively and sometimes intense devotion, quite in contrast with the sameness and heaviness which have proved the death of so many meetings of this sort. Of it the Doctor thus speaks in his twentieth Annual Report : —

"Simultaneous with the opening of the church, a noon prayer-meeting was inaugurated in the vestry. This has been most blessedly sustained, led at first by Dr. Cullis and his co-laborers, but taken up in the summer months during the Doctor's absence by a beloved brother, Mr. West. His spirit, witnessing with God, has made these daily gatherings a power ; mingled with praise, the testimonies give evidence to the full gospel teaching received ; and we trust Beacon-Hill noon prayer-meeting shall continue, as it really is, a centre for the radiating of gospel truth to the healing of sin-sick souls and bodies."

And now appears the reason for treating of the Tuesday meeting and the Beacon-Hill Church in the same chapter. Their history is a common one; without the former, the latter would not have existed. Thus the church has a broad and deep foundation in the laying-out of the Divine providence; for, instead of owing its rise to sectarian zeal or the harmony of human opinions, its walls were built by prayer, and its gates were set up by praise. Herein on Tuesday afternoons the multitude of written requests for prayer which Dr. Cullis has received during the week are laid by him before the Lord, in the presence of a large assembly of believing ones; the place is therefore one of the great prayer-centres of North America, at which hundreds of lines of supplication continually converge on their way to the mercy-seat : no wonder, then, that this should be a Bethesda of healing for the body, and a mount of vision for the soul.

Thus the increasing needs of the Tuesday consecration-meeting have been the occasion of other great and precious additions to the Faith-work; and if the necessity for its expansion should a fourth time occur, by the same law of proportion what an outburst of glad alms-giving, and what an opening-out of helps and powers and blessings, there would be !

CHAPTER XXI.

CITY MISSIONS.

"Go out quickly into the streets and lanes of the city, and bring in hither the poor and the maimed and the halt and the blind."

IN the Lord's own plan for the spread of his gospel, benefactions to men's bodies and benedictions to their souls go hand in hand : it is therefore just what would be expected, that, along with this work of faith for the care of the sick, there should be a work for the saving of sinners.

And so it has been. While the Consumptives' Home was yet in its infancy, a lady missionary with the modest title of Bible-reader was sent out into the streets and lanes of the North End of Boston, to teach and practise the gospel. It was at first a house-to-house ministry, until the chapel in Willard Street was opened; and thereafter, until the removal of the Home to Grove Hall, this little sanctuary was the headquarters of an enterprising campaign among the "unchurched masses" of that region ; the gospel being carried to those who did not want it enough to go after it, and the scanty supplies sent to the Home being also shared with the poor outside its walls.   Under date of Nov. 2, 1867, occurs the following note in the journal :—

"To-day the lady appointed as Bible-reader for the ward in which the Home is located commenced her labors.   May the Lord go with her, and give her grace and wisdom !   I am praying for means to support this branch of the work.   Not only is the Bible to be *read*, but *given* to those who have none ; and the necessities of life supplied so far as the Lord shall send the means."

At this time the Doctor had begun to pray for the money to buy or rent a house for a chapel ; and a few days after the above announcement, the first gift for that object was received.   It was only thirty-nine cents, accompanied by the direction, "to be used for what you have been praying for more particularly to-day ;" and, the chapel answering to that description, these few cents were laid aside as the commencement of a fund for that purpose.

The next step was the opening of an evening school in one of the rooms of the Orphan House, a gentleman having offered his services as teacher.   The room was very soon crowded with pupils, mostly young persons employed in shops and stores during the day, or from other causes debarred the privileges of the public schools.   With the close of this year, the house in Willard Street had been bought, and refitted as a chapel ; and the force of workers in connection therewith was increased by the addition of a voluntary missionary, Mr. L. R. Bumpus, — whose name appears in the Reports as a beloved and valued helper first at Willard Street, and afterwards for several years at Grove Hall, — and a second Bible-woman, one of the Deaconesses, that sisterhood which has furnished such a large proportion of hands and hearts for this great circle of charities and missions both at home and abroad.

No part of the early history of the Faith-work is of more stirring interest than that of the mission in this little chapel. Reference has already been made to it in the chapter on Beacon-Hill Church, but the mission has a precious record of its own. At the outset the Lord gave evidence of his favor in the awakening and conversion of sinners, and the Devil gave evidence of his disfavor by stirring up some of his young servants to disturb and break up the meetings. A chief reason for this seems to have been the temperance prayer-meetings, which were held on Tuesday evenings, at one of which, presided over by that patriarch of this reform, the Rev. Dr. Chickering, no less than forty-one persons signed the total-abstinence pledge. The rum-devil is particularly spiteful, impudent, and outrageous, and it was probably he who set the *gamins* to break the windows of the chapel, and do other mischief; which assaults became at length so serious that it was necessary to call on the police for protection, who by a few arrests soon put an end to the disturbances. The incident shows that Satan is particularly opposed to temperance prayer-meetings, especially in the neighborhood where his drinking-dens abound.

But another sore trial came to the friends of this new enterprise. The chapel, like most of the other property of this Faith-work, was purchased on credit; and when the first instalment of money became due, there was nothing wherewith to meet it. Week after week passed by, and still the prayers for the requisite funds were not answered. The creditor then became pressing; and after asking and obtaining still further allowance of time, which passed without bringing relief, the Doctor advertised the chapel for sale in order to pay the debt. Yet neither did this desperate measure bring any help; for only one person came to examine the property, and he would not buy it. So there remained nothing to do but to pray and wait. Little by little the needed money came, with no other asking than asking of God; and by the payment of a portion of the debt, the danger was averted for the present. In the midst of this heavy strain upon his faith, the Doctor avows his unfailing courage, and relates a touching incident as follows: —

"The dear Lord has given me grace to insert the advertisement."

"JUNE 20. Peace reigns within. Praise his holy name, who hath given me the victory through our Lord Jesus Christ. I know the dear Lord will spare the precious chapel, and not only that, but enlarge it. O my dear Christian reader, take God at his word, and when he tries your faith, cling to him ; for 'the word of our God shall stand forever.' Never doubt it ! A dear friend gave me twenty dollars this afternoon in aid of the chapel, and I felt as sure of the safety of the work as if he had put twenty thousand in my hand.

"JUNE 23. This morning, as I visited a patient at the south part of the city, who had but a short time to live, she inquired about the chapel ; and as I told her it had not been sold, but was in the market, she took from under the bed-clothes a one-hundred-dollar United States bond, saying, ' I want to give this to the chapel.' Being confident that she had but small means, and perhaps this might be her all, I said, 'But you will need this.' She replied, ' No ; ' to which I answered, ' Your sister may need it.' Her reply was, ' She is just as anxious as I am that you should have it.' I could only thank her, and as I knelt we thanked God together."

The report of the first year's work in connection with the Willard street Chapel shows one thousand and eighty-two families visited ; over ten thousand Bibles, books, papers, and tracts distributed ; the receipt of thirty-five hundred dollars for building, alterations, and current expenses ; and, better than all, an almost constant succession of awakenings and conversions, some of them of persons very far from God.

Early in the next year (the sixth fiscal year of the Home, beginning Oct. 1, 1870), another considerable instalment of the debt was paid, and the possession of the premises was thus assured ; though not for long, as the good Lord had it in view to transfer the entire

institution to more spacious and attractive quarters.
The following extracts from the final report of the missionary, brother Bumpus, show the manner, spirit, and
results of this kind of service for Jesus. They commence with Oct. 31, 1870.

"The precious promise of the dear Master, 'I will guide
thee with mine eye,' has been fulfilled in labor for him during
the past month.

" A gentleman called one day, and requested me to visit his
aged mother, some miles distant, who was in spiritual darkness
and bondage through fear and doubt. I called, and, after con-
versing with her, read some passages from the Word, and prayed
with her. God blessed her with faith in a loving Saviour. I
have since learned that she is kept in ' perfect peace.' "

Under date of Nov. 31 he reports : —

"As the cold season is upon us, the wants of the poor are
increasing ; and in answer to prayer the Lord has sent the
means to meet some of these demands.

" One evening a stranger came to the prayer-meeting, attracted by hearing the singing as he passed. The Lord spoke
to his heart, and at the close of the meeting with tears he
requested prayers. We trust he gave his heart to Jesus. He
was from the West, and stopped in the city only for the night."

" DEC. 2. Visited twenty families to-day. There is much
of sameness in visiting the poor, many of the rooms are so alike
in their coldness, filth, and scanty furniture ; and the wants of
one family are the counterpart of the wants of many. Coal,
clothing, and food, they will tell you they need ; you cannot
doubt this as you feel the chill air, look in their thin faces, and
scan their worn garments. We pray for more means to help
the deserving poor.

"I find an eagerness for religious reading, which shows that God is working in the hearts of many. While talking with one poor woman who asked for a Bible, the attention of a Roman-Catholic woman in the room seemed awakened. I turned to her, and after conversation repeated the twenty-third Psalm, and prayed. The woman then said, 'No Protestant ever talked with me before about the Saviour.' This she said with tears. I furnished the family with a Bible."

"DEC. 3. I have found several inquirers who request prayers for their conversion. In the Bible-class of the sabbath school, adults are blessed with light on Bible truths, and remain to converse after the session about the faith that saves fully."

"JANUARY, 1871. I love to record the sweet leading of God's Spirit. He led me to go to a neighboring city, and visit in a locality where I had never been before. In almost every house I found blessed work to do for Jesus. Near the close of one day I called at a house, and conversed with a young lady who said she wanted to be a Christian. That night she found the Saviour. I afterwards learned that her mother had been praying that some one might be led of the Lord to talk with her daughter."

"JAN. 20. Visited a family for whom I have felt a deep interest for weeks past. The father has been out of employment some time, and they have lacked food and clothing. Much of their trouble has been caused by the intemperance of the mother. Her husband has borne long and patiently with her; and although she would for a short time leave off drinking, it was only to fall again still lower. While furnishing them with clothing, and assisting them in other ways, I besought the mother to give her heart to Jesus, knowing that he could keep her from falling. She has become a constant attendant at our meetings, and seems really to have found the Saviour. She says *Jesus has taken her love for drink all away.* One of her little ones, who is just beginning to talk, said the other day,

'Mamma, *you don't drink beer now.*' They are a happy family, and their home is greatly changed.

"Recently, finding so many families needing coal, I prayed the Lord to send it; when he inclined the heart of one of his dear children who has assisted the mission much before, to give an order for five tons. For this we feel thankful, as it will cheer many a heart."

"FEBRUARY. The Lord has answered prayer in saving souls.

"One snowy night several weeks ago, a young woman came to the chapel asking aid. She said it was the first time she had ever asked for help. She was lame, and held her babe in her arms. She said her husband was willing to work, but had only one hand, as the other had been crushed under a pile-driving hammer. He could find no work to do. They had pawned their clothing for food. I went to their house, and found her story more than true; assisted them with clothing, food, groceries, and coal; found a place of business where the husband could work, and earn good wages; invited them to our prayer-meeting. They came regularly, and were soon rejoicing in the Saviour's love. With thankful hearts, they received their trials as sent of God to bring them to Himself. Shortly afterward they brought another young man and his wife to the meetings, who requested prayers, and we trust they have given their hearts to Jesus."

"APRIL 23. Last meeting in our chapel. The hearts of those who have so often met together seemed melted, and in the sweetest union and sympathy recounted the blessings God had given us. Ever since the chapel was opened, scarcely a meeting has closed without the evidence that sinners were pricked in their hearts and led to Jesus, while many a dear disciple has here found a complete Saviour. Our deepest gratitude is due to God's servants who have kindly volunteered to preach the gospel to the people here."

Thus closes a record of loving labor among the poor in a section of the city which had not then so many mission-stations as now; if, indeed, there were any others at all except Father Taylor's famous Seamen's Chapel, since given over to the Italian Catholics.

For the next six years, the great enlargement of the Consumptives' Home, the church at Grove Hall, and the outburst of zeal for foreign missions, gave full employment to all the force then at hand; but in January, 1877, the city-mission work was revived in a little low building at 125 Brighton Street, at the West End of Boston, under the charge of Mr. H. L. Babbitt, a retired sea-captain, and the Rev. Benjamin B. Scott, a young Methodist preacher from Iowa, — both of whom were men with families, but who joined the staff of Dr. Cullis, trusting wholly in God for support. Trying times had these brethren and their households. Capt. Babbitt mentions having to walk five miles from his home to the mission, because he had no money for a street-car fare. The captain, at the solicitation of his wife, had abandoned the sea, and settled in business on shore, but the land-sharks were too much for him; and, having lost all through frauds that were practised on him, he devoted himself to the work of the Lord, and great blessing attended his labors. At length, having passed through the time of trial to the good of his soul, the way opened for him to re-enter his old profession; and at the date of this writing he is a godly and successful seaman with a heart as big as his body.

The entrance of the Rev. Mr. Scott upon the life and work of faith is an event deserving more than a passing notice. Coming first as a student in the Faith Training College, a notice of which he had seen in some newspaper; taking next the charge of the little church which was formed of the converts at the Brighton-street mission; returning, after another brief pastorate, to become the general superintendent at Grove Hall, — he is at the date of this writing (September, 1885) on the voyage to India with his wife and their youngest child, and two lady missionaries, one a physician and the other a graduate of the Training College, all of whom go out to re-enforce the picket-line which the Faith-work under Dr. Cullis has established in that foreign field.

Having no taste for an Iowa farm, and being of a wild and enterprising temper, young Scott was sent by his father to the naval school at Annapolis, Md. Here the temptations were so many and so strong that the young man went on from bad to worse, till evil habits had become fastened upon him, and he was far on the road to destruction. But God had a work for him; and he was arrested by the Holy Spirit in the midst of his sins, was radically and soundly converted, the appetite for strong drink was at the same time wholly taken away from him, and, being now a trophy of the gospel, he felt strongly moved to preach it. For this work an opening was found among the Methodists; and it was while supplying a charge at Sioux City, Ia., that he first heard of Dr. Cullis and the Faith Training College.

Writing to the Doctor, and saying that he wished to take the course of study there, and that he had a wife and child, reply was sent to him not to come; but one morning he made his appearance at the Doctor's office, saying that his little family were at the railway-station, and that he had spent his last dollar in coming to Boston. He had done this under an impression that such was the will of the Lord; and in view of this fact he was received, and with some difficulty himself and family were provided with a snug little home on the outskirts of the city, not far from the new mission which had been opened at Brighton Street.

From the first it was evident that God was with him. He and Capt. Babbitt wrought together in cultivating that patch of the Lord's vineyard, faithfully assisted by two of the Deaconesses, Miss Wheeler and Mrs. Renshaw; and within six months a little church with the watchword "Jesus only" was organized, and Mr. Scott was ordained as its pastor. However, the little society was a short-lived affair; for its members moved away, and the locality soon filled up with foreigners who were Romanists in religion, and thus the church became extinct. For a time Mr. Scott filled a Baptist pulpit in a town of Western Massachusetts, but presently swung back to the centre towards which his heart was gravitating; and after serving as a helper at the Homes and a preacher at the different chapels connected with the work, he was promoted to the office of general superintendent at Grove Hall.

His three years of service in this responsible station furnished further proof of his ability and devotion. Especially was he blessed with the power to open and explain the word of God; and so rare and helpful was this gift in him, that, while it gave occasion for deep regret at his departure, it also gave evidence of his peculiar fitness for the work of teaching to the heathen the mysteries of the kingdom of God.

But we must return to the history of the city missions. Having now a sufficient staff of workers to allow of extending this line of service, two more missions were opened the following year (i.e., in 1878), — one in the hall of the Dorchester Athenæum on Cottage Street, at the request of members of several churches of the locality which had been closed either through misfortune or dissension; and the other in the city, on Fulton Street, chiefly for seamen. The former of these was only maintained until the churches got out of their troubles, and were ready to resume their work; but the latter proved a worthy successor of the old Willard-street Mission, and in its better quarters on Lewis Street, near by, still rejoices in the demonstration of the Spirit and the manifest power of God.

The Cottage-street enterprise introduces another

name which has of late become a familiar one on the list of these faith-workers ; viz., that of F. D. Sandford, now an evangelist in Great Britain, but still reckoned as a member of the Doctor's staff. The history of this first pastor at Cottage Street is one of the wonders of grace. He is the son of a clergyman in Central Massachusetts. But, unlike the majority of ministers' sons, — the slander to the contrary notwithstanding, since it is the very singularity of such cases that makes them conspicuous, — this young man for a time utterly departed from the ways of the Lord, and plunged into the depths and excesses of wickedness. Recalled at length by the Spirit of God, to a sense of his sins and a remembrance of the Saviour, he turned to God with all his heart, and began to preach the great salvation which had been able even to meet his case.

It was at one of the Faith Conventions held at South Framingham, Mass., before the meetings at Old Orchard Beach, that young Sandford sought and found the blessing of full salvation, of which he has since been such a successful teacher, first at the Dorchester Athenæum, and afterwards at Beacon-street Church, and in evangelistic meetings elsewhere. It was his high privilege to represent the Faith-work of Dr. Cullis at the Faith Convention in London in the spring of the present year (1885), which was called and led by that venerable apostle of faith-healing, the Rev. Dr. Boardman, whose honored name appears so often in these pages.

This chapter may be appropriately closed with an aphorism reported in one of the addresses of brother Sandford, who has felt in himself the need of a vital and thorough experience of grace, in the work of teaching the high experiences of the Christian life : —

"We never can lead a soul any nearer to Christ than we are ourselves."

CHAPTER XXII.

THE MISSION TO THE SEAMEN.

" Carest thou not that we perish ? "

CHIEF among the city missions which have sprung up under the hand of Dr. Cullis, and well deserving a chapter to itself, is the work among the seamen, first at Fulton Street and now at Lewis Street at the old North End, a portion of the city of Boston which suggests the remark of Mr. Moody concerning a section of the British capital : " The East End of London is the nearest to hell of any place I ever saw."

The gospel-loft in Fulton Street was opened by Rev. D. M. Stearns ; and so great was the blessing of God upon his labors, that for the first six months he was able to report a hundred and twelve signers of the temperance pledge, and no less than eighty-nine cases of professed conversion.

The removal to Lewis Street was on this wise : The hall at the corner of Lewis and Commercial Streets had, years ago, been used by the Boston Bethel Union, and on the removal of that mission had been kept as a Mariners' Exchange ; but, having now again fallen vacant, Dr. Cullis took a lease of the dirty and dilapidated premises, and, having cleaned them up and fitted them up, re-dedicated them to their former holy use on the 25th of February, 1879. Chaplain Stearns, who had given his services in connection with the Fulton-street mission, transferred his love and labor to the new post at Lewis Street; and assisted by Miss Meek, one of the Grove-Hall Deaconesses, the work went grandly on.

The following extracts from the first year's report of these devoted missionaries show the depth and power of the work under their hands. Chaplain Stearns says, —

"Every week, without an exception, we have seen souls coming to Christ, and abandoning themselves to him; and sometimes we have seen this at every meeting for three or four days in succession. All glory to Jesus be given!

"Dear sister Meek is heart and soul in the work, and every noon-time is out on the street with her handful of tracts or papers, visiting the shipping-offices and sailors' boarding-houses, and urging all who will listen to her to come into the meeting, and hear of Jesus, — mighty to save unto the uttermost all who will come unto him. She also does this at the boarding-houses and on the street on Wednesday and Friday evenings, and three times on Sunday; and, when they refuse to come, the gospel is preached to them by our dear sister, there on the street or in the house or office. And such is the power of the Spirit through her, that often, when they have refused her invitation and gone away, they have had to turn and come back, and in many cases have accepted Christ.

"Brother H. I. Pearson, who has been for some months with

us in the work, is also skilful in gathering them in from the street."

Miss Meek speaks thus of the same year's work : —

" Rejoicing daily that the Lord was working with me, and trusting him to give the word, I have visited the saloons, boarding-houses, and shipping-offices, distributing tracts and the word of life, and inviting those whom I met in these places and on the street to attend the meetings at the mission. I do not remember a single instance in which none have accepted the invitation ; sometimes about a dozen will come together, oftener five or six. Sometimes those who have said they could not go to the meeting, and have gone away, have returned, being impressed by the word given them. Many times they have left card-playing and other amusements, and even their dinners, to go to the mission. . . .

" The great number who have accepted the invitation have been persuaded to do so by no other inducement than that they would hear about the Lord Jesus, and be saved by receiving him as their Saviour.

'Lord, if I may, I'll serve another day;'

and year, should the Lord tarry."

The summary of this report for the year ending Sept. 30, 1879, shows that three hundred and eighty-four professed to accept Christ as their Saviour. In the year's work, nearly twelve thousand copies of the word of life were distributed, and over five thousand tracts : about one thousand of these were kindly furnished by the American Tract Society of Boston. There were also over six hundred Bibles, Testaments, and Bible-portions distributed, these being in nine different languages ; all of which were given by the American Bible Society.

In the summer of 1880, chaplain Stearns accepted a call to a Presbyterian pastorate at the South End of Boston ; and the work among the sailors and their rude companions was continued by Miss Meek, sometimes with the help of a missionary brother, sometimes alone, but always with the same calm, sweet, straightforward devotion which won the homage and courtesy of the roughest men and the rudest women.   The following incident will show her power over those turbulent spirits, so many of whom she was able to lead to Christ.

One day, as she was entering a house to visit a sick woman, she found the door surrounded by some men who said to her, —

"You can't go in there."

"Why not ? "

"Well, you can't go in.   There are two men going to fight."

"Ah! then I must go in."   So she entered the hall, and hearing in one of the rooms the noise of moving chairs, tables, etc., she rapped at the door.   Getting no response, she rapped louder ; and presently the door was opened a little, and a harsh voice began to say, "You can't come in," but stopped short in the middle of the sentence, and finished with the words, addressed to those within : "It is the missionary woman."

Taking advantage of the surprise and embarrassment caused by her unlooked-for appearance, she pushed the door open a little wider, and entered the room, where she found the middle of the floor cleared for the fight, and two wrathy sailors with coats off, just ready to begin.   Stepping between them, and calmly fixing her black eyes upon the face of one of them, she said, —

"What are you going to do?"

"I'm going to lick that fellow," was the reply.

"What for?"

"Because he called me bad names."

"Is that the way Jesus would do if some one were rude to him?"

At the tender and reverent mention of that holy name, the man was struck with astonishment; his anger began to cool; and as the "missionary woman" went on with her gentle reproof, both men yielded to the invisible power which accompanied her words, gave up the idea of fighting, put on their coats, and accepted an invitation to come to the mission; and two or three days after, they both sailed aboard the same ship, the best of friends, and each with a Bible which he had gladly accepted from the hands of the "missionary woman."

The Report for the first half of the year 1881 contains the following among other incidents of this forbidding but strangely profitable line of service for Jesus. It will be seen, that to the mission-hall, with its daily noon prayer-meeting, its all-day services on Sunday, and its Wednesday and Friday evening prayer-meetings, a coffee-room had been added ; and besides this, by the kindness of a Christian lady, several lodging-rooms were joined to the gospel outfit, which proved a blessed means of grace in providing a refuge for some of the homeless ones who were struggling to break away from their bondage to Satan, and who must otherwise have herded with the motley crew to be found in the cheap sailors' lodging-houses, roaring with blasphemy, and reeking with every form of vice, or have sought temporary shelter at the station-houses among the captures of the police.

"Last summer a young man came into one of the meetings, and one of the workers asked him if he might pray with him ; he assented, and he prayed that he might have no rest until he gave his heart to God. The expression followed him ; and he was angry that such a prayer had been offered, and made it the subject of conversation after he went home. But it was a nail in a sure place ; and in September he came to us again, and was converted. The 1st of November, a man came in, and introduced himself as the young man's father, and with tears in his eyes thanked God that through the instrumentality of this mission his boy had been saved.

"An interesting case was that of a young man, the son of a minister, a college graduate, who became addicted to the use of intoxicating liquors, and had sunk very low. He came into the mission intoxicated, and was at times very noisy ; but the Lord gave us patience with him. One Friday his father sent him fifty dollars for clothes, and he immediately went on a drunken spree ; on Sunday morning he came to himself, his money all gone, and Saturday was a blank to him. He says that from that time until Thursday his mind was full of thoughts of himself and his condition. We furnished him with food, and also lodging, to the extent of our ability. On Thursday, at noon meeting, he gave himself to the Lord ; and he has kept thus far for two weeks, steadfast and immovable amid the temptations that surround one who steps upon a higher and better plane of life after having given loose rein to all the vices of an immoral life.

"One day in going into the coffee-room, I met an infidel who was loud in his denunciations of God and the Bible ; he said he did not believe in any such stuff. After some persuasion he came into the noon meeting, and during its progress God was pleased to give him conviction of sin ; it came with such force that he cried for mercy, and asked us to pray for him. He staid after the close of the meeting, for conversation and prayer, and went away rejoicing in the Lord.

"George W. S. from Norfolk, Va., was converted April 26. He replied, when we spoke to him, 'I am a castaway ; all my people are Christians, but I am a vile, bad boy.' We think that his was a clear case of conversion ; he attended to the meetings until he sailed in May.

"The whole number who have professed conversion from Jan. 1 to July 23, 1881, is one hundred and thirty-one ; a large majority of these we have reason to believe are truly saved. *Thirty-four* of this number have either returned, and given evidence of their faith in Christ, and have shown the fruits of the religion of Jesus Christ in their lives, or we have heard from them by letters.

"One hundred and twenty-two have signed the pledge. We think our pledge one of the best ever used, and it reads thus :

MY PLEDGE.

" ' Believing that the Lord Jesus Christ is able to save me from strong drink, I yield myself to him to be kept from it, and delivered from the appetite for it ; promising in his strength to shun it as I would a deadly poison.' "

And now the earthly mission of this faithful hand-maid of the Lord draws to a close, and she is to be taken to her reward. This fearless and tireless woman, who had become the chief apostle to the sailors, and a missionary at large to all sorts of lost men and women of that fearful region, — whom she searched out with a zeal and love that must have been a direct and mighty inspiration of the Spirit of the Master himself, — this devoted member of the Grove Hall Deaconess sister-hood is now ready to be translated from the midst of the degradation and wickedness which seethed and surged among the streets and rookeries of the "old North End," to the peace and rest that remain for those who have worked hard enough for the Lord to be honestly tired ; tired not of the work, but by it.

The following tribute is paid to her memory by Dr. Cullis, in the Report for 1881 : —

"Our dear sister Miss Meek, whose work was recorded in last year's report of Lewis-street Mission, finished her course quite suddenly to us all. Early in February she went to her rest. It seems scarcely possible that our eyes shall behold her no more in the flesh. Her strong personality so impressed itself, that when in the places where we were wont to meet, it seems as though we had only to turn, and meet her earnest, speaking gaze. All who ever listened to her will also remember how her convictions could be summed up in the words, 'I *believed*, therefore have I spoken.' Her zeal in the work was great; she was a sacrifice to this zeal. Often when remonstrated with, and asked during the heated season to leave for a while the unhealthy localities in which she labored, her invariable reply was, 'I feel perfectly well, and able to work steadily on.' Her sense of adequacy for the work made her refuse the help offered her; and we were indeed surprised, when the summer had passed, to learn that the little visit she had commenced at her home in Salem was prolonged from the effects of a cough which she could not throw off. Soon after this, how great was our astonishment, on visiting her, to find that human help could avail nothing for her recovery! What could we say, when after her faith united with ours in asking for healing, and we were far away across the Atlantic, the news came of her departure 'to be with Christ'? Only with Paul, 'It is far better.' 'The Lord gave, and the Lord hath taken away: blessed be the name of the Lord!'"

After the death of Miss Meek, the guild of Deaconesses furnished another "missionary woman" to take up the work, in the person of that bright, active, fluent little lady, Miss Flora Blinn, whose labors, assisted by one and another masculine worker, were attended with the same Divine approval and success. It is evident, as one studies the reports of this work, that strong drink is the great curse of seafaring men; as, indeed, it is of multitudes of others, though perhaps no whole class of persons are so unfortunate in this respect. Thus it was that almost every meeting was a

temperance-meeting, and that the pledge and the gospel
went hand in hand.

Twenty years ago, if any reformed drunkard had
claimed to be wholly saved from the very appetite for
liquor, it would have been regarded as both false and
foolish, "nothing less than a miracle." Neither is it
any thing less than a miracle ; but whoever has carefully followed the trend of the great revivals and re-
forms which of late years have astonished the Church,
and aroused the world, has seen, that so far from the
day of miracles having passed, as some slow theologians
affirm, there are more miracles transpiring now than
ever. Especially frequent has become that blessed miracle, the deliverance of the hopeless slave to drink from
the taste and appetite therefor. And these with other
marvels of saving grace are constantly passing before
the eyes of all the most successful workers in city
missions, especially seamen's missions ; for the reason
above mentioned, — that they are as a class particularly
given to drink. These two cases, from among those
reported for the year 1882, suffice to tell the story of
ruin by rum, and of salvation from its curse through
the regenerating grace of God : —

"James H. A. was passing the Mission, heard the singing,
came in, was convicted ; wept when I spoke to him of his
mother ; said, 'I never did any thing wrong until my mother
died, but after that I fell into sin, and am going to sea to get
rid of rum.' He was with us after this two or three days ;

seemed to be trusting in Jesus to keep him. He shipped at last on a whaling vessel, to go on a two-years' voyage. He said, as we talked with him before he left, ' I feel I am a different man from what I was the first day I came in here. I was entirely discouraged that day ; would have drowned myself if I had had courage ; do not know but that I should if I had not come in here. But now I have none of those feelings. I must hold on to God, and will, with his help.'

" W. C., of G., had been a drunkard for many years ; came into our Mission careless ; was converted, and saved from the desire for liquor so completely that the smell of it became offensive to him. Obtained a pass for him, and sent him home to tell his friends the good news. Has since returned, and given blessed testimony and proof of what the Lord has done for him."

This interesting field was afterwards in charge of Mr. James E. Dee, a man who has himself experienced the power of Christ to save lost men. In his former profession of negro-minstrel, he formed vicious acquaintances and vicious habits ; and for the crime of a companion, in which he had no immediate hand, he was committed to the Connecticut State Prison for a term of years. While there the Spirit of the Lord found him, and he was soundly converted to God. After his release, with no other preparation than his experience, his well-read Bible, and his voice, — a big voice for such a little man, — he devoted himself to evangelistic work, assisted by his Christian wife, wherever the Lord opened their way. Through one of his friends he was brought to the notice of Dr. Cullis, who

placed him in charge of the Lewis-street mission, where
he both sung and preached the gospel with all his
might, superintended the little gospel restaurant in the
room under the hall, and rejoiced at seeing men as wild
as his former self coming to his Saviour for pardon and
a new heart.

God is still with this blessed mission, in which, it is
said, more sinners have been saved since its foundation than in any first-class church in Boston.

A NEW HOME.

In the Report for the nineteenth year of the work,
the Doctor partially reveals a secret, and partly keeps
it to himself. There must always be something repul-
sive, to a woman in whom there is still enough of the
Divine image even to wish for salvation from a life of
shame, in being put into a "Magdalen asylum" among
a crowd of victims like herself. (Mr. Moody protests
against the use of the name of that particular Mary in
this sad connection; for, he says, if the Magdalen had
been a fallen woman reclaimed, the tender care of the
Master for women more sinned against than sinning
would have caused him forever to conceal her name
instead of letting it be made prominent in his gospel,
— a view of the case in which the editor of this
volume heartily concurs.)

The sorrows of this class of God's lost ones have not
failed to awaken the sympathy of his servant. But

they could not be admitted to any of the Homes ; and it was not his mind to make prominent any charity of this sort, which, of all others, ought to be done in secret, both for the Lord's sake and for the sake of the poor and unhappy ones who are rescued and saved. The following is all that is said in the Report, concerning this department of city missions, and all that needs to be said in these pages. Under the title of "A New Home," the Doctor writes : —

" This branch of the work of faith has been doing its work quietly, almost unseen of men, but not of God. Souls and bodies of unfortunate girls have been saved, and have heard the blessed message from the Master, 'Neither do I condemn thee. Go, and sin no more.' "

" DEC. 2. This morning I received the following letter : —

Dec. 1, 1882.

DR. CULLIS.

Dear Sir, — Perhaps you may think it strange to receive a letter like this ; but I feel as if I must write to some one, and as I have heard of your kindness I thought perhaps you might be willing to help me in the right direction.

My heart is heavy. I do *long* to be a true follower of Christ ; but I have been a bad, yes, a wicked girl, and it seems to me that I dare not go to him, for I have sinned against him so deeply. Will he accept me? Long ago there went into one of your Tuesday meetings a request for prayer for a young girl, an orphan, who had gone astray. I am the girl. I knew that request was to be carried in to you by a lady who cared for my soul. She is now far away. I then laughed at the idea of any one praying for me : now I earnestly desire it. Can I be saved? Oh, it seems as if I would be willing to do any thing !

May I come and see you? And will you pray for me? Ask God to help me go to him. You will please excuse me for writing you as I have; but I knew no one to whom I could write, that I felt sure would help me, but you. Tell me, do you think God will reject me after so long trifling with his mercy?

Yours respectfully,

"I wrote her that Jesus Christ came to the world to save sinners, and he was ready and willing to save to the uttermost all who would come unto him. I urged her to go to Jesus just as she was, and that I too would pray for her. I asked her to go to the Tuesday meeting, and to remain after the meeting. She did so; and after talking with her she gave herself, just as she was, to Jesus. I prayed with her, when the joy of the Lord came into her life, and she went away with the peace of God in her heart.

"While we have a house for this branch of the work, occupied by one of the workers with his family, we have thus far been able to provide for such cases as have come to us, without receiving them in the Home.

"The following gifts have been given during the year: From Stevens Point, Wis., $15; Genesee, N.Y., $1; Somerville, N.Y., $5; Milton Mills, N.H., $1; Somerville, 25 cents; Eastham, $2; North Wilmington, $2."

At the date of this writing, the Lewis-street mission and the private one just mentioned comprise all there is of the city mission-work. The former is a "survival of the fittest," and the latter has yet to stand the test of time and use: yet the presence of any and all of these institutions, supported by the prayer of faith, in unbelieving Boston, is of itself a mighty missionary agency, whereby the gospel, which is larger than any possible statement˝of it, is freed from the limitations of doubt and naturalism, and brought before the Church of God as a means of doing for lost souls and bodies all that needs to be done for them till the Lord himself shall return.

CHAPTER XXIII.

FOREIGN MISSIONS.

" Behold, I send you forth as sheep in the midst of wolves."

THE outbreak of missionary zeal in January, 1874, being in the tenth year of the history of the faith-charities, has already been mentioned in the chapter on the Grove-Hall Church. It was not a mere spasm of interest, but the beginning of a permanent and important section of the Work of Faith.

With the first gifts for this object, the members of the little church began to pray that God would raise up among them some one who should go forth to preach the gospel in foreign lands ; and notwithstanding all the difficulties in the way, — the want of funds, the need of money and service at home, and the startling nature of a foreign mission on a faith-basis, — the matter was taken hold of in right good earnest, and it was not long before the prayer was answered. On the 31st of October, 1875, Miss Lucy R. Drake, one of the Deaconesses, who had begun to feel an intense desire to enter the foreign field, was set apart thereto by the laying-on of hands, and prayer ; and a week later she sailed from New York for Bombay.

Her first residence, as a student of Marathi, — the
native language of Central India, — was at Ellickpoor;
but she afterwards removed to Bassein (or Basim) in
the province of Berar, a point two or three hundred
miles east from Bombay, in the very heart of India, and
among a mass of people whose native heathenism had
been still further corrupted by the worst abominations
of the Mohammedan religion.   It was new missionary
ground, and as fair a field as one could wish for testing
the virtues of the faith-plan among heathen populations.   Self-supporting missions along the coasts and in
the commercial cities of Asia and Africa had already
been successfully established by Rev. William Taylor,
now Bishop Taylor of Africa; but this woman with no
base of supplies, and no "communications" with any
missionary society, struck out boldly into the enemy's
country, and was at least so far successful in this solitary invasion in the name of the Lord, that the mission
which she commenced has now become the centre of
operations for the Faith-work in India, in which country
ten devoted women, who pray their way through all
sorts of dangers and trials, are now spreading the gospel both by the voice of the preacher, the training of
the teacher, and the circulation of the printed page.

Does any one call this single-handed onset upon the
myriad powers of darkness a piece of fanaticism, the
wild scheme of a deluded dreamer?   Let such a one
know that it is by such pioneering as this, that the

gospel has always been extended into "the regions
beyond:" more commonly by men than by women, indeed, because the initial work in most cases could be
better done by men than by women, especially with
women to help them ; but in India, where the religion
of the country enslaves and degrades its wives and
mothers, and shuts them away from the knowledge of
Christ except as it may be carried to them by persons
of their own sex, the prophesying of the "daughters "
and "hand-maidens " is both fitting and essential.
Thus does the blessed Lord break into the house of
this strong Paganism and this stronger Mohammedan-
ism, spoil the idols, unloose the fetters of venerable
tradition, and bring out of their prison the hopeless
captives, who, except by the hands of angels or of
women, could never be set free.

The successor of Miss Drake — whose marriage led
to her return to America — was Miss Laura Wheeler,
for years the leading spirit, humanly speaking, in the
thriving work in the province of Berar, a woman who
was evidently raised up and appointed to this work by
the hand and voice of the Lord himself. With few
literary advantages, and at first no special fitness for
any thing beyond the common lot of hard-working
Christian women, she was brought out by the Spirit
into "a large place." Her capacity for heroic work
became more and more apparent as she performed the
humbler duties of a Deaconess at Grove Hall, gave

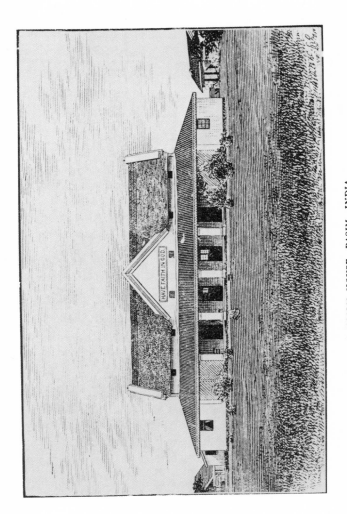

MISSION HOUSE, BASIM, INDIA.

close attention to the teaching at the Faith Training College, and sought in prayer the deep experiences of a consecrated and sanctified soul. So eager was she for instruction, that when she had no money she would walk to the evening lectures of the college, nearly four miles distant. Rapidly the qualities required in a faith-missionary developed in her; and, after two years of training in the home work, she was ready to enter on her novitiate at Basim, where she became the Lord's own ambassador to the heathen.

Miss Wheeler's comrade in this little outpost of Christ's army in India is Miss Lottie Sisson, a quiet, cultivated lady, who left her duties as a teacher of Christian children, to set up a school for heathen orphans at Basim. These two missionaries sailed together, and reached Bombay on the last day of the year 1877. Many were the privations endured by those three pioneers of faith-missions in foreign lands, — or, at least, the advance-guard of American missions of this sort; there being some notable examples of this same heroic devotion on the part of the faithful from other and older countries, — and so sore was the trial of their faith, that at times they were actually on short allowance of food. Still their confidence in God remained unshaken; and by reason of their courage and devotion this little mission-station at Basim, West Berar, Central India, — in which province, swarming with Pagans and Mohammedans, there were then only six English families, —

became first an object of wonder, then an argument
in favor of the faith which had such representatives.
Then the missionaries began to receive occasional gifts
from the natives, which their English friends told them
was a perfect marvel; and now, with a spacious mission-house (or bungalow), a preaching-shed near the
great bazaar, and an orphanage large enough to hold
forty homeless children, it has come to be the headquarters of one of the most promising gospel enterprises in all heathendom. It is grandly evident that
God is with these his faithful and fearless handmaidens,
and that faith in him is a real and substantial bond
between the power of the Almighty and the work they
are doing in his name.

There is a perfect fascination about the letters and
reports of these two young women, who, after the
departure of Miss Drake for America, were left to push
on the work of setting up the worship of the true God
in this ungospelled region. It was a year and a half
before they were mistresses of the Marathi language
so as to preach therein; but in a few weeks Miss
Wheeler began to sing the gospel, having learned a few
songs that had been translated into the Marathi tongue.
At first they found a residence in a shed made of tin,
which belonged to the British garrison; and when,
after they had endured the heats of an Indian summer
under it, they were told that it was to be torn down,
they were forced to take refuge in an old tent. This

too presently failed them ; for when the rains commenced, they and the little orphan girls whom they had
already adopted were but poorly sheltered, and at last,
one terrible night, the tempest actually demolished the
tent over their heads ; and in their efforts to protect
the children from the storm, Miss Wheeler was so
drenched with the rain that the next day she was down
with rheumatism and the terrible Indian fever.

So great were their sufferings, that for a little while
they entertained the question of removal, and asked
the Lord to show them his will ; which he did, as Miss
Wheeler says, "by not giving us money enough to get
away with."

The rise and progress of the new bungalow is charm-
ingly told ; as if the struggles with poverty, the bad
faith of the builder, the slow coming of small sums to
pay for materials and labor, the occupancy of the roof-
less walls in the rainy season, and at one time the
giving-out of provisions, except a little native meal and
a box of macaroni, were but a series of problems under
the rule of faith, which they were sent to this school to
solve. The temptation is a strong one, to embody in
these pages the full report of their hand-to-hand fight
for possession of this camp within the enemy's lines ;
but want of space forbids. The following incident will
serve to show that the life of faith is taught, in all its
simplicity and fulness, to those Hindoo waifs in the
Basim orphanage, and that they learn the lesson quite

as well as some of God's older children in more favored climes. Under date of Sept. 20 and 21, 1879, Miss Wheeler writes : —

"About a week ago we purchased a buffalo, that we might be able to give the girls some milk. We kept it as a surprise to them ; and when she was led into the compound, their delight knew no bounds. They clapped their hands, and danced about in very joy. But their joy has been short-lived, for night before last the buffalo disappeared. Whether she broke loose, and has wandered away, or whether some one has stolen her, we know not. We have searched all about for her, but up to this afternoon she has not been found. While sitting this afternoon with the girls gathered about us for their daily singing and conversation, we said, 'Children, the buffalo is gone, we do not know where ; but we are asking God to bring her back again to us. You too should ask God about this.' . . . This afternoon the girls prayed, 'O God, our buffalo having found, back to us send ;' and the words had scarcely died on their lips, ere they began clapping their hands, saying, 'Now she *surely, surely* will come back, for we have asked God to send her ;' and our faith was strengthened, for they really seemed to have received the assurance of faith.

"SEPT. 21. The girls went to bed last night with tearful faces, saying, 'Mamma, the buffalo has not come.' We bade them 'have faith in God,' or, as the Marathi has it, 'on God faith put,' that God would in his own time surely send her back to us. And all the morning, one here, and another there, they have been silently praying God to hear them, and send back the lost buffalo. The trial of their faith is very hard for them to bear ; but, thank God, *all* our children are being taught of the Lord.

" (Afternoon.) Sitting with the children, as is our custom, for a little chat and sing, we saw the man who takes care of the buffalo, coming toward the house with bounding steps; and we knew at once that she was found. The girls, when we told them, seemed unable to find sufficient expression for their joy; they laughed, clapped their hands, and danced about the room, crying, ' *God* our buffalo back has sent, *because we asked him.*' After a little they became more quiet, and gathering them about us, we all kneeled before God, and in unison offered this simple prayer, or rather praise : ' O God, thou our prayer hast heard, and our lost buffalo back to us sent; on account of this we thy praise do. Amen.' God has surely by this simple means taught our children to pray, as we could never have done by simple precept, without the co-working of the Divine Spirit. To him be all the glory."

Here is an entry that reminds one of the Doctor's trials in the early years of the Consumptives' Home :—

"This morning the children's food all gone, also the box of corn-flour and macaroni, upon which we have been living for the last ten days. The girls have known all about this strait, and have begged us to eat some of their food, also to give them less; but we have felt to feed them as long as food remained, sure that in his own good time God's deliverance would come. The sweet spirit which this trial produced in the children was beautiful to behold. They seemed to recognize it as a means of discipline. They pray thus :—

"'O God, to you is known that in our house very little food is, in our house no money is; O God, to us faith is, or is not, this to see, you our trial do. O God, if it is thy will that we suffer hunger, do not let us be like the children of Israel, who when they had plenty of food were very happy, but when thou to try their faith didst take away their food, murmured against *thee.* But, oh! make us like Abraham, who never lost faith in thee. For ourselves we would just say that it is written that

the SON OF GOD *was an hungered,* and we *thank God* for
fellowship in *his sufferings.'*

"Just at the time of our greatest need, one of the servants
came in, and said that the buffaloes, which we have been using
for work on the house, had had nothing to eat for two days.
After some thought, we decided to sell them if we could find a
purchaser, which is quite difficult at this time of the year. We
were, however, helped, a purchaser being found that same day.
The money received from their sale kept us until the full deliverance came."

Of the work of the Holy Spirit upon the hearts of
these girls, this sweet record is given by Miss Sisson.
The time is early in the year 1880. The girls were sitting about their teacher, who was speaking to them of
the difficulties of a holy life, and of Christ's power to
save and keep as well as to forgive all who come to him
in faith. But let the teacher herself tell the story : —

"Oh, how often does God surprise us beyond our faith !
As though an arrow had been shot in our midst, the eldest
sprang to her feet and left the room, the others following her
example, one in one place, one in another ; and, awed in the
presence of God, we sank our heads in our hands, praying that
what we were not able to teach, and too feebly illustrated by our
lives, the blessed Holy Spirit would do. In a short time they
returned ; and upon the countenances of our three oldest girls,
as though the sweet Dove had flown into their hearts, and taken
up his abode there, beamed a heavenly light of joy and peace.
They tried to express the joy they felt. One said, drawing a
circle around her heart, 'Such joy sits here, there is no room !'
Did not this seem like 'filled with joy in the Holy Ghost'?
One said, holding her hands loosely, ' No more will our faith

hold Christ like *this ;* but ' — suddenly clinching her hands with a tightening grip — ' *like this!* ' We sang ' There is a fountain,' and prayed our evening prayer, then dismissed them. They showered kisses upon us, and could hardly be content to go to their rest for the night ; even then, one hymn after another rang out on the night air, till we bade them sleep, and in obedience they were quiet. As we look upon the still radiant faces, and feel the refreshment of the blessing that came to our own souls yester-eve, we ask this morning, ' What has been the work of the Spirit in their hearts ? ' God keep us from undervaluing or overvaluing the work that may have been done at this time ; but sure we feel, there has been another *divine touch,* — that the great Sculptor's hand is upon the rough-hewn stones, to fashion them into polished ones that will shine forth in resplendent glory in the New Jerusalem."

The same " presumption " and " rashness " and " foolhardiness " marked the doings of these pioneer believers, as that which, in the early days of their friend and teacher Dr. Cullis, so disturbed the timid souls of his friends in Boston. Here is a case in point : —

" FEB. 4. This evening our cook said to me in broken English, ' Many little children at the jail to give away.' Upon further inquiry we found that several kidnappers of children had been arrested in Basim district, and about forty children rescued from a life worse than death. We felt at once that God meant something for us in this, as we are told that nothing of the kind has ever before been known to occur in the Berars. We are asking God to show us his will in regard to these poor little children, who are to be given away to any one who will take them. Among the number are eleven girls. Our hearts long to take all these in ; and we are asking God to suffer no one to take them, if it is his will for us to have them."

"FEB. 5. To-day have made further inquiries about the children; for, although we have only a small tent for ourselves, we feel that it is quite roomy enough to take in as many of Jesus' little ones as he will give us. The girls are to be given away to-day. The order of the government is, that they be given to those of their own caste."

"APRIL 28. To-day we have heard more of the children. One of the officers wrote us, asking if we still desired the girls who remain unclaimed by their own caste. Although we did not know how many there were, and we were in great straits for means to meet our own needs, we felt at once that God would have us take all who remained, as we had asked him three months before to keep his chosen ones for us. See now the way of the Lord, for ' Whoso is *wise*, and will *observe these things*, even he shall understand the loving-kindness of the Lord.' Three months before, we had asked for those girls, when we were in circumstances of comparative plenty. Now that we are reduced to almost a rupee, God again offers us the gift of these souls, thus leading us to cast ourselves anew upon his faithfulness, and making this, our first work in India, so purely one of faith. We sent our answer to the officer in question; and in the evening the children came to us, five in all, bright, active girls."

And now appear two tokens of the benediction of Heaven; a little church established in this heathen city, and a re-enforcement coming.

"DEC. 4, 1880. Sabbath. A memorable day. Our seven girls have to-day, in this heathen land, testified to their faith in Christ by receiving baptism. In the early dawn we gathered by the banks of the river, sang our hymns of praise, and besought God's favor and blessing on the hour. We felt his blessed presence with us, and his smile of approval upon us. It was with fulness of joy that we beheld these the first-fruits of our ministry in Christ, and praised him for the little church in our own house. May he add many more unto it of such as shall be saved !

"After the baptism, a little church was formed in our own house ; and then, with faces on which shone the light of God's Spirit, in solemn awe, they each came forward to the breaking of bread in remembrance of Him who was wounded for their transgressions and bruised for their iniquities ; and we praised God with all our hearts for this seed of his Church in Basim, while for the future our souls rest back upon his own word of promise concerning his vineyard, 'I the Lord do keep it ; I will water it every moment ; lest any hurt it, I will keep it night and day.' "

"Jan. 26, 1881. Nearly one month of the new year has slipped away ; and, loaded with benefits, we are about entering upon the second with a prospect of re-enforcement ere it close. Miss Lizzie Sisson is now in England on her way to join us. Three years, without any break, we have 'held the fort' here for Jesus, and now one more soldier of the cross is marching on to join our ranks. Praise God ! Some may ask, What are one or two more against such odds? In themselves, nothing ; but in the power of Him who has said, 'One shall chase a thousand, and two put ten thousand to flight,' EVERY THING.

"The gifts for Basim Mission have been, for the year, twenty-two hundred and seventy dollars and fifty cents."

Let it be remembered by those who may further follow the history of this centre of radiating light in that region of darkness, that the truth of God and the reality of faith were built into the very foundation-walls of this mission. It will be no wonder, then, if the structure rises large and fair, a joy and a praise throughout the camps of Israel, and a watchword of victory all along the line.

Having become mistress of the Marathi language, Miss Wheeler caused a "gospel-shed" to be erected near the great bazaar in Basim, and there preached to congregations of varying size, sometimes fifty or more; but when the people would not come for the gospel, she carried it to them. Having some Methodist traditions about her, she next asked the Lord for a horse, and soon found herself in possession of a fine trusty pony; whereupon she organized a work of some forty miles in extent, and began to "ride the circuit," after the manner of the "saddle-bags men" on the Western frontiers of America. This "circuit" included the market-town of Nagardash, where is held an annual fair in honor of the goddess Bhwani, one of the thirty million gods and goddesses to which the devout Hindoo pays homage. This fair afforded a grand opportunity for spreading the truth, and most eagerly did she improve it. But holding five or six services daily for eight days proved too much for her strength; and for three months she suffered again the burnings of the Indian fever, looking death in the face, and seeing the gates of heaven opening before her. But God had further work for his brave and faithful handmaiden; and she was again restored to health, none too soon to take the entire charge of the mission, as she was compelled to do by the break-ing-down of the health of her devoted comrade Miss Sisson, who in the hot season of 1882 was obliged to return to America.

At home once more, Miss Sisson began to beat up recruits for India ; and almost immediately two of the Deaconesses offered themselves for the work, — Miss Harriet N. Millett, a lady in middle life, then in charge of the Tract Repository in Boston ; and Miss Mary French, who had once been a missionary to India, but had returned on account of ill health. Miss Millett had been healed in answer to prayer, and Miss French was now fit for service again. The Divine leading in their cases was too plain to be mistaken ; and in May, 1883, they sailed to re-enforce the outpost of the faith-missions on the other side of the world.

On the 7th of October of the same year, Miss Sisson returned to India, taking with her three more Christian devotees, — Miss Ella Beardsley (who had been the Doctor's stenographer), Miss Addie Smith, and Miss Nettie Ballou.

In Bombay a branch of the Willard Tract Repository has been established by Miss Millett, who also labors as an evangelist, preaching in English to Europeans and Eurasians, and doing an important work in spread-ing the gospel by means of the printed page. Hers is the only book-house in India where literature on the subject of holiness is supplied. In addition to this, she has opened a Faith-cure House, thus preaching and practising the gospel in both its great departments, — wholeness for the body, and wholeness (or holiness) for the soul.

The patient and loving work of that blessed yet afflicted Christian lady, Miss E. A. Folsom, among English-speaking people at Balasore, was carried on for two or three years under the auspices of "the Faith-mission;" the names, also, of Miss E. Sisson and of Mr. and Mrs. M. B. Fuller appear as for a longer or shorter time connected with the work in India.

And now, while these pages are passing through the press, another missionary party, consisting of the ex-superintendent at Grove Hall, the Rev. and Mrs. B. B. Scott, and their little son Rankin, Miss Alice B. Condict, M.D., and Miss Carrie Palmer, are sailing towards Bombay to open out the missions in Central India on a larger scale. A sketch of Mr. Scott has already been given in the chapter on "Home Missions." A man better fitted to represent the gospel of Christ in all its fulness, as a salvation both for body and soul, could hardly be found in this land. And let the mothers who read these pages bethink themselves whether they could break their households in twain, leaving two children of tender years in America and taking one to India with them, as Mrs. Scott and her husband are doing, for the sake of Jesus Christ and his blessed kingdom. Is there not a good deal of martyrdom in such an experience, as well as in actually dying for the Lord?

The address of Dr. Condict in the farewell meeting at Beacon Hill on the 14th of July, 1885, showed not only her exceptionally thorough training as a physician, but a power of effective speaking hitherto but little used. This lady had not been personally acquainted with the Faith-work of Dr. Cullis until shortly before her departure, but was received, with the right hand of fellowship, as a good Presbyterian, and sent forth with the other faith-workers to do, as may well be hoped, great and precious service in Jesus' name.

Miss Palmer is one of the younger Deaconesses from Grove Hall, who goes out from this her only home, to give herself to God in that far-off land. The destination of Mr. and Mrs. Scott is Basim, that of Dr. Condict and Miss Palmer is Bombay.

Thus far these Deaconesses have given a noble account of themselves: it is now the proper thing for women to go forth to preach the gospel abroad, as well as to teach and illustrate it at home. On this point the following final extract from the report of the Basim Mission — alas that these pages have room for no more! — will be read with interest. It is from the fourth annual report of Miss Wheeler: the Italics are her own.

"Oct. 15. Preached in the big bazaar to-day, for the first time since I have been alone. Took with me four of the

Christian girls to form a singing-band.   Crowds gathered at the
sound of the gospel songs to their own native tunes, and afterwards listened attentively for half or three-quarters of an hour
to the truths of the gospel.   Removing to another place, we
were soon surrounded by an entirely different crowd of all
classes, who listened for about the same length of time.   Came
home more and more burdened in heart for the millions of
Berar alone, who know nothing of the true Saviour Jesus Christ.
I often think how worse than ridiculous must appear our position here, as we, a few women, lift up our voices against their
hoary systems of religion.   They doubtless look upon us much
as Goliath and the Philistine host looked upon the youthful
David.   Yet the 'stripling,' by simple faith in God, put them
all to rout.   'Not by might nor by power, but by my Spirit,
saith the Lord.'   'The kingdom of heaven is like unto leaven,
which a *woman* took, and hid in three measures of meal, till
the whole was leavened.'"

The marriage of Miss Wheeler to the Rev. Mr. Moore,
a Eurasian, instead of removing her from the work,
brings her husband into it; and they will set up their
new home as another mission-station in some one of the
centres of population within supporting distance of
Basim.

Still another gospel enterprise is to be inaugurated
under this system at Nagpur, the chief town of the
province adjoining Berar on the east; where, under the
direction of Rev. Dr. Frazer, a Scotchman of piety,
learning, and fortune, who is about to join the Faith-
mission, a training-school for native missionaries is to be
established.   "Open thy mouth wide, and I will fill it."

This chapter may appropriately close with the follow-ing statement made by Dr. Cullis in the fourth annual report of the Indian Missions. It shows that these are " faith-missions " in fact as well as name. The question having been asked, " Is not Dr. Cullis morally bound to supply these missionaries so that neither they nor the work shall suffer ? " the answer was as follows : —

" These sisters," and the same is true of the breth-ren, " go from us without any salary or any visible means of support, depending only upon the exceeding great and precious promises." And again the pub-lished statement declares : " Dr. Cullis is not bound to support these missionaries any further than God enables him to do so, by prompting his children to give for this work ; and that these gifts fall below the actual expenses of the mission, a glance at the financial report will show."

It seems a strange thing to expect Pagans to help pull down their own ancient faith by giving money for the support of Christian missions ; but it will be remembered that there is a great amount of unrest among those heathen populations, some of whom wel-come the coming of " the Jesus doctrine." There are also great numbers of Eurasians, children of European fathers and Asiatic mothers, who may be said to have both religions and yet neither ; these, moved by the Holy Spirit, do sometimes help on the good work. Be-sides, there are numbers of English residents, some of whom have not forgotten the Christian faith of the homes they have left behind. And there are missionaries of different societies in the country, who, strange as it may seem, do really help one another. There is, then, nothing absurd in establishing missions in Bombay or Basim on the faith-basis just the same as in Boston : the possibilities are not outrun ; and in point of fact these adventurous believers, in spite of their trials, are blessed of God with very large success. Thus to the dull ears of slow believers the promises of God's word come with twofold emphasis; they are neither temporary nor local, but stand for all time, and are good in all the world.

BOYDTON INSTITUTE.

CHAPTER XXIV.

THE BOYDTON INSTITUTE, ETC.

" The last shall be first, and the first last."

IN all the history of this circle of charities, nothing is more manifestly providential than the line of events which led to the purchase, by Dr. Cullis, of the college property at Boydton, Va., and the re-opening of its halls for the higher education of colored people.

For some time the Doctor had been praying that the Lord would give him a work at the South, but said nothing of his wish to any other friend. One day, at the close of the Tuesday meeting, a clergyman who had been present came to him, and asked him if he had heard that the old Randolph-Macon College was offered for sale; mentioning that the building and grounds, which cost somewhere about a hundred and fifty thousand dollars, could now be bought for seven thousand. The college building was in a dilapidated condition, having been occupied by both armies in the late civil war; but it was not beyond repair.

The brother had been trying to persuade his Baptist friends to buy it, and open a school for the freedmen in it; but, failing to awaken an interest among his own people, he thus opened the way to "the man that believes in God."

For a few days the Doctor prayed and counselled over the matter, though he made no public statement or appeal. But a lady friend who was interested in the scheme laid it before a benevolent gentleman of her acquaintance; and he, approving of her plan, came to the Doctor, and said, "If you want the Boydton College property, I will give you ten thousand dollars to buy it." The terrible shrinkage of land values at the South, after the war, has perhaps no more striking illustration than this, — that the great brick edifice which had cost some eighty thousand dollars, the magnificent campus of ninety acres, and over three hundred acres of forest for the supply of fuel, were all sold to Dr. Cullis, and by him deeded to "The Trustees of Faith Missions at Home and Abroad," for the sum of six thousand two hundred dollars! The remainder of the gift of ten thousand dollars was used to repair and furnish the building. Thus the Boydton Institute, as it is now called, came to be another striking instance of the practical value of prayer.

The following is a description of the place, by one whom Dr. Cullis sent to examine and report upon the question of its purchase: —

"The property is situate about a mile south of the village of Boydton, in Mecklenburg County, Virginia, some twenty miles north of the North-Carolina line, and about a hundred and fifty miles west of Norfolk, and nearly a hundred and ten miles south-west from Richmond. The small town of Boydton, containing two or three churches, a few stores, etc., lies in the centre of what was once a rich section of the country, where large tobacco-plantations, worked by slave-labor, yielded handsome fortunes to their owners; although the culture was carried on at exhaustive cost to the soil, and many hundreds of acres which were once used for this purpose are now growing up to timber, which in this country grows rapidly. . . . It is in the centre of the famous 'South-side Virginia' district, which, with a belt of the adjacent northern counties of North Carolina, comprised the largest slave-holding sections of these two States; and the wealth of the planters enabled them to furnish from their families a large proportion of the former students of the college. Hidden away among these woods, shut out from sight of the traveller on the public roads, are a great many large plantations, containing, even now, thousands of cleared acres devoted mainly to tobacco-raising; and all through the country are hundreds and hundreds of cabins of the colored people, who, in this part of the State, comprise about three-fifths of the entire population. . . .

"Upon a slight knoll, on which is a fine oak-grove, and from which a fairly extensive view is obtained, stands the main building of what was once the Randolph and Macon College of Virginia, now removed to another locality, — an institution which in its day was a prominent one among the educational foundations of the South. . . . The building is a large four-story brick structure, with two wings and a main portion, which latter is surmounded by a small belfry, and contains, first a chapel capable of accommodating some two hundred persons; then, thirteen large rooms formerly used as lecture and recitation rooms, and which are perfectly adapted to such uses; and, lastly, forty-eight rooms, twenty-four in each wing, which were used as sleeping and study apartments, and which could conveniently contain three students each.

"At a short distance from this building stands a second, smaller one, which was formerly the steward's hall, or mess-room of the college, and which comprises, upon the first floor, a large room, with seating capacity at tables for a hundred or more persons, and five other rooms similar to the study-rooms in the college. The kitchen (detached from the house, as all are in Virginia) has been taken down."

In reference to the spiritual darkness of these people, the report has these startling statements : —

"Their own native preachers are, in the main, ignorant men, who, deceived themselves, can only deceive others ; and hence it is, that in the 'native churches' the truth of the gospel is no more taught or known than in the interior of Africa. And what the density of ignorance must be, you can judge when I say that during a so-called 'revival-meeting' held in one of the native churches recently, and which lasted ten days, there was not either a Bible or a hymn-book used, and yet they claimed a large number of conversions. Indeed, they discard the use of the Bible, saying that they have no need of it, as God tells them directly what he would have them know."

Surely there is need of the missionary teacher among this population in the very midst of "a Christian country."

The fifteenth anniversary of "Dedication Day" — Sept. 27, 1879 — was worthily celebrated by the re-opening of these desolated halls as a training-school for teachers and preachers among that unfortunate race which, in that region, was once regarded as neither entitled to, nor capable of, any extensive literary culture. The Lord, who had sent the money to buy the college, sent also a man and a woman to open it, in the persons of the Rev. and Mrs. C. W. Sharp, from the State of Connecticut, who were already experienced teachers among the freedmen, and who entered upon this new branch of the work with a new spirit of devotion. The following notes from Principal Sharp's account of the opening services are full of interest. It is proof of the good-will of the ministers of Boydton and vicinity, that so many of them should appear at such a remarkable service for that section of country ; and their names may well adorn the page of this history of God's work of grace. Here is the record : —

"Rev. Messrs. Leach (Baptist), Goodwin (Episcopal), August (Methodist), Clark (United Presbyterian), and Smithy (Methodist) ; Mr. Ashenhurst, principal of the United Presbyterian Mission School; our good friend Capt. Hughes (Confederate), the clerk of the county ; Capt. Sloan, county sheriff; Drs. Laird and Jones ; and a few other old and prominent citizens of Virginia, — besides some good *Northern* friends and citizens of Boydton and Chase City, — were present. There was also a goodly company of ladies, the wives and families of those mentioned."

It was a unique college "commencement," indeed, with negroes comprising the audience, and their own brightest sons and daughters about to become the students of an institution within whose favored precincts, in its former state, no one of that race might venture

to appear except for menial service. The following
extract from the report shows the fraternal and Chris-
tion spirit which prevailed : —

" I cannot give you any adequate idea of the warmth and
intense interest, felt and expressed, excited by the occasion. It
was a thorough *Christian union* of all hearts in the one work
of our Lord and Master, and wholly to the praise of his name.
You would have rejoiced, could you have been here, to see so
auspicious a beginning of our work. It should be remembered,
that the majority of our visitors and speakers were Southern
men, representatives of the liberal and Christian element in this
portion of Virginia. This is what gives especial significance to
the occasion. Both Northern and Southern persons expressed
to me their gratification and surprise at what they had heard,
and the colored people cannot find words to express their un-
bounded delight."

In his address on this memorable day, Principal
Sharp fitly responded to the kind Christian words
spoken by his Southern neighbors and friends, from
which address the following sentences are taken. Under
the topic, " The Spirit of Our Work," he said, —

" We have no theories to propagate, except that the strong
should help the weak ; that those who know the power of the
gospel and the value of Christian education should give of these
precious things to those in darkness, and powerless to help
themselves. We come not as Northerners, but as Christians ;
and we do not depend on the appreciation of our work by the
colored people, or on the approbation of the community generally : we are working for God. But I have no doubt that our
undertaking will command the interest and good-will of the

best Christian people, and of all liberal and enlightened men. Furthermore, we cannot lift up one portion of the community without benefiting the rest.

"We are not Methodists, Baptists, Congregationalists, Presbyterians, etc., but all of these, united in Christ for a common work, with the words behind the platform for our motto, ' Jesus only.' "

At first only a day-school was attempted, as the dormitories and stewards' hall were not in readiness for use. It began with fifteen scholars, which number by the first of January had increased to fifty. Concerning the pupils and their studies, the following from the principal's first report is worthy of special notice : —

"The especial care of the Lord was not more clearly shown to us than in the selection of these students. They were much above the average of the colored people, and of such material as the Lord could best use in his service. Our plan has been to make the study of the Word the most prominent feature of our work. We found religion among the colored people, for the most part, merely a matter of the emotions, full of superstitious notions, having little or no foundation in the Bible. Their preachers are mostly ignorant men, who can read but little, or not at all. . . . In our day school, the first half-hour of the morning was devoted to Bible-study, — the passage explained, applications made to daily life, followed by questions from the students, answered by the instructor. These half-hours were wonderfully blessed of God, the allotted time frequently running over into an hour, so eager and interested were they to know more of the blessed teachings of our Lord."

Thanks be to God ! At last there is one "school of higher learning" in this Christian country, where the

highest learning of all has a respectable place on the
list of studies.   No wonder Boydton Institute has
been so wonderfully favored from above.

During the second year, so many students came from
a distance, that it was determined to give them the use
of the empty rooms, hire a cook, and let them make
the best of it.   In this rude fashion, twenty students
became inmates of the college itself.   It was on these
that the first baptism of the Spirit descended, and
from among these that the little church with the
watchword " JESUS ONLY" was organized.   Of this, and
other matters of vital interest, the principal thus
speaks : —

" The power of the Spirit of the Lord, so manifest to *us* in
the work, since the beginning, began to show in the students ;
first, two were converted, then another and another, until nineteen out of the twenty within our walls were trusting in Christ,
and the few who were nominal Christians when they came were
awakened, and built up in the blessed life of faith.   The question then arose among them, Can we go back to our own
churches, so full of ignorance and superstitions, and join?
The answer to this question resulted in the organization of a
church, in April, of seventeen members, consisting simply of a
band of believers joined together without denominational name,
for mutual helpfulness and the spread of the gospel, our faith
centred in ' Jesus only.'   God gave us a wonderful day ; that
sabbath we gathered by the side of a little stream where our
students were baptized, then, repairing to the chapel, made our
covenant with him.   The blessing that fell upon all made the
day one to be long remembered.

"Each sabbath one or more of the students went out and

preached in neighborhoods more or less distant, rehearsing to other hearts the lessons from the gospel learned here. Numbers were converted from these ministrations. One instance I remember. We had had the parable of the Prodigal Son. The idea that God had such compassion on sinners was a new one to them. One of the students got leave to go home twenty miles to preach it to his people. He was greatly blessed, and seven of his people were converted by that one effort. . . .

"Since the war, the slaves being free, and the price of their chief staple, tobacco, being low, the price of labor has been low. Working-men get from two and a half to five dollars per month and rations, or by the day from thirty to fifty cents without rations. Women get from one dollar and a half to three dollars per month, or from fifteen to thirty cents per day. To support families out of these wages, is a hard matter at the best ; and the sick, crippled, helpless, and orphaned ones suffer for the necessaries of life. Clothing is a luxury too expensive to be much indulged in. In our distress at the sight of so many children over the fireplaces at home, because they hadn't clothing to enable them to go to school, and old people in rags, without shoes or stockings, we cried unto the Lord. The answer was, first, two barrels of clothing ; others soon followed. While giving out these supplies, we gratefully thanked the good Father who cares for all, and asked for more. In four months we distributed sixty barrels of clothing."

The second Christmas holiday season in the history of the Institute was saddened by the news of the death of Principal Sharp in his New-England home. Of this faithful servant of the Lord, his successor, Rev. John T. James, thus speaks in his report for the school year 1880–81 : —

"Just as we were closing for the Christmas holidays, came the news of his departure to his rest. The school and community were stricken with grief. He had done a good work already, in one single year, in the improvements made and excellent grading given to the Institute. His last year's work was in connection with great bodily infirmity, and how sweet the rest into which he entered ! Almost all the time since the close of the war, he had labored for the education of the colored race, sometimes at the risk of his life. How true it is now of those who enjoy working for that people in comparative safety and quietness, 'Other men labored, and ye are entered into their labors' ! "

Mrs. Sharp, after the departure of her husband from the land of the dying to the land of the living, returned to her chosen field of labor in the power of a new devotion. A woman of sagacity as well as of piety, she is the ideal matron and preceptress for such a school. She and her husband had asked for a field "where others would not go," and "where it was not crowded:" here at Boydton she has her wish gratified, and, what is more, the constant and sensible presence of the Lord attends her work in his name. Some of the practical as well as educational items of the report relative to the school and its belongings claim a place in these pages : —

"We have among these students some of the finest speci- mens of the race to be found in the South. Before the war, this section made a business of raising and selling slaves South. Their soil was exhausted by raising tobacco ; and it became, as *they* thought, a necessity. Whenever one became unruly or troublesome, or was hopelessly dull, he was sold for the cotton and rice plantations farther South.   So for years they have been culled, the choicest left behind.   We had only three pure Africans in our school, some of them so bleached as to lose all traces of colored parentage.   Besides this, we ask the Lord to select the students for us, and, when they come, we take them from him. . . .

"We are often asked, Do the students study without much urging?   I am very glad to say, that in the twenty years in which I have been teaching, both at the North and South, I have never seen such application, and so much accomplished, as among these students.   They have made better progress, as a whole, than any other school I have ever seen. . . . The college bell rings at six in the morning through the winter, but nine out of ten of the students are up and have been studying an hour before that time.   They carry their books into the field when they go to work, to catch the spare moments, and sometimes even to the dinner-table ; but the latter we felt obliged to forbid.

"Discipline is almost unknown ; they govern themselves. Perfect love and good-will abound.   In all these months there hasn't come to our knowledge one case of angry dispute or alienation among the students.   Their love and gratitude to us, and their prayers for us and for Dr. Cullis, are most touching."

But the spiritual side of the work is still more impressive.   In addition to what has already been quoted from the records of the school, these following extracts open out a wide range of fair prospects before the colored race in the South, — a simple, believing people, whose enforced ignorance has been, in one sense, blessed to them, since it has kept them from doubting the Lord their God, and shut them up to the only faith he ever delivered to his saints. With learning will come the special temptations thereof : may grace be given them to save them from the small conceits which have inflated with rationalism and atheism so many dabblers in science and philosophy !

During the second year, every unconverted student was brought to Christ, including the only one who had stood out against the Lord the year before ; and the work of grace overflowed into the surrounding country, through the vacation-work of the student preachers and teachers. Principal James gives, among others, the following interesting cases : —

" During the vacation, even while writing this brief sketch of the year's work, news has come of the success of these students in their labors. One preacher has preached regularly to his church of over four hundred members, and held meetings in five other places ; converts in every place, and the Word quickening and building up believers. Another told me he had had revivals in his four churches ; converts in one a hundred and thirteen, in another seventy-three, in another forty-four, and in another thirteen. A letter last evening from a young girl, now teaching, formerly a pupil and converted at the Institute, writes that she has a large sabbath school of old and young, and she has such joy and blessing in teaching the Word to them that she cannot afford to lose one Sunday to come home for a visit. One and another all over this part of the country are the beacon-lights shining, the blessed gospel carried by these students. My heart gets full as I hear and know of these things, and of the wonderful contrast in the lives of these taught by the Word, compared with those under the almost heathen worship, believing and following dreams, signs, etc.; and I almost wish I had a dozen lives to give to this work."

And who is this brother whose heart so warms toward these sons and daughters of former slaves?

An ex-Confederate soldier; a Southern man by birth and education; a former member of a Southern Methodist conference; a man full of faith and of the Holy Ghost; able to trust God for himself and his school; able to face his Southern friends, and not be ashamed of his position as teacher of negroes (the lowest office, in their eyes, in which one of "the superior race" could be engaged); able to heal the sick by the prayer of faith, and able to preach the Word with power. Such men are the true bond of union between the two sections of our once-divided country. May their tribe increase! He who, like so many of his Southern brethren, once fought for his State, now fights for the Kingdom; of which he strikingly says, "I am determined to do as much for Jesus Christ as I ever did for Jeff Davis." Of such soldiers, the heavenly Captain will never have cause to be ashamed.

The influence of this school among the colored people far and near is matter of devout thanksgiving. Here is an incident related by Principal James, which is worthy of special attention.

"A young man came to us last fall, from North Carolina, whose mind seemed under a strange pressure of religious con-

viction, while the most receive their convictions after they come.
It was ascertained about him, that his school-trustees had told
him that they would dispense with his services until he could
become a true believer in the Lord Jesus Christ. And so the
poor fellow came to Boydton, ostensibly for mental instruction,
but really to realize the new birth. When finally converted, as
he was soon after entering, he was almost beside himself for
joy, and in a few months was back in his school. A blessing
on such trustees ! . . . Where are the schools among us whose
patrons demand truly religious persons as teachers of their children ? And yet this is a common and growing sentiment among
the newly liberated people."

The third year was like the second, only much more
abundant. These extracts from the report of the preceptress, Mrs. Sharp, will tell the story better than any
re-casting of it by other hands. The date is May 1,
1883.

" The year opened with signal answers to prayer. We met
in the chapel every day after the school · closed, the year previous, to ask God to finish the repairs on the building, furnish
the rooms, and fill them with students at the next session.
About forty rooms needed repairs ; over fifty needed furnishing.
School opened in the fall with the repairs under full headway,
and wagon-loads of furniture coming from the depot, that soon
put all the rooms in nice order. The number of students was
double that of the last year, reaching a hundred and four.
Most of these were young men and women from fifteen to
twenty-five years of age. The funds for repairs and furniture
came without solicitation from any one but our dear Father.

" The increase of students was just as much in answer to
prayer as the funds ; for the crops had been cut off by drought,
and every one in this part of the country predicted a small

THE BOYDTON INSTITUTE, ETC.

school, as there was almost no money in the country. God knew how to answer prayer, in spite of outward circumstances. . . . Our blessings in temporal matters were not greater than in spiritual things. The daily teaching of the Word brought forth its fruits in the conversion of all those unconverted, some twenty-five in number, and the quickening and growth of all those already converted. Quietly and surely the leaven worked, blessing in the Bible lesson, blessing in the evening meetings, the students uniting their faith with ours until all were brought in. Then came the higher grace of sanctification. One day, early in January, we invited all of the students that wanted to give themselves entirely to the Lord, seeking a deeper work in their hearts, to meet us in the evening at the house. About thirty came to the first meeting. The Lord was present with power. . . . They sought in good earnest ; but the doctrine is so wholly unknown in this country, they were a little slow in grasping by faith the Comforter. . . . One morning at the gospel lesson, one (a young preacher) received the baptism of the Holy Ghost. The cloud broke on the whole school : seven or eight ' entered in ' that same week, and almost the entire school were seeking the blessing. One morning the Spirit seemed so manifestly present, that we stopped in the gospel lesson, and invited all that were ready to receive the fulness to come forward and occupy the front seats. All but four came. We engaged in prayer. A large number were blessed. The meeting continued almost through the time of the morning session, closing a little before noon. Most of the sanctified ones went on, and received a special anointing for service.

" This the Lord most signally sanctioned, and almost imme- diately our numbers began to diminish rapidly ; one called to teach in this direction, another in that, opening sabbath schools in connection with day teaching. During the summer there have been twenty-five of these schools opened in districts where there were no Sunday schools ; and in them over fifteen hun- dred persons, old and young, received Bible instruction, — the gospel lessons of the Institute rehearsed again. Several of these had revivals in them, conducted by the students; two of these, the converts of the winter before. One of these, a young girl of eighteen, writes: 'He gave me his word, and I gave it to the children. It was the means of bringing many of them to him. Seventeen of them confessed and were baptized two weeks ago.' And so the light is spreading all through this dark region.

"Beside teaching, the Lord let us do some most precious work in caring for the poor. The crops were nearly all cut off by the drought; the poor must starve unless some help could be obtained. We went to their dear Father, whose tender love lets not a sparrow fall without his notice. Having both of us received a little money for Christmas presents, we took out enough to buy a barrel of meal; this we gave to the Lord, asking him not to let that barrel be empty while there were any hungry ones. This was during the Christmas vacation. From that time until the wheat-crop came in, in June, the barrel never failed. Before it was empty the first time, we received a letter from a lady, an entire stranger, enclosing twenty dollars, ten for personal use and the rest to invest for Jesus. This bought enough to fill the barrel twice. Just as that was getting toward the last, another dear friend wrote, enclosing five dollars, saying she had usually collected a barrel of clothing every fall, but, not succeeding this year, would send the money to be used for the poor. Then a good friend from Portland sent ten dollars, suggesting that I might find some use for it. None of these knew any thing about the barrel, or the want of the people."

In the report for the fourth year, the same blessed testimony is borne, that the Lord has never permitted a student to remain at the Institute any length of time without being converted; while, in addition to the religious life in the school, some of the pupils were organized into "praying-bands," and thus extended the blessed work in the region round about.

During this fourth year, an orphanage was built; probably the first house for colored orphans in the State of Virginia if not in the whole South. These friendless ones, cared for in the name of their Father in heaven, give promise of great usefulness among their own people, going forth in due time as the examples of what can be made of children who are raised in a cultivated Christian home.

During the six years of its existence, the Boydton Institute has sent out eighty teachers, thirteen preachers, and one evangelist. At present it has reached the full capacity of its buildings, and greatly needs enlargement. Its graduates are in request over a wide region of Virginia and the Carolinas, and take first rank in their profession. Forty of these teachers are adding to their day-school work the charge of Sunday schools, in which, without aspiring to the title of "preacher," they teach the Word very effectively. Thus this school has come to be as a city set on a hill, whose light cannot be hid.

The Institute is, of a truth, one of the "Faith-missions." Its seven instructors work directly for the Lord, and look directly to him for their support; as, inded, must be the case in a school with no endowments, where the entire advantages of the institution, including board, rooms, fuel, lights, and tuition, are furnished to its students at the rate of thirty-five dollars for the thirty-five weeks of the school year!   How small a sum is this with which to rescue from ignorance and superstition one of the children of this hitherto unfortunate race, and to put him or her into a position of life-long power and usefulness!   Here is a chance for larger profit than even that attending the purchase of this college ; and those who invest therein may hope to hear the heavenly Master say, "Inasmuch as ye have done it unto one of the least of these my brethren, ye have done it unto me."

OTHER MISSIONS SOUTH AND WEST.

There are four young missions in what may be called the home department of the Faith-work, whose beginnings deserve a mention in these pages.

First, that at Renick's Valley, W. Va., where Mr. R. C. Loveridge has consecrated his house and farm to the Lord for a school and preaching house among the white people of that tobacco-cursed region.

Second, the evangelistic work among the colored people, by one of the Deaconesses, Miss Bessie Hockin, at Oxford, N.C.

Third, a Chinese gospel-school at Monterey, near San Francisco, Cal., in charge of Mrs. E. L. Wilson, assisted by one more of the Grove Hall Deaconesses,

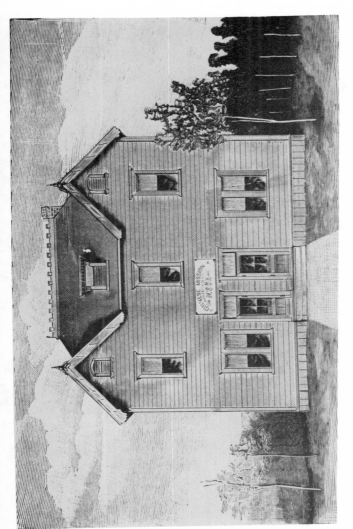

CHINESE MISSION.

Miss North.   It is slow work learning the Chinese language ; and those people are so migratory, both from
choice and from fear of violence at the hands of ruffians,
that there are few ascertained results to publish.   Before the difficulties which have beset the work, none
but a fully consecrated, trusting soul would have been
able to stand.   The Lord has put it into the heart of a
lady in New York to devote eight hundred dollars for
a mission-house, which contains a little chapel and a
snug home for the workers.

Fourth, at Santa Barbara, Cal., is a Faith-mission,
opened by the Rev. Messrs. E. J. Scudder and Samuel
Chafe with their wives.   Before they are fairly under
way, comes the announcement of the call of Mr. Scudder to a place nearer to the throne.   A suffering body
will no longer check his glad and grateful service, and
his bereaved wife and comrades will have a holy joy
in the thought that their newly planted mission
has already a representative in the presence of the
King.

During the present summer (1885), another work of
faith is opening at Los Angeles, Cal., under the direction and generous care of the Rev. H. R. Stevens, for
years a successful minister in the California Methodist
Conference ; a man who has been permitted to build no
less than fifteen churches, to witness the conversion of
many sinners, and to take a prominent part in the
spreading of " gospel holiness " over that Western

coast.   With him are to be associated two more of the
Grove Hall Deaconesses, Miss Carrie Smith and Mrs.
Christie Goodwin, the former a graduate of the Faith
Training College.

So swiftly sweeps this blessed work along, that deliberate history cannot keep pace with it.   East and
West, by sea and land, the Lord is moving out his
trained and chosen workers, who, whatever else they
lack, do yet possess the two great preparations for his
service ; viz., a full consecration of soul and body, and
absolute faith in the Master's word.

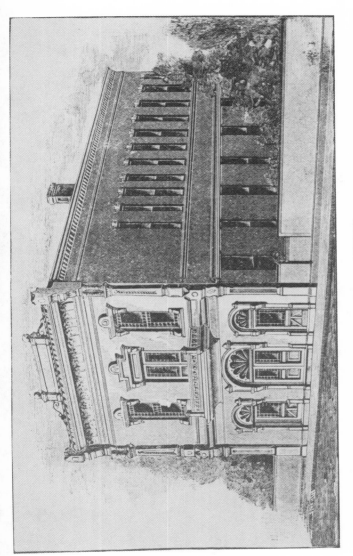

SANTA BARBARA MISSION.

CHAPTER XXV.

THE FAITH-CURE.

"Who healeth all thy diseases."

IN the Annual Report of the Consumptives' Home for the year ending Sept. 30, 1873, Dr. Cullis first makes public the call of the Lord which had come to him to use his faith in praying for the healing of the sick. He gives as the first instance the case of one of his patients, a Christian lady, who had long been suffering from a tumor for which there was no human remedy but the knife. He had for several years been exercised in his mind over the promise in the fifth chapter of the Epistle of St. James, which says, "Is any sick among you? let him call for the elders of the church; and let them pray over him, anointing him with oil in the name of the Lord: and the prayer of faith shall save the sick, and the Lord shall raise him up; and if he have committed sins, they shall be forgiven him." Reading these words to this poor sufferer, he asked if she had faith to be healed according to the promise. She replied, "I have no particular faith about it, but am willing to trust the Lord for it." The Doctor then prayed for her recovery, and, according to the scriptural direction, anointed her with oil in the name of the Lord. "Soon after I left," he says, "she got up, and walked three miles. From that time the tumor rapidly lessened, until all traces of it at length disappeared." Two years afterwards this same lady is again mentioned as continuing "perfectly well."

In the summer of 1873, as previously noted, the Doctor and his wife visited the house of healing at Mannedorf, on Lake Zurich, in Switzerland, — erected under the direction of the saintly Dorothea Trüdel, and now under the management of Mr. Zeller, her chosen successor, — the fame whereof has gone out into a very large part of the earth, but which at that time had scarcely been heard of by the Christian public in America. Here they found about a hundred and fifty persons who had come to be healed in answer to prayer; including thirty insane persons, on which unfortunate class the prayer of faith seemed particularly efficacious. The presence of the Holy Ghost in this work was evidenced by the rich spiritual blessings which accompanied the physical ones; and, on inquiry as to whether *all* were healed who were prayed for, the answer was, "No; but none die until the *soul* is healed."

The casting-out of devils from lunatics, and the salvation of souls appointed to speedy death, are classes of "cures" which at once lift this wonderful work of faith entirely out of the range of "animal magnetism," "mesmerism," "electric phenomena," "Christian (?) science," "spiritualism," and the like, to some of which causes unbelievers in the gospel for the body are wont to attribute all cases of alleged healing in answer to prayer; but the presence and work of the Holy Spirit upon the soul, in co-operation with the work of the Great Physician upon the body as here witnessed, affords an unerring proof that these cures are wrought by supernatural and not subternatural means.

Returning home from his tour among the wonders of grace, as well as of nature, in the Old World, Dr. Cullis devoted himself anew to the office of healing in the name of the Lord; of which he says, in his tenth Annual Report, —

" During the past year many have come to me, and claimed the promise contained in Jas. v. 14, 15. Requests for prayer for the healing of the body have also reached me from hundreds, afflicted in most cases with diseases that the physicians have given up as hopeless. A great proportion of these have been entirely healed."

So greatly did this department of his labors increase, and so many requests for prayer did he receive from all over this country, and even from across the sea, and so marked were the answers to those prayers, that there began to be no small stir about the matter; though,

strangely enough, instead of rejoicing over the good
that was done, many, especially among professing
Christians, began to denounce the instrument of it.
At first it was easy to deny the facts, on the general
ground that they were incredible : so indeed they were
if nothing is to be believed but what can be accounted
for on natural principles, and if the personal hand of a
personal God is to be shut out from all work for the
benefit of his people. But as the number of faith-cures
multiplied, it became rather difficult to frown down the
movement ; and then some of its opponents had re-
course to theology, — not to Bible theology, for that is
all on the side of supernatural healing, but to that sort
of theology which has been invented since the Bible
was written ; which includes, among other unfounded
dogmas, the assertion that "the day of miracles is
past," a notion as false in logic as it is in fact.

One can readily see a reason for hostility to the
prayer-cure, on the part of doctors of medicine ; but
how can it damage the doctors of divinity, to have
a Christian physician practise according to the gospel
school ?

Why a simple act of faith in a perfectly plain promise
contained in the Word of God should have roused such
a storm of opposition against this well-known apostle of
faith-charities, is one of the unaccountable things in the
workings of human nature. All Christians pray for the
healing of the sick, and many such prayers are an-

swered. What, then, should hinder Dr. Cullis or any other believer from doing the same? Setting forth some of the answers to his prayers for money to carry on his hospitals and homes, he was applauded and assisted: setting forth some of the answers to his prayers for the healing of diseases, he was slandered and denounced. Can any one explain this riddle?

Viewed from a Bible standpoint, such opposition to the scriptural use of Scripture promises is wicked: viewed from a rational standpoint, it is absurd. Is health a blessing to the sick only when it comes through drugs or surgery? Has any one a right to insist that sick people shall be cured only in some particular way? If a man can pray away disease, ought he not to do it? If sick people prefer faith to physic, is it not their undoubted right to use it? And is it not an impertinence, as well as an absurdity, to complain of the sick for coming to be healed, or of the man who is the instrument of such healing? Is disease better than health which is obtained in answer to prayer? How ridiculous it seems, when considered in cold blood, or read in "cold type," that multitudes of persons claiming to be Bible Christians are stoutly opposing the exercise of a gift distinctly promised in the Bible; even though it is used in precisely the way the Bible prescribes, and is followed by the identical benefits which the Bible leads us to expect!

Alas for the mental condition of those who think to

put a statute of limitations on the promises of God's Word, and say that payment was stopped on them shortly after they were made!

It was in the original plan of this volume, to set forth at large the Scripture doctrine in respect to the healing of the sick, and to follow this with ample citations of unquestionable instances of cures within the editor's own personal knowledge, both in England and America. But of what avail is exegesis with those who set up theological opinions against plain texts of Scripture? or of what use are facts, to those who, for the sake of theories to which they are committed, can doubt what they actually know to be true?

So exceeding many and mighty are the works of faith in these days, upon human bodies as well as upon human souls, that a few cases cited might be put aside as "exceptions to the rule;" while to recount those cases by multitudes would only be repeating what has already repeatedly appeared in the ample list of publications of the Willard Tract Repository, and in other advanced Christian literature, thus needlessly extending this volume now drawing to a close. Only general reference to a few great classes of cures wrought by means of the prayer-power, by Dr. Cullis and his co-laborers, will therefore be made in these pages.

In the first place, it will be noticed that most of those who have come to be healed through prayer have been given over by medical men. Internal cancers, chronic cases of spinal disease, pulmonary consumption, paralysis of many years' standing, total blindness, — in one case amounting to a partial disintegration of the eyes themselves, — these and other such hopeless cases comprise a large majority of the ailments which the Doctor is asked to pray away. Now, let us suppose that a physician of some new school were to open an office in Boston, and that few if any but confessedly incurable patients should come to him. If, out of the multitudes of such cases, a larger proportion were to be cured than in the ordinary practice of his medical neighbors, would not that new school of medicine be heralded as a new dispensation of blessing? Precisely this is the state of the case in respect to the faith-cure, — as for convenience it is commonly called, — with the exception that the practice is old instead of new, and is a revelation of God instead of a scientific discovery of men. "For envy" the Pharisees condemned the Lord. Is that the basis of the objections to the prayer-cure?

In the second place, it is a joy to see that a class of physical sufferings closely interwoven with moral and spiritual evils, and which have been thought to be beyond the reach of human aid, are constantly being cured in connection with a radical work of saving grace. This class includes the alcohol appetite, the opium-habit, the tobacco craze, and other ungovernable passions. It is quite the usual thing for lost men, utterly under the power of strong drink, to experience

instant and complete deliverance from that awful bondage, in connection with their conversion to God. At
the Lewis-Street Mission, and in other such places
where people of that description so often appear, salvation for the body is as fully expected as is salvation for
the soul : it is fully understood that these men need
new nerves and new stomachs, as well as new hearts ;
and God seems to be just as willing to give the one as
the other.

In the third place, as has already been seen in the
brief reference to the work of Mr. Zeller at Mannedorf,
the prayer of faith is reaching the cases of many who
are possessed with devils, — a form of madness not by
any means confined to those who are commonly called
insane. An honored representative of the house of
healing in London, under the charge of that eminent
man of God, Dr. W. E. Boardman, brings the information that it is a frequent occurrence in the testimony-
meetings at Bethshan, for persons who have been
insane to bear witness to the blessing of a rational
mind, to which they have been restored in answer to
the prayer of the Doctor, in unison with the faith of
their relatives or near friends. Such cases are not
wholly wanting on this side of the ocean. And when
one considers the source of this sort of infirmity, which
is certainly satanic, whatever may be thought of ordinary forms of disease, the use of prayer in the name of
Him who gave his disciples power to "cast out devils"

seems to be the most reasonable and proper thing to do : indeed, so feeble is the success of medical science in dealing with this form of disease, which is terribly on the increase, that the Bible method of saving men from the power of demons seems to be the only one that offers any hope of general and ultimate success. Devils that will not go out by physic do go out by prayer.

Finally, in the ordinary kinds of sickness a very large proportion of cases are the immediate result of sin. Fast living, fashionable dissipation, imprudence, and idleness, to say nothing of the grosser sins, bring on diseases which can never be cured, though they may be temporarily relieved, by medicine. Their seat is deeper than muscles or nerves, and the only cure is to be found in a change of habit which will only be brought about by a change of heart. Now, the very first thing in the diagnosis which precedes the faith-treatment is to determine whether the patient is in harmony with the Spirit of God and the Word of God. If not, the first prescription is repentance ; the next, consecration ; the third, faith in Jesus for pardon and regeneration : then, when the status of a true Christian believer has been reached, the cure of the physical ailment may begin. Such cures are radical and permanent, and not a mere temporary check to the currents of disease which will break out again with greater violence when the evil has attained greater volume and power.

Beyond all dispute, then, these four classes of sickness, which comprise the great majority of all sickness amongst mankind, are directly within the range and scope of the prayer-cure. If there be infirmity that is wholly a misfortune, prayer is surely good for it; and if there be disease which has been sent as a punishment or a corrective, surely that will yield to prayer and penitence quite as readily as to powders and pills.

Looking at the subject from still another point of view, it is seen that medical science is founded upon ascertained and classified facts. From the days of Galen and Æsculapius until now, certain sicknesses have sometimes been relieved by certain treatments; and the accumulating mass of such facts has given to certain roots and herbs and balsams and minerals a well-established reputation as means for healing. Physicians cannot agree upon the philosophy of the cures, and the failures to cure, which occur under their practice. There are no actual specifics: none but quacks ever claim to possess a "universal remedy;" and aside from surgery, which has its basis in anatomy, there are few if any certainties in the science of healing.

In like manner the faith-cure has its basis of ascertained and classified facts. From the days of Peter and Paul, certain exercises of faith in certain promises of the Bible have resulted in the removal of diseases; and the accumulating mass of cases, gathered from the testimony of Christian believers and Christian teachers in all the ages, has given to "the prayer of faith" a well-established reputation as a means of healing. Thoughtful people believe in medicines, for what they have been known to do. For the self-same reason, candid people believe in prayer for healing, for what it has been known to do. Are not facts in the one case as good a basis for doctrine as are facts in the other? When all the smoke and dust raised by medical and theological polemics has cleared away, the increasing multitude of cases under the gospel school of healing will be found adequate to establish the truth that Jehovah Rophi is still the Healer, and that Jesus Christ is still as good as his word.

FAITH-CURE HOUSE.

On the 8th of November, 1881, several persons testified at the Tuesday meeting, to the healing of the body by the prayer of faith ; and at that time Dr. Cullis felt moved to appoint an hour, eleven o'clock on Thursday mornings, when he would meet, in the chapel at Beacon Hill, all persons who desired to seek for health by prayer. From that day to this, the meeting has been continued, and people in large numbers have been healed ; some at once, but more by slower processes which were, however, wholly outside of what are called natural causes and effects.

So many of these came from a distance, some of whom were not in a state of mind to understand and

grasp at once the privilege of health as well as grace
in Jesus Christ, that a house where they could rest and
study and pray for a season seemed to be an important
need of the work.   This need was made known in the
same general manner with all other needs of the great
system of faith-charities ; and funds were voluntarily
given with which the Faith-cure House, on the beauti-
tiful estate at Grove Hall, was erected.   On the 23d of
May, 1882, it was opened as a house of healing ; a modest beginning in the same direction as the great establishments of Dorothea Trüdel at Mannedorf, and Pastor
Blumhardt at Bad Boll.

The following notes from the nineteenth Annual
Report are selected, because they show the approbation of God in the most unmistakable manner ; viz.,
the conversion of sinners who come to the Lord for
bodily healing, which work of grace upon the soul has
been followed by a work of health upon the body.   Indeed, in all cases the healing by faith is accompanied
with great spiritual blessing, leaving no room for doubt
that the work is indeed wrought by the good hand of
the Lord.   On this point Dr. Cullis says, —

"There is one very interesting feature connected with the
truth of faith-cures ; and that is, the many persons who have
been converted through the presentation of the Word of God
on this subject.   This morning at the meeting, I asked if there
were any present who were not Christians, when four raised
their hands.   I then explained that the promise for healing was

only to the Church of God, and that they as unconverted persons had no claim upon the promises until they gave themselves to the Lord, and were washed in the blood of the Lamb. After a talk on this matter, as one would plead with an unsaved soul, they all yielded themselves to the Lord, first for the pardon of their sin. The meeting then went on ; and when the four persons alluded to came to be prayed with separately, they confessed that the Lord had saved them, and went their way rejoicing, counting their sins forgiven, and claiming healing by faith.

" 'Bless the Lord, O my soul, and forget not all his benefits ; who forgiveth all thine *iniquities ;* who *healeth* all thy diseases.'

" This work of soul-saving has been such a joy to me ! Many, many strangers come to me, and first seek pardon and then healing ; so much so that scarcely a day passes that one or more are not brought into the kingdom of his dear Son."

" Nov. 23. Our new house is filled to overflowing. Three persons who came last evening had to be cared for in one of the other buildings. This leads me to pray for the enlarging of the house. At the Thursday meeting, another heart was brought low at Jesus' feet for forgiveness before she claimed healing. Thus the Lord brings many a weary one into the light of his love."

This chapter may appropriately close with the following statement by Dr. Cullis, in the twentieth Annual Report. It gives practical information which may be of value to the readers of this volume, and bears testimony to the power and goodness of the Lord as the Saviour both of soul and body : —

" I have the proof in thousands of cases, that God heals the sick in answer to his own promise. Last year our Faith-cure

House opened its doors for the reception and care of those desiring to come under its roof for healing. Upwards of a hundred during the year availed themselves of the privilege of spending days and weeks under its shelter. We begin this year crying to God for the means to enlarge the building, as we are often crowded to overflowing. . . .

"Our charge for board is one dollar per day, to cover the household expenses. Some ask why we do even this. The answer is, because people of ample means come to the city seeking board (while they receive the prayer of faith), but can find none in the city unless among adverse surroundings, discouraging to faith. For such we have opened this Faith-cure House. I visit it nearly every day, and charge nothing for my time. But some do respond with thanksgiving to God, and a desire to minister to my necessities and those of the Faith-Work. For the sick and poor throughout the Work of Faith, every thing is free, and received from the hand of our Father in answer to prayer."

CHAPTER XXVI.

THE THEOLOGY OF THE INSTITUTION. — THE COLLEGE. THE CONVENTIONS.

" Thou shalt see greater things than these."

IF there be any respect in which, more than another, the faith of the Church is at fault, it is expressed by the one word *littleness*. The gospel of the kingdom is doubtless greater than any possible statement of it; yet multitudes stand aghast at the faith of advanced believers, as if they were actually believing and expecting too much of God! Modern and mediæval theology have, alike, this calamity : they are cursed with limitations which their finite logic has sought to fix upon infinite truths. From these artificial bonds and bounds, it has pleased the Lord to deliver some of his people, who, in view of the ocean which opens out before them, have ceased to enclose their theology within the dogmatic headlands of this or that little bay. Creeds are always wrong, because they are always human; but in nothing are they more human — and therefore farther wrong — than when they lay off certain zones of truth, and say to their believers, "This is all." For, out be-

yond the widest range of human thought and human
speech, extend the purpose of God, the salvation of his
Son, and the operation of his Spirit.   Blessed is the
man whose faith has no smaller measure than God and
his Word.

It is in this respect alone that the theology of the
rapidly increasing school of advanced believers is peculiar. They do not believe differently from the common
faith of Christendom, but they believe with more large-
ness and freedom.

Whoever has studied the theological situation carefully has discovered a painful increase in the number
of things which are alleged to be "irrational," "unphil-
osophical," "fanatical," and "impossible," in the literal
statements of the Bible ; and a consequent toning-down
of the hopes and efforts of the victims of this theology,
to harmonize with the pretensions of self-appointed
biblical critics.   The faith of all advanced believers
resists the belittling efforts of all such critics in their
impudent work of "rectifying" the Holy Scriptures,
because they have more confidence in the Scriptures
than they have in the critics.   They insist that God
is to be taken as meaning just what he says by the
mouth or pen of his prophets and apostles.   They
do not find it needful to make any of the great works
therein recorded, any easier for the Almighty.   They
believe in God as God, and not as a being who is
himself governed by the laws which he makes for the

government of his creation.   They regard faith as a faculty of the soul expressly given for the purpose of apprehending truths which are beyond the reach of all the other faculties : therefore, when " logic " or " law " or " science " bids them halt at this and that arbitrary frontier, because it is not possible for logic or law or science to go any farther, they cheerfully take leave of these plodding powers whose functions are bounded by the natural world, and boldly strike out to walk by faith. Here, then, is the point of divergence.   Modern theology is rationalistic, and thinks to limit God and his people by the bounds of the natural understanding : advanced believers find that where the world of observation ends, the world of faith begins.   Alas for the theology which teaches a little God, and a little revelation no bigger than it can understand !

Under this general principle of a boundless faith in an infinite Deity, it is to be expected of all advanced believers, that they will accept the largest and fullest views of all scriptural promises and provisions ; knowing as they do that God is infinitely more and better than any thing which human words can say.   If it be a promise of healing for the body, they do not stop to ask the doctors whether they shall believe or not : they take their fill of the boundless blessings, just as they do of the air.   If it be a promise of salvation for the soul, through faith in the Divine Redeemer, they take plentifully of it, and do not worry over the possible exhausting of the supply. Human souls are not so big as to give the Infinite One any trouble in filling them full, so they believe in "full salvation;" and since man is the measure of sin, and God the measure of grace, they have reason as well as revelation on their side. If it be a question of Divine providence, they do not stop to think how great a task it must be for God to count the hairs on the heads of all his people, and how difficult it seems to sort out and correct and answer all the myriad prayers that are continually coming up to his throne: they assume, that, since God is God, he cannot have any difficulty with any thing, however appalling the idea may be to our little minds; and so they believe, and pray, and get the answer in due time, and are not surprised at it either.

Such, briefly stated, is the faith of the school of advanced believers, in our times, to which the saints of all ages have belonged.

In harmony with this general principle of believing in God's word as the word of God, and not as a word of man, the school of advanced believers look for the coming of the kingdom of Christ on earth, in the person of the King himself. They know he once was here in person, and they have full faith in the promise of his coming back again "in like manner." To them there is no more difficulty in the actual and visible reign of the Son of God on earth than there is in any thing else which he might be pleased to do. They do not regulate their faith by their politics, but bring up their politics to their faith. They see the powers of government, large and small, in the hands of men who govern for themselves ; and this, instead of being a discouragement, is a pledge of the millennium, for the coming King is to destroy the power of Satan by battle, and bring in peace through victory.

For the rest, it does not signify. He who takes God as his Father, Jesus as his divine Saviour and Redeemer, the Holy Spirit as his Sanctifier, and the kingdom of God as his allegiance, is not likely to go far astray in the minor matters of religion. Advanced believers do not grieve over the intellectual divergence among God's people. They know that all opinions must be faulty, because they are human ; and a variety of faults is no worse than a uniformity thereof. They see people dying in faith, and going to glory not by means of, but in spite of, their opinions : hence they conclude that opinions are trifles, like the different forms of leaves and grass, no two of which are exactly alike, but all are in some sort "orthodox" so long as they take in the air, the rain, and the sun. To advanced believers, "the unity of the faith" does not signify that every voice must sing the same notes, but that all voices shall sing in the same key, and thus pour forth together not a stentorian melody, but a grand and heavenly harmony. This, as they take it, is the true "communion of saints."

It is this large catholicity which has helped to make the Tuesday consecration-meeting a blessing to so many believers of different sects. Perhaps there are no topics on which there is a greater variety of teaching, i.e., in the details thereof, than on the topic of "holiness;" but here, as elsewhere, the divergence of doctrine begins when believers attempt to explain the word of God in the light of their own experience, thus reversing the proper order of testing one's experience by the word of God.   The teaching of Dr. Cullis and of those associated with him is neither more nor less than the presentation of doctrines and facts as they are presented in the Scriptures.   Inferential theories are rarely heard from his lips : there are no catch-words or stock phrases in his Bible-readings, by means of which certain doctrinaires label their particular brand of holiness ; and it may be doubted if, from one year's end to another, there could be found in his exposition and application of the Word any trace whatever of that small ambition, sometimes so painfully conspicuous, of impressing *himself* upon people, or of winning *for himself* a large personal following.   An advanced believer he certainly is, a pioneer of advanced believers, a trusted and honored apostle of the high things and the deep things which belong to the Christian life ; but no one can point to any peculiarity of faith or feeling, and say, "This is the Dr. Cullis style of faith," or, "This is the Beacon Hill style of 'higher life.'"

The most transparent genuineness and simplicity, and the closest possible adhesion to the Scripture, are the two great characteristics which mark the theology taught and practised in this circle of faith charities, and in these missions at home and abroad.

FAITH TRAINING COLLEGE.

This is a kind of theological seminary, in which persons of both sexes and all ages are taught the actual work of ministers, missionaries, evangelists, and teachers. It has little form, but considerable substance, and in a modest way is putting a great many "helps" into a great many hands. It was as a "help," and not as a defender of any particular creed or order in the Church, that it was at first projected; and as such it has ever since been maintained.

In the month of February, 1875, the legal foundation was laid by incorporating the Board of Trustees of Faith Training College under the laws of the State of Massachusetts. The names of the Board are as follows: Rev. Daniel Steele, D.D., Rev. Samuel Cutler, J. C. Hartshorn, B. E. Perry, B. F. Redfern, Charles Cullis, Lucretia A. Cullis. At the first meeting of the Board, resolutions were recorded resting the sole management of the institution in the hands of the one man who had been the Lord's instrument in bringing it into existence; thus at the outset providing against divided counsels, and recognizing the evident hand and mind of God in the singular line of providences by which his chosen servant has been distinguished.

The first public announcement of this gospel school, in the autumn of 1876, was as follows : —

FAITH TRAINING COLLEGE, BEACON HILL PLACE, BOSTON.

BOARD OF INSTRUCTION.

Charles Cullis, M.D., President, and Professor of Christian Work; Rev. W. E. Boardman, Professor of Christian Life; Rev. A. B. Earle, Professor of Revival Work; Rev. Daniel Steele, D.D., Professor of Systematic Theology; Rev. Edmund Squire, Professor of Spiritual Philosophy; Rev. Marcus Ames, Professor of Pastoral Theology; Rev. E. Payson Thwing, Professor of Sacred Rhetoric and Vocal Culture, including singing; Mrs. L. A. Cullis, Professor of Christian Work for Women; Fred. A. Sawtelle, Professor of Natural Theology.

The faculty issue this circular announcing the organization of Faith Training College, for the purpose of publishing information on the following points : —

I.   THE DESIGN

Of the college is to train for Christian work such consecrated men and women as are unable to pursue an extended and thorough course of theological study in the various denominational seminaries, but are desirous of fitting themselves for the highest efficiency in the widening fields of lay activity which the Head of the Church is wonderfully opening in our age, such as Sunday-school instruction, Christian Association work, Bible exposition, exhortation, lay preaching, lay evangelism, home and foreign missionary labor.

2. ITS UNSECTARIAN CHARACTER.

The College is undenominational in its spirit and aims. It is the design of the founder, to call to the various chairs of instruction men and women full of faith and the Holy Ghost, who believe that Jesus Christ, our glorified Redeemer, is able to save to the uttermost all that come unto God by him, and that it is the office of the Sanctifier to purify all believers.

3. THE COURSE OF STUDY

Comprises only those subjects most necessary to be known by Christian workers who have no time to acquire a knowledge of the original tongues in which the Bible was written.

4. THE RECITATIONS AND LECTURES

Will be in the evening, between the hours of seven and nine o'clock, to accommodate those who are engaged in business in the day. Special arrangements for day classes can be made, if desired, with the professors. None but enrolled persons are admitted to the lectures and recitations.

5. THE TUITION IS FREE

To all who may be deemed by the faculty suitable to be enrolled as students. A diploma will be given to each student who honorably completes the two-years' course.

6. ENDOWMENT AND FUNDS.

The College has no other endowment than the "many and exceeding great and precious promises" of Him who stands pledged to supply all our need.

7. CALENDAR.

The College year will begin on Oct. 4, 1875, and close on the last Wednesday of April following. Application may be made to the President, No. 2 Beacon Hill Place, Boston.

When it is remembered that the faculty of this college receive no compensation for their services, it will be matter of special pleasure that so many eminent scholars have held these honorable and honorary posts. The Rev. Dr. Earle, that veteran prince of evangelists; Dr. Daniel Steele, who has a fame among advanced believers throughout the world; Prof. C. W. Emerson, who is one of the few elocutionists fit to be trusted to teach people how to speak in the name of the Lord; Dr. D. G. Woodvine, the Christian physician, whose name did not appear in the first announcement, but whose work as professor of natural theology has honored both his head and heart from the beginning; and Rev. William McDonald, D.D., whose name has been a household word in many lands, as an aggressive teacher and leader along the line of "the higher life," — these, with Dr. Cullis the president, and other ministers of Christ, have wrought steadily, generously, faithfully, admirably; giving to this unpretentious school of practical Christian learning a status not to be despised by any seminary in the land.

The numbers in attendance at these lectures have never been large, say from twenty to thirty; the present year has opened with a class of twenty-five. The deeply spiritual work contemplated in this institution precludes the expectation of large membership; but the college has for this very reason become a widely recognized spiritual power, and its students are in request both at home and a

CONVENTION WORK.

Another method of disseminating the truth as preached and practised in these homes, schools, and missions, is by the annual Faith-conventions, which have come to be a recognized feature of the religious life of New England; and which, first at Framingham, Mass., in 1874, afterwards at Old Orchard Beach, Me., and now for two summers at Intervale Park, N.H., among the glorious scenery of the White Mountains, have called together multitudes of Christians from the United States and Canada, to study and seek after the larger possibilities of saving grace. In 1885 a mid-winter convention was held at Beacon-Hill Church, Boston, which in its way was fully the equal of the summer assemblies, and at which there were wonderful displays of the salvation which is through faith in the gospel of Jesus Christ.

The limits of this volume having now been reached, this department of the Faith-work, so promising and powerful, can only receive a passing notice; and therewith must close the record of twenty years of blessing in answer to prayer.[1] The writer desires to remind his readers that his work has been simply that of an editor, and not that of an author. The facts, as they have been furnished him, have been plainly set forth in their own light; and if at times the editor has become the

[1] The twenty years ended Sept. 30, 1884. It will be seen that the annual report for 1885 has been anticipated in these pages at several points.

advocate, it is because of the influence upon his mind of these amazing facts themselves. For a whole summer at Grove Hall and Beacon Hill, in the midst of the work he has had the privilege to set forth, he here records his devout thanksgiving to Almighty God, and joyfully adds his personal testimony to the power of faith to heal the sick, as well as to save the soul. In this world, now so long in possession of the enemy of God and of his people, some of the sharpest conflicts are with disease. With so many of the Lord's host in hospital, his kingdom comes but slowly; but with the opening of this dispensation of health, through faith in the Great Physician, a measureless impetus seems about to be given to the elect of God, who with a new sense of Divine power pulsing through every nerve and fibre, as well as through every thought and feeling, are girding themselves anew for battle in the blessed name of the King. "Thanks be to God, who giveth us the victory through our Lord Jesus Christ." Truly these are days of power and of blessing: yet they are but the beginning of the new era. Mighty works on every hand are wrought by "them that believe;" wonders multiply, miracles increase. But let not the sluggish faith of the Church recoil before them, as if some strange thing had happened : all this has been set forth in the unfailing Word of God ; and still there stands the glorious promise, "Greater things than these shall ye do, because I go unto the Father."

TITLES in THIS SERIES

1. THE HIGHER CHRISTIAN LIFE; A BIBLIOGRAPHICAL OVERVIEW. Donald W. Dayton, *THE AMERICAN HOLINESS MOVEMENT: A BIBLIOGRAPHICAL INTRODUCTION*. (Wilmore, Ky., 1971) *bound with* David W. Faupel, *THE AMERICAN PENTECOSTAL MOVEMENT: A BIBLIOGRAPHICAL ESSAY*. (Wilmore, Ky., 1972) *bound with* David D. Bundy, *Keswick: A BIBLIOGRAPHIC INTRODUCTION TO THE HIGHER LIFE MOVEMENTS*. (Wilmore, Ky., 1975)

2. *ACCOUNT OF THE UNION MEETING FOR THE PROMOTION OF SCRIPTURAL HOLINESS, HELD AT OXFORD, AUGUST 29 TO SEPTEMBER 7, 1874*. (Boston, n. d.)

3. Baker, Elizabeth V., and Co-workers, *CHRONICLES OF A FAITH LIFE*.

4. THE WORK OF T. B. BARRATT. T. B. Barratt, *IN THE DAYS OF THE LATTER RAIN*. (London, 1909) *WHEN THE FIRE FELL AND AN OUTLINE OF MY LIFE*, (Oslo, 1927)

5. WITNESS TO PENTECOST: THE LIFE OF FRANK BARTLEMAN. Frank Bartleman, *FROM PLOW TO PULPIT—FROM MAINE TO CALIFORNIA* (Los Angeles, n. d.), *HOW PENTECOST CAME TO LOS ANGELES* (Los An-

geles, 1925), *AROUND THE WORLD BY FA.*
WEEKS IN THE HOLY LAND (Los Angeles,
YEARS MISSION WORK IN EUROPE JUST BL   .HE
WORLD WAR, 1912-14 (Los Angeles, [1926],

6. Boardman, W. E., *THE HIGHER CHRISTIAN LIFE*
    (Boston, 1858)

7. Girvin, E. A., *PHINEAS F. BRESEE: A PRINCE IN ISRAEL*
    (Kansas City, Mo., [1916])

8. Brooks, John P., *THE DIVINE CHURCH* (Columbia,
    Mo., 1891)

9. RUSSELL KELSO CARTER ON "FAITH HEALING."
    R. Kelso Carter, *THE ATONEMENT FOR SIN AND SICK-
    NESS* (Boston, 1884) *"FAITH HEALING" REVIEWED
    AFTER TWENTY YEARS* (Boston, 1897)

10. Daniels, W. H., *DR. CULLIS AND HIS WORK* (Boston,
    [1885])

11. HOLINESS TRACTS DEFENDING THE MINISTRY OF
    WOMEN. Luther Lee, *"WOMAN'S RIGHT TO PREACH
    THE GOSPEL; A SERMON, AT THE ORDINATION OF REV.
    MISS ANTOINETTE L. BROWN, AT SOUTH BUTLER,
    WAYNE COUNTY, N. Y., SEPT. 15, 1853"* (Syracuse,
    1853) *bound with* B. T. Roberts, *ORDAINING WOMEN*
    (Rochester, 1891) *bound with* Catherine (Mumford)
    Booth, *"FEMALE MINISTRY; OR, WOMAN'S RIGHT TO
    PREACH THE GOSPEL . . ."* (London, n. d.) *bound
    with* Fannie (McDowell) Hunter, *WOMEN PREACH-
    ERS* (Dallas, 1905)

12. LATE NINETEENTH CENTURY REVIVALIST TEACHINGS
    ON THE HOLY SPIRIT. D. L. Moody, *SECRET POWER
    OR THE SECRET OF SUCCESS IN CHRISTIAN LIFE AND*

WORK (New York, [1881]) *bound with* J. Wilbur
Chapman, RECEIVED YE THE HOLY GHOST? (New
York, [1894]) *bound with* R. A. Torrey, THE BAPTISM
WITH THE HOLY SPIRIT (New York, 1895 & 1897)

13. SEVEN "JESUS ONLY" TRACTS. Andrew D. Urshan,
THE DOCTRINE OF THE NEW BIRTH, OR, THE PERFECT
WAY TO ETERNAL LIFE (Cochrane, Wis., 1921) *bound
with* Andrew Urshan, THE ALMIGHTY GOD IN THE
LORD JESUS CHRIST (Los Angeles, 1919) *bound with*
Frank J. Ewart, THE REVELATION OF JESUS CHRIST (St.
Louis, n. d.) *bound with* G. T. Haywood, THE BIRTH
OF THE SPIRIT IN THE DAYS OF THE APOSTLES (Indian-
apolis, n. d.) DIVINE NAMES AND TITLES OF JEHOVAH
(Indianapolis, n. d.) THE FINEST OF THE WHEAT (In-
dianapolis, n. d.) THE VICTIM OF THE FLAMING
SWORD (Indianapolis, n. d.)

14. THREE EARLY PENTECOSTAL TRACTS. D. Wesley My-
land, THE LATTER RAIN COVENANT AND PEN-
TECOSTAL POWER (Chicago, 1910) *bound with* G. F.
Taylor, THE SPIRIT AND THE BRIDE (n. p., [1907?])
bound with B. F. Laurence, THE APOSTOLIC FAITH
RESTORED (St. Louis, 1916)

15. Fairchild, James H., OBERLIN: THE COLONY AND THE
COLLEGE, 1833-1883 (Oberlin, 1883)

16. Figgis, John B., KESWICK FROM WITHIN (London,
[1914])

17. Finney, Charles G., LECTURES TO PROFESSING CHRIS-
TIANS (New York, 1837)

18. Fleisch, Paul, DIE MODERNE GEMEINSCHAFTS-
BEWEGUNG IN DEUTSCHLAND (Leipzig, 1912)

19. SIX TRACTS BY W. B. GODBEY. *SPIRITUAL* (*GRACES* (Cincinnati, [1895]) *THE RETURN* ..s (Cincinnati, [1899?]) *WORK OF THE HOLY SPIRIT* (Louisville, [1902]) *CHURCH—BRIDE—KINGDOM* (Cincinnati, [1905]) *DIVINE HEALING* (Greensboro, [1909]) *TONGUE MOVEMENT, SATANIC* (Zarephath, N. J., 1918)

20. Gordon, Earnest B., *ADONIRAM JUDSON GORDON* (New York, [1896])

21. Hills, A. M., *HOLINESS AND POWER FOR THE CHURCH AND THE MINISTRY* (Cincinnati, [1897])

22. Horner, Ralph C., *FROM THE ALTAR TO THE UPPER ROOM* (Toronto, [1891])

23. McDonald, William and John E. Searles, *THE LIFE OF REV. JOHN S. INSKIP* (Boston, [1885])

24. LaBerge, Agnes N. O., *WHAT GOD HATH WROUGHT* (Chicago, n. d.)

25. Lee, Luther, *AUTOBIOGRAPHY OF THE REV. LUTHER LEE* (New York, 1882)

26. McLean, A. and J. W. Easton, *PENUEL; OR, FACE TO FACE WITH GOD* (New York, 1869)

27. McPherson, Aimee Semple, *THIS IS THAT: PERSONAL EXPERIENCES SERMONS AND WRITINGS* (Los Angeles, [1919])

28. Mahan, Asa, *OUT OF DARKNESS INTO LIGHT* (London, 1877)

29. THE LIFE AND TEACHING OF CARRIE JUDD MONTGOMERY Carrie Judd Montgomery, *"UNDER HIS WINGS": THE STORY OF MY LIFE* (Oakland,

[1936]) Carrie F. Judd, *THE PRAYER OF FAITH* (New York, 1880)

30. THE DEVOTIONAL WRITINGS OF PHOEBE PALMER Phoebe Palmer, *THE WAY OF HOLINESS* (52nd ed., New York, 1867) *FAITH AND ITS EFFECTS* (27th ed., New York, n. d., orig. pub. 1854)

31. Wheatley, Richard, *THE LIFE AND LETTERS OF MRS. PHOEBE PALMER* (New York, 1881)

32. Palmer, Phoebe, ed., *PIONEER EXPERIENCES* (New York, 1868)

33. Palmer, Phoebe, *THE PROMISE OF THE FATHER* (Boston, 1859)

34. Pardington, G. P., *TWENTY-FIVE WONDERFUL YEARS, 1889-1914: A POPULAR SKETCH OF THE CHRISTIAN AND MISSIONARY ALLIANCE* (New York, [1914])

35. Parham, Sarah E., *THE LIFE OF CHARLES F. PARHAM, FOUNDER OF THE APOSTOLIC FAITH MOVEMENT* (Joplin, [1930])

36. THE SERMONS OF CHARLES F. PARHAM. Charles F. Parham, *A VOICE CRYING IN THE WILDERNESS* (4th ed., Baxter Springs, Kan., 1944, orig. pub. 1902) *THE EVERLASTING GOSPEL* (n.p., n.d., orig. pub. 1911)

37. Pierson, Arthur Tappan, *FORWARD MOVEMENTS OF THE LAST HALF CENTURY* (New York, 1905)

38. *PROCEEDINGS OF HOLINESS CONFERENCES, HELD AT CINCINNATI, NOVEMBER 26TH, 1877, AND AT NEW YORK, DECEMBER 17TH, 1877* (Philadelphia, 1878)

39. *RECORD OF THE CONVENTION FOR THE PROMOTION OF*

SCRIPTURAL HOLINESS HELD AT BRIGHT   ..AY 29TH, TO JUNE 7TH, 1875 (Brighton, [1896?])

40. Rees, Seth Cook, *MIRACLES IN THE SLUMS* (Chicago, [1905?])

41. Roberts, B. T., *WHY ANOTHER SECT* (Rochester, 1879)

42. Shaw, S. B., ed., *ECHOES OF THE GENERAL HOLINESS ASSEMBLY* (Chicago, [1901])

43. THE DEVOTIONAL WRITINGS OF ROBERT PEARSALL SMITH AND HANNAH WHITALL SMITH. [R]obert [P]earsall [S]mith, *HOLINESS THROUGH FAITH: LIGHT ON THE WAY OF HOLINESS* (New York, [1870]) [H]annah [W]hitall [S]mith, *THE CHRISTIAN'S SECRET OF A HAPPY LIFE,* (Boston and Chicago, [1885])

44. [S]mith, [H]annah [W]hitall, *THE UNSELFISHNESS OF GOD AND HOW I DISCOVERED IT* (New York, [1903])

45. Steele, Daniel, *A SUBSTITUTE FOR HOLINESS; OR, ANTINOMIANISM REVIVED* (Chicago and Boston, [1899])

46. Tomlinson, A. J., *THE LAST GREAT CONFLICT* (Cleveland, 1913)

47. Upham, Thomas C., *THE LIFE OF FAITH* (Boston, 1845)

48. Washburn, Josephine M., *HISTORY AND REMINIS-CENCES OF THE HOLINESS CHURCH WORK IN SOUTH-ERN CALIFORNIA AND ARIZONA* (South Pasadena, [1912?])